Cataloging and Catalogs

HANDBOOKS FOR LIBRARY MANAGEMENT

Administration, Personnel, Buildings and Equipment
Acquisitions, Collection Development, and Collection Use
Reference Services and Library Instruction
Cataloging and Catalogs
Circulation, Interlibrary Loan, Patron Use, and Collection Maintenance
Library Education and Professional Issues

Cataloging and Catalogs
A Handbook for Library Management

David F. Kohl

Foreword by Sanford Berman

ABC-CLIO

Santa Barbara, California
Oxford, England

©1986 by David F. Kohl

*This book is Smyth sewn and printed on acid-free paper to
meet library standards.*

Library of Congress Cataloging in Publication Data

Kohl, David F., 1942–
   Cataloging and catalogs.

   (Handbooks for library management)
   Bibliography: p.
   Includes index.
   1. Cataloging–Handbooks, manuals, etc. 2. Library
catalogs–Handbooks, manuals, etc. I. Title.
II. Series: Kohl, David F., 1942–   . Handbooks for
library management.
Z693.K6 1985   025.3   85-15835
ISBN 0-87436-434-5 (v.4)
ISBN 0-87436-399-3 (set)

10 9 8 7 6 5 4 3 2 1

ABC-Clio, Inc.
2040 Alameda Padre Serra, Box 4397
Santa Barbara, California 93103

Clio Press Ltd.
55 St. Thomas Street
Oxford OX1 1JG, England

Manufactured in the United States of America

CONTENTS

1. ⎯⎯⎯⎯⎯⎯⎯⎯⎯⎯⎯⎯⎯⎯⎯⎯⎯

Cataloging

2.

Catalogs

Contents

FOREWORD

This compendium of quantitative study results concerning catalogs and cat-aloging contains much information—especially on relative "hit rates" for various copy sources, format and classification switching, and such basic maintenance operations as filing, revising, and cross-referencing—that should prove useful to efficiency-conscious technical services administrators. Knowing about comparable libraries' experiences can save money and increase productivity. But the data also suggest—to anyone who wants to know what's really happening in cataloging and what makes catalogs "work"—some variously remarkable, important, and even disturbing trends and implications. For instance:

It appears, despite the enormous attention devoted to online catalogs in professional meetings and publishing, that *card* catalogs still overwhelmingly predominate in libraries.

Subject access represents a frequent "problem" for catalog users in all types of libraries.

Users experience a serious degree of search failure for items actually *in* collections but either not cataloged or undercataloged. Ancillary findings pinpoint government documents and non-English language items as two kinds of material often cataloged selectively, if at all.

A notably low percentage of catalog users seems to ask for searching help, and errors (e.g., in name spelling) continue to plague LC- as well as utility-supplied copy, which implies that, for maximum "do-it-yourself" success, catalogs should be heavily cross-referenced (including "see" references from misspelled terms) and employ "first hit" name forms and subject terminology. However, related evidence reveals that many libraries do not extensively add cross-references nor alter inappropriate subject tracings, but *do* allow "blind" cross-references to accumulate. On the "plus" side, however, more libraries (particularly academic) deliberately "tinker" with "outside copy" than is generally assumed, e.g., verifying LC or network-member authority terms and *adding* subject tracings.

Audiovisual and print records apparently remain segregated in most catalogs in spite of repeated and persuasive pro-integration arguments.

To be truly practical and valid, research should be more rigorous, focused, comparative, and explanatory. For example, several studies indicate whether COM catalog users in a given library find that format acceptable, but don't examine why. Might acceptability hinge on publicity? On the number and quality of fiche/film readers? On the extent of user instruction? On staff attitudes? On the layout and legibility of the fiche or film product itself?

Some "findings" should not be accepted as sufficient bases for either continuing or changing current policies because they (a) haven't been successfully replicated, or (b) originated from poorly conceived and executed studies (for two critiques, see my "Research," in *Joy of Cataloging* [Oryx Press, 1981], pp. 197-200).

Several crucial areas seem to lack much, if any research. For instance:
How well do library users—and staff—comprehend standard and ISBD abbreviations and punctuation? (Surveys conducted during the 1970s in both Wisconsin and Minnesota found that such conventional abbreviations as "min.," "pt.," "in.," "c," "d.," "b.," "ed.," "v.," and "ill." are *not* well understood by a majority of catalog users, while anecdotal evidence plus common sense dictate the same conclusion for those beloved slashes, brackets, and equals signs, as well as the Latin-derived "s.l." and "s.n." It may be that these elements of the bibliographic record directly contribute to mystification and dissatisfaction.)

Would more notes describing contents and special features (a) better enable catalog users to decide whether to actually seek a cited item and (b) enhance term searching in online catalogs?

Is it still true—as earlier research reported—that many catalog searchers will not make a second lookup? If so, has this fact—coupled with the known tendency of many users to avoid asking for staff help—prompted any libraries to consciously strive for "first hits" by augmenting and/or changing standard LCSH, MeSH, or Sears subject headings and AACR2 name forms (e.g., replacing NEAR EAST with MIDDLE EAST, "Fast" with "Cunningham" for Masao Masuto mysteries, and GRUNEN with GREENS, as well as innovating—as necessary—rubrics like MAGNET SCHOOLS, NUCLEAR WINTER, SUSTAINABLE AGRICULTURE, and SPACE-BASED MISSILE DEFENSES)?

What about school library needs and practices? Do they differ markedly from other types of libraries?

In sum: We now know about catalogs and cataloging. But we surely need to know a lot more in order to make sensible, objective, and functional decisions. Far too often, policy—local, national, and global—has been established merely on the basis of guesses, convention, caprice, or bias (e.g., toward making things easier for machines than for people). And that's not good enough. Not any more.

> —*Sanford Berman*
> Hennepin County Library, Minnetonka, Minnesota

INTRODUCTION

The *Handbooks for Library Management* have been designed for library managers and decision makers who regularly need information, but who are chronically too short of time to do involved and time-consuming literature searches each time specific, quantitative information is desired. This unusual tool, rather than abstracting complete studies or providing only citations to research, instead presents summaries of individual research findings, grouped by subject. By looking under the appropriate subject heading in the *Handbook*, librarians can find summaries detailing the research findings on that topic. For example, what percentage of reference questions are answered correctly, and does it make a difference whether professional or nonprofessional staff are doing the answering? As a result, helpful information can be found in minutes and without an extensive literature review. Furthermore, if a more complete look at the study is desired, the user is referred to the bibliographic citation number so that the full study can be consulted.

Arrangement

The series consists of six volumes, with each volume covering two or more of the sixteen basic subject areas that divide the volumes into parts. While most of these basic subject divisions reflect such traditional administrative division of library work as administration, circulation, and reference, at least two subject areas go somewhat further. "Library Education" may be of interest, not just to library school administrators, but to faculty and students as well, and "Professional Issues" should be of interest to all career-oriented library professionals. Each basic subject division is further divided by specific subject headings, which are further subdivided by type of library: General (more than one library type), Academic, Public, School, and Special. For example, readers seeking information on book loss rates in academic libraries would consult the basic subject division "Collection Maintenance" and look under the specific subject heading "Loss Rates (Books)," in the "Academic" libraries subdivision. There they would find the summarized results of studies on book loss rates in academic libraries followed by the number referring to the full citation in the Bibliography of Articles.

Each volume in the series follows the same basic pattern: The introduction; a list of the journals surveyed; a detailed table of contents listing all subject headings used in that volume; the research findings arranged by subject; the complete bibliography of articles surveyed for the series with page numbers indicating locations of corresponding research summaries in the text; and an alphabetically arranged author index to the Bibliography of Articles.

The summaries of the research findings also tend to follow a standard format. First the study is briefly described by giving location, date, and, when appropriate, population or survey size and response rate. This information is provided to help users determine the nature, scope, and relevance of the study to their needs. The actual findings, signaled by an italicized *"showed that,"* follow and include, when appropriate, such supporting data as significance level and confidence interval. Information in brackets represents editorial comment, for example "[significance level not given]" or "[remaining cases not accounted for]," while information in parentheses merely represents additional data taken from the article.

The Sample Entries on page xix identify the elements and illustrate the interrelationships between the subject organization of the volume, research summaries of the text, corresponding article citations in the bibliography, and the author index entries.

Scope

In order to keep the *Handbook* series manageable, a number of scope limitations were necessary. The time period, 1960 through 1983, was selected since it covers the time when quantitative research began to come of age in library research. Only journal literature has been surveyed, because the bulk of quantitative library research is reported in that medium, and because the bulk of editorial and refereeing process required by most journals helps ensure the quality of the research reported. This limitation does ignore a number of important studies reported in monographic form, however, and we hope to cover this area at a later date. Further, only North American journals and research were reviewed since they constitute the main body of quantitative library research reported. Again, this ignores several journals reporting significant library research, particularly journals from Great Britain. We plan to expand our focus and include these in later editions or updates of the *Handbook* series.

Although we generally followed the principle that research good enough to publish was research worth including in the *Handbook* series, several caveats must be stated. First, no research findings with statistical significance exceeding .05 were reported. This follows general Social Science practice and, in recent years, almost universal library research practice. Second, occasional findings, and sometimes whole studies, were not reported in the *Handbook* series when there were serious problems with internal consistency and/or ambiguous and confusing text. At issue here is not the occasional typographical error or arithmetical miscalculation, but those situations where charts and text purportedly presenting the same information differed in substantial and unaccountable ways. Fortunately, such problems were not excessive. And third, as a general rule, only original and supported findings were used in the *Handbook* series. Findings that were reported second-hand, or where the study documentation was reported elsewhere (often the case with doctoral research), were generally not used in the series. Only in those instances when the second-hand data were used to show a pattern or otherwise resulted in new data by their juxtaposition, were such findings reported.

Finally, under the category of unsought limitations, we, like many library users, were not always able to find all the journal articles we needed in the time available to us. However, the excellent holdings and services of the University of Illinois Library Science Library provided us with access to almost all of the journal issues actually published and received by March 1984—a fact that should probably be listed as a record rather than as a limitation.

Acknowledgements

As might be expected, a project of this size required assistance from many quarters. Both the University of Illinois Library Research and Publication Committee and the University of Illinois Research Board provided invaluable assistance in the form of financial support for graduate assistants. The assistants themselves, Becky Rutter, Nicki Varyu, and Bruce Olsen, constituted a dedicated, bright, and hardworking team. The Undergraduate Library staff deserve special thanks for their support and cooperation, as do the Library Science Library staff, who were unfailingly courteous and helpful in making their truly outstanding collection available. The staff at ABC-Clio, particularly Gail Schlachter and Barbara Pope, provided much needed encouragement and good advice, even in the face of several delays and at least one nasty shock. And last, but by no means least, I would like to acknowledge the patience and support of my wife, Marilyn, and my son, Nathaniel, who have given up much in the way of a husband and father so that this *Handbook* series could be completed on schedule.

—*David F. Kohl*
Urbana, Illinois

SAMPLE ENTRIES

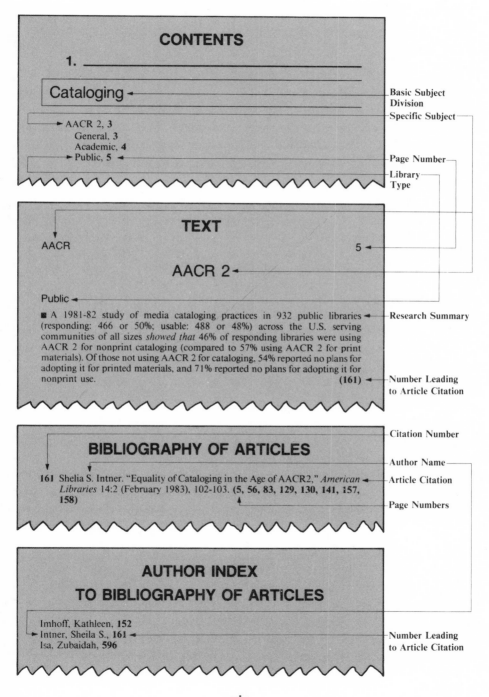

CONTENTS

1. _____

Cataloging ← ————————————— Basic Subject Division

————————————————————— Specific Subject

→ AACR 2, 3
   General, 3
   Academic, 4
→ Public, 5 ←

————————————— Page Number

Library Type

TEXT

AACR ←

AACR 2 ←

5 ←

Public ←

■ A 1981-82 study of media cataloging practices in 932 public libraries ← ——— Research Summary
(responding: 466 or 50%; usable: 488 or 48%) across the U.S. serving
communities of all sizes *showed that* 46% of responding libraries were using
AACR 2 for nonprint cataloging (compared to 57% using AACR 2 for print
materials). Of those not using AACR 2 for cataloging, 54% reported no plans for
adopting it for printed materials, and 71% reported no plans for adopting it for
nonprint use. **(161)** ← ——— Number Leading to Article Citation

————————————— Citation Number

BIBLIOGRAPHY OF ARTICLES

————————————— Author Name

161 Shelia S. Intner. "Equality of Cataloging in the Age of AACR2," *American* ← ——— Article Citation
Libraries 14:2 (February 1983), 102-103. **(5, 56, 83, 129, 130, 141, 157,
158)**

————————————— Page Numbers

AUTHOR INDEX

TO BIBLIOGRAPHY OF ARTICLES

Imhoff, Kathleen, **152**
→ Intner, Sheila S., **161** ←
Isa, Zubaidah, **596**

————————————— Number Leading to Article Citation

LIST OF JOURNALS SURVEYED

American Libraries. Chicago: American Library Association, 1970– . Monthly. LC 70-21767. ISSN 0002-9769. (Formerly *ALA Bulletin, 1907–1969.*)

American Society for Information Science. Journal. (JASIS) New York: John Wiley & Sons, 1970– . Bimonthly. LC 75-640174. ISSN 0002-8231. (Formerly *American Documentation, 1950–1969.*)

Canadian Library Journal. Ottawa: Canadian Library Association, 1969– . Bimonthly. LC 77-309891. ISSN 0008-4352. (Formerly *Bulletin, 1944–* March 1960; *Canadian Library, 1960–1968.*)

Catholic Library World. Haverford, PA: Catholic Library Association, 1929– . Monthly. LC 39-41. ISSN 0008-820X.

Collection Building. New York: Schuman, 1978– . Quarterly. LC 78-645190. ISSN 0160-4953.

Collection Management. New York: Haworth Press, 1975– . Quarterly. LC 78-640677. ISSN 0146-2679.

College and Research Libraries. Chicago: American Library Association, 1939– . Bimonthly. LC 42-16492. ISSN 0010-0870.

Drexel Library Quarterly. Philadelphia: Centrum Philadelphia, 1965– . Quarterly. LC 65-9911. ISSN 0012-6160.

Harvard Library Bulletin. Cambridge: Harvard University Library, 1947– . Quarterly. LC 49-1965//R802. ISSN 0017-8136.

International Journal of Legal Information. Camden, NJ: International Association of Law Libraries, 1982– . 6/yr. LC 82-643460. ISSN 0731-1265. (Formerly *Bulletin. International Association of Law Libraries, 1960–1972; International Journal of Law Libraries, 1973–1979.*)

International Library Review. London: Academic Press, 1969– . Quarterly. LC 76-10110. ISSN 0020-7837.

Journal of Academic Librarianship. Ann Arbor, MI: Mountainside Publishing, 1975– . Bimonthly. LC 75-647252. ISSN 0099-1333.

Journal of Education for Librarianship. State College, PA: Association of American Library Schools, 1960– . 5/yr. LC 63-24347. ISSN 0022-0604.

Journal of Library Administration. New York: Haworth Press, 1980– . Monthly. LC 80-644826. ISSN 0193-0826.

Journal of Library Automation. Chicago: American Library Association, 1968–. Quarterly. LC 68-6437//R82. ISSN 0022-2240.

Journal of Library History, Philosophy and Comparative Librarianship. Austin, TX: 1966–. Quarterly. LC 65-9989. ISSN 0275-3650. (Formerly *Journal of Library History,* 1966-1975.)

Law Library Journal. Chicago: American Association of Law Libraries, 1908–. Quarterly. LC 41-21688//R6. ISSN 0023-9283.

Library Acquisitions: Practice and Theory. Elmsford, NY: Pergamon Press, 1977–. Quarterly. LC 77-647728. ISSN 0364-6408.

Library Journal. New York: R.R. Bowker, 1876–. Semimonthly, except July–August. LC 76-645271. ISSN 0363-0277.

Library Quarterly. Chicago: University of Chicago, 1931–. Quarterly. LC 32-12448. ISSN 0024-2519.

Library Research. Norwood, NJ: Ablex Publishing, 1979–. Quarterly. LC 79-643718. ISSN 0164-0763.

Library Resources and Technical Services. Chicago: American Library Association, 1957–. Quarterly. LC 59-3198. ISSN 0024-2527. (Formed by the merger of *Serial Slants* and *Journal of Cataloging and Classification.*)

Library Trends. Champaign: University of Illinois at Urbana-Champaign, 1952–. Quarterly. LC 54-62638. ISSN 0024-2594.

Medical Library Association. Bulletin. Chicago: Medical Library Association, 1911–. Quarterly. LC 16-76616. ISSN 0025-7338.

Microform Review. Westport, CT: Meckler Publishing, 1972–. Quarterly. LC 72-620299. ISSN 0002-6530.

Notes. Philadelphia: Music Library Association, 1942–. Quarterly. LC 43-45299//R542. ISSN 0027-4380.

Online. Weston, CT: Online, 1977–. Quarterly. LC 78-640551. ISSN 0416-5422.

Public Libraries. Chicago: American Library Association, 1978–. 4/yr. ISSN 0163-5506. (Formerly *Just Between Ourselves,* 1962-1969; *PLA Newsletter,* 1962-1977.)

RQ. Chicago: American Library Association, 1960–. Quarterly. LC 77-23834. ISSN 0033-7072.

RSR Reference Services Review. Ann Arbor, MI: Perian Press, 1972–. LC 73-642283//R74. ISSN 0090-7324.

School Library Journal. New York: R.R. Bowker, 1954–. Monthly except June and July. LC 77-646483. ISSN 0362-8930.

School Library Media Quarterly. Chicago: American Library Association, 1981–. 4/yr. LC 82-640987. ISSN 0278-4823. (Formerly *School Libraries,* 1951-1972; *School Media Quarterly,* 1972-1980.)

Special Libraries. New York: Special Libraries Association, 1910– . 4/yr. LC 11-25280rev2*. ISSN 0038-6723.

Wilson Library Bulletin. Bronx, NY: H.W. Wilson, 1914– . Monthly except July and August. LC 80-9008(rev.42). ISSN 0043-5651.

1.

Cataloging

AACR 2

General

■ A 1978 study of OCLC's online union catalog preparatory to converting to AACR 2 form of name headings and uniform titles, involving a 1% test file (41,212 records) and a thorough review of AACR 2 rules, *showed that* AACR 2 contained 454 "significant" rule changes or new rules, of which 56% would benefit neither librarian nor patron, 23% of which would benefit librarians, and 21% of which would benefit patrons. **(337)**

Ibid. . . . *showed that* 39% of the total records in the online union catalog were ultimately converted to AACR 2 form. **(337)**

■ A survey reported in 1982 of Canadian libraries selected from the *CLA Directory* and its supplement (sample size: 203; responding: 85; usable: 69 or 34.0%) concerning implementation of AACR 2 *showed that* 53 (77%) respondents had adopted AACR 2 either in full or in part. Adopting AACR 2 in full were 94% of the academic libraries, 57% of the school libraries, 78% of the public libraries, and 71% of the special libraries. **(299)**

Ibid. . . . *showed that* of the 16 libraries that did not adopt AACR 2 the following reasons were given (multiple responses allowed): lack of staff to deal with the transition (69%), cost (56%), fear of causing patron confusion (31%). **(299)**

Ibid. . . . *showed that* of the 53 libraries who adopted AACR 2, 94% planned to use it to catalog monographs, 62% for serials, 57% for audiovisuals, and 51% for microforms. **(299)**

Ibid. . . . *showed that* of the 53 libraries who adopted AACR 2, 77% reported they would interfile the AACR 2 entries in their old catalogs, 7 [%] reported they would freeze their catalogs, and 9% reported they would close their catalogs. **(299)**

Ibid. . . . *showed that* of the 53 libraries who adopted AACR 2, 60% reported they were able to manage implementation with regular staff during regular hours, while 9% reported they had to hire extra staff. [The actions of the remaining libraries were not reported.] **(299)**

Academic

■ A study reported in 1980 of 2 card catalogs (University of Wisconsin, Whitewater, 170,000 titles; University of Illinois, Urbana, 3,000,000 titles) investigating the number of personal authors for which there was only 1 title in the collection (sample size: Whitewater, 2,762 authors; Urbana, 2,345 authors), *showed that* a sample of 1,366 personal authors selected from 6 months of recent cataloging revealed that 52.12% had established headings. Based on Library of Congress estimates that 11% of the headings would have to be revised under AACR 2, 5.7% of all headings for new titles would have to be revised initially so that different works by the same author would file together.   **(758)**

■ A study reported in 1982 concerning the impact of AACR 2 on the card catalog in a medium-sized (740,000 volumes) academic library, based on a random sample of 909 catalog records (1,714 headings) taken from a year's pre-AACR 2 OCLC archival tapes and searched in the post-AACR 2 OCLC LC name authority file, *showed that* 217 (12.7%) different headings required changes under AACR 2 rules. 43% of these "unique" headings were verified in the online name authority file as of January 1981.   **(770)**

Ibid. . . . *showed that* the distribution of changes to be made by type of heading was as follows:

personal (1,246 headings)	98 (7.9%) changes
corporate (125 headings)	53 (42.4%) changes
geographical (153 headings)	20 (13.1%) changes
uniform title (34 headings)	1 (2.9%) changes
series (156 headings)	45 (28.8%) changes

However, since not every heading that required a change under AACR 2 was already represented in the catalog, the number of conflicts was less than the number of changes. The number of conflicts by type of heading was as follows:

personal (1,246 headings)	85 (6.8%) conflicts
corporate (125 headings)	27 (21.6%) conflicts
geographical (153 headings)	15 (9.8%) conflicts
uniform title (34 headings)	1 (2.9%) conflicts
series (156 headings)	42 (26.9%) conflicts **(770)**

Ibid. . . . *showed that* not all conflicts needed to be changed in order to interfile with pre-AACR 2 entries in the card catalog. Specifically, assuming that 5 kinds of differences could be ignored (punctuation, abbreviation, spelling, qualifier, and forname), 31.8% of the conflicts could be interfiled.

(770)

Ibid. . . . *showed that* a summary review of the literature came up with the following rates of difference ("headings which would be constructed differently under AACR 2") and rates of conflict ("AACR 2 headings for names already entered in the catalog under a different form"):

of 295 records and 541 headings studied at Johns Hopkins University, the rate of difference was 17.3% and the rate of conflict was 11%;

of 484 records studied at Duke University the rate of conflict was 15.5%;

of 330 titles and 577 headings at Emory University the rate of difference was 15%;

of 300 titles and 447 headings at the University of Minnesota the rate of difference was 3%;

of 258 headings at the University of Washington the rate of difference was 30%;

of 325 titles and 644 entries at Southern Illinois University, Carbondale, the rate of difference was 20.3%. **(770)**

Public

■ A 1981-82 study of media cataloging practices in 932 public libraries (responding: 466 or 50%; usable: 488 or 48%) across the U.S. serving communities of all sizes *showed that* 46% of responding libraries were using AACR 2 for nonprint cataloging (compared to 57% using AACR 2 for print materials). Of those not using AACR 2 for cataloging, 54% reported no plans for adopting it for printed materials, and 71% reported no plans for adopting it for nonprint use. **(161)**

Backlogs

Academic

■ A 1968 survey of Association of Research Libraries, some larger Canadian university libraries, and some libraries "where novel treatment of arrearages was known to exist" concerning cataloging arrearages (survey size: 91; responding: 86 or 95%) *showed that* 53 libraries reported arrearages without qualification, while 14 others qualified their reports of arrearages. Thus 67 (78%) respondents reported arrearages, including 83% of the ARL libraries and 62% of the Canadian libraries. **(604)**

Ibid. . . . *showed that*, of the 67 libraries reporting arrearages, the 3 most frequent factors used to determine whether to include a book in an arrearage were (multiple responses allowed):

lack of Library of Congress catalog copy (49 or 73.1% respondents),

publication of a book in a non-Roman alphabet (37 or 55.2%) and provenance,

including receipt by gift (11 or 16.4%),

by block purchase including PL 480 (10 or 14.9%),

or by approval plans (4 or 6.0%). **(604)**

Ibid. . . . *showed that*, of the 67 libraries reporting arrearages, 36 (53.7%) reported providing entries in the public card catalog for some or all of the books in the arrearage. The remaining 31 respondents reported no such display. **(604)**

Ibid. . . . *showed that*, of the 67 libraries reporting arrearages, 40 (59.7%) libraries reported that they expected the arrearages to continue and increase, while 26 (38.8%) reported that they considered the arrearages temporary. 1 library did not respond to this question. **(604)**

Ibid. . . . *showed that*, of the 67 libraries reporting arrearages, the majority did not consider permanent cataloging below "LC standard" for books a good idea. Specifically, only 11 (16.4%) respondents reported adopting or planning to adopt such a procedure, while only 3 libraries "indicated clearly" that they were actually implementing permanent cataloging below LC standard. **(604)**

■ A 1979 survey of academic libraries listed in the 1979 edition of *OCLC Participating Libraries Arranged by Network and Institution* (survey size: 200 libraries; responding: 166 or 83%) *showed that* of 163 respondents the number of backlogged titles awaiting cataloging was as follows:

less than 1,000 titles   125 (76.7%) libraries
1,000-4,999 titles   22 (13.5%) libraries

continued

5,000-9,999 titles   5 (3.1%) libraries
10,000 or more titles   11 (6.7%) libraries   **(764)**

Bibliographic Utilities

General

■ A 1977 study comparing the use of the Blackwell North America and OCLC data bases as sources of cataloging copy for 344 English-language imprints received on the B/NA approval program during a 3-month period [library not reported] *showed that*, after 2 searches about 2 months apart, 247 (72%) of the items were found in the B/NA data base and 315 (92%) were found in the OCLC data base. Further, 232 (67%) were located in both data bases, while 14 (4.1%) were located in neither data base. Neither place nor date of publication affected the hit rate. **(448)**

■ A study reported in 1981, of 45 monographs in microform format (randomly selected from the 1979 *Microforms in Print*) searched in RLIN, OCLC, and the *National Union Catalog*, *showed that*:

exact copy was found for 17.7% of the microform items searched of which 4.4% was Library of Congress cataloging and 13.3% was shared cataloging;

variant copy was found for 22.3% of the microform items searched of which 6.7% was Library of Congress cataloging and 15.6% was shared cataloging;

exact copy was found for 55.5% of the hard copy editions of the items of which 31.1% was Library of Congress cataloging and 24.4% was shared cataloging;

variant copy was found for 17.7% of the hard copy editions of the 45 items of which 13.3% was Library of Congress cataloging and 4.4% was shared cataloging. **(768)**

Ibid. . . . *showed that* of the exact copy that was found for 17.7% of the microforms, RLIN provided no exact matches, OCLC provided 11.1% of the matches (all shared cataloging), and the *National Union Catalog* provided 8.8% of the matches (evenly divided between LC and shared cataloging). **(768)**

Academic

■ A 1977 survey of academic libraries with collections of 300,000 volumes or more that were also OCLC members concerning cataloging practices (survey size: 147 libraries; responding: 121 or 82.3%) *showed that* the following sources of cataloging copy were used in addition to OCLC (large libraries = 900,000 volumes or more; small libraries = less than 900,000 volumes):

National Union Catalog	100.0% large;	100.0% small libraries
Mansell	95.0% large;	97.0% small libraries
MCRS	13.2% large;	5.0% small libraries
MARCFICHE	8.5% large;	2.0% small libraries
other	0.0% large;	4.0% small libraries

(760)

■ A 1977 survey of U.S. law libraries over 10,000 volumes taken from the 1976 *Directory of Law Libraries* (sample size: 1,080; responding: 373 or 35%) *showed that*, of 123 academic law libraries and 250 other law libraries, use of a bibliographic utility was highest among academic law libraries (43 or 35% compared to 15 or 6% in all other types of law libraries combined). Of the academic law libraries using a bibliographic utility 36 used OCLC, 6 used BALLOTS, and 1 used Blackwell North America; of the remaining law libraries 13 used OCLC, and 2 used BALLOTS.

(366)

■ A 1978 study of RLIN cataloging at the Law School Library, UC Berkeley over a 6-month period *showed that*, of 2,748 titles for which no MARC or RLIN copy cataloging was found, 1,099 (40%) were published in or after 1970.   **(368)**

Ibid. . . . *showed that* of 1,282 records found in the RLIN data base the hit rate in each subject area was as follows:

religious law	153 (18.4%)	titles found
Roman law	15 (18.8%)	titles found
comparative law	102 (38.0%)	titles found
foreign, civil law	332 (35.9%)	titles found
Anglo-American law	548 (34.5%)	titles found
international law	132 (39.2%)	titles found **(368)**

Ibid. . . . *showed that*, of 781 full MARC records in the RLIN data base, 51% required no modification, while of 91 standard Contributed Data File records 55% required no modification.   **(368)**

■ A 1979 survey of U.S. community college libraries selected from the 1978 *Community, Junior and Technical College Directory* (sample size: 98;

responding: 52; usable: 48 or 48.98%) *showed that*, of 46 respondents, 39 (84.8%) reported that they did not participate in computerized cataloging networks. Of the 39, 23 (59.0%) reported they did not plan to join such a network, while 7 (17.9%) said they did, 8 (20.5%) said they were undecided, and 3 (7.7%) did not respond. Of the 7 libraries that did participate in such networks, 6 (85.7%) used OCLC, while 1 (14.3%) used the Washington Library Network. **(498)**

■ A 1979 survey of academic libraries listed in the 1979 edition of *OCLC Participating Libraries Arranged by Network and Institution* (survey size: 200 libraries; responding: 166 or 83%) *showed that* 164 (98.8%) respondents reported using OCLC to produce catalog cards. Further, of 163 respondents, 73 (44.8%) reported use of another card production system as well. The 3 most common additional methods used were (in descending order of importance): use of a photocopier (37 libraries), typing complete card sets (17 libraries), and purchasing commercially available cards, including Library of Congress cards (15 libraries). **(764)**

■ A 1980 survey of North American medical school libraries concerning automation of internal library operations (population: 139; responding: 93 or 69%) *showed that* 81 (87.1%) libraries participated in 1 or more of the major bibliographic utilities (OCLC, RLIN, or UTLAS) for shared cataloging. **(741)**

Special

■ A 1977 survey of U.S. law libraries over 10,000 volumes taken from the 1976 *Directory of Law Libraries* (sample size: 1,080; responding: 373 or 35%) *showed that*, of 123 academic law libraries and 250 other law libraries, use of a bibliographic utility was highest among academic law libraries (43 or 35% compared to 15 or 6% in all other types of law libraries combined). Of the academic law libraries using a bibliographic utility 36 used OCLC, 6 used BALLOTS, and 1 used Blackwell North America; of the remaining law libraries 13 used OCLC, and 2 used BALLOTS. **(366)**

■ A 1978 study of RLIN cataloging at the Law School Library, UC Berkeley over a 6-month period *showed that*, of 2,748 titles for which no MARC or RLIN copy cataloging was found, 1,099 (40%) were published in or after 1970. **(368)**

Ibid. . . . *showed that* of 1,282 records found in the RLIN data base the hit rate in each subject area was as follows:

religious law	153 (18.4%) titles found
Roman law	15 (18.8%) titles found
comparative law	102 (38.0%) titles found
foreign, civil law	332 (35.9%) titles found
Anglo-American law	548 (34.5%) titles found
international law	132 (39.2%) titles found

Ibid. . . . *showed that*, of 781 full MARC records in the RLIN data base, 51% required no modification, while of 91 standard Contributed Data File records 55% required no modification.   **(368)**

■ A 1978 study at the General Electric Research and Development Center (Schenectady, New York) comparing the availability of cataloging copy in OCLC vs. Inforonics, which involved searching 3 months of monograph acquisitions (183 titles) in both data bases, *showed that* cataloging copy was found for 153 titles in the OCLC data base compared to 101 titles found in the Inforonics data base. Further, the hit rate in OCLC was better than in Inforonics regardless of country of publication, date of publication, or availability of LC card number.   **(433)**

■ A 1980 survey of North American medical school libraries concerning automation of internal library operations (population: 139; responding: 93 or 69%) *showed that* 81 (87.1%) libraries participated in 1 or more of the major bibliographic utilities (OCLC, RLIN, or UTLAS) for shared cataloging.   **(741)**

Brief versus Full

Academic

■ A 1979 survey of U.S. community college libraries selected from the 1978 *Community, Junior and Technical College Directory* (sample size: 98; responding: 52; usable: 48 or 48.98%) *showed that* for audiovisual materials:

24 (50.0%) libraries did full cataloging and interfiled entries in the central catalog;

8 (16.7%) libraries did full cataloging but filed audiovisual entries in a separate catalog;

1 (2.1%) library did full cataloging and filed audiovisual entries in separate drawers of the central catalog;

6 (12.5%) libraries did full cataloging but filed audiovisual entries in a separate catalog in the AV center;

9 (18.8%) libraries did full cataloging and filed audiovisual entries both in the central catalog and in a separate catalog in the AV center. **(498)**

Public

■ A 1969 survey of Canadian public libraries serving populations of more than 10,000 people as well as all county and regional libraries belonging to the Canadian Library Association concerning holdings and use of non-English collections (survey size: 203; responding: 83 or 41%) *showed that*, of 74 respondents, 56 (75.7%) libraries reported they fully cataloged books in non-English languages. In 52 (70.3%) libraries the cataloging was handled by library staff. **(534)**

Card Production

Academic

■ A 1971 study at the University of Utah concerning the actual time required to obtain Library of Congress card sets based on 523 orders sent during a 1-month period *showed that* the number of working days between the time the order was sent and the receipt of the cards was as follows (cumulative percentages given):

returned by 20 working days	7.1% orders
returned by 25 working days	43.4% orders
returned by 40 working days, 2 months	63.8% orders
returned by 80 working days, 4 months	91.7% orders
returned at the end of 5 months	93.3% orders **(602)**

■ A study reported in 1972 at the University of British Columbia (Canada) of 7 different methods of catalog card production (including duplication of cards and "finishing" the cards with tracings, etc.) over a 2-year period *showed that* the relative combined labor and materials costs for an average set of cards (13.2 cards) was as follows:

Flexowriter	$1.31 per set
Itek typed stencil, 10-up	$ .86 per set
Itek pasted stencil, 10-up	$ .65 per set
Xerox 914 typed stencil, 8-up	$ .81 per set
Xerox 914 pasted stencil, 8-up	$ .60 per set
Xerox 3600 typed stencil, 4-up	$ .78 per set
Xerox 3600 pasted stencil, 4-up	$ .57 per set

(599)

■ A 1973 study at the University of Colorado Medical Center of cataloging and card production costs of English-language monographs with 1972-73 imprints that required complete cataloging (sample size: 319 items) *showed that* unit costs of in-library processing were as follows (estimated unit cost of purchased card method in parentheses):

bibliographic searching	$ .26 (.31) per item
cataloging	$1.33 (.66) per item
card production	$ .62 (1.08) per item
book preparation	$ .63 (.63) per item
TOTAL UNIT COST	$2.84 (2.68) per item

(706)

Ibid. . . . *showed that* the average number of days before the books were available to users was 16.07 days (26.97 days estimated for the purchase card method), while the average number of days before the cards were filed in the catalog was 19.88 days (34.11 days estimated for the purchase card method). **(706)**

■ A 1979 survey of academic libraries listed in the 1979 edition of *OCLC Participating Libraries Arranged by Network and Institution* (survey size: 200 libraries; responding: 166 or 83%) *showed that* 164 (98.8%) respondents reported using OCLC to produce catalog cards. Further, of 163 respondents, 73 (44.8%) reported use of another card production system as well. The 3 most common additional methods used were (in descending order of importance): use of a photocopier (37 libraries), typing complete card sets (17 libraries), and purchasing commercially available cards, including Library of Congress cards (15 libraries). **(764)**

Ibid. . . . *showed that*, of 71 respondents, non-OCLC card production systems were used to produce cards for the following 3 most frequently mentioned types of materials (multiple responses allowed):

audiovisual material	22 (31.0%) libraries
non-Roman alphabet texts	17 (23.9%) libraries
local ephemera (including	
student theses and papers)	15 (21.1%) libraries

Further, the number of titles per year for which cards were produced using an alternate (to OCLC) system based on responses from 67 libraries ranged from 10 titles to 31,200 titles with a median of 450 titles per year.

(764)

Special

■ A 1973 study at the University of Colorado Medical Center of cataloging and card production costs of English-language monographs with 1972-73 imprints that required complete cataloging (sample size: 319 items) *showed that* unit costs of in-library processing were as follows (estimated unit cost of purchased card method in parentheses):

bibliographic searching	$ .26 (.31) per item
cataloging	$1.33 (.66) per item
card production	$ .62 (1.08) per item
book preparation	$ .63 (.63) per item
TOTAL UNIT COST	$2.84 (2.68) per item **(706)**

Ibid. . . . *showed that* the average number of days before the books were available to users was 16.07 days (26.97 days estimated for the purchase card method), while the average number of days before the cards were filed in the catalog was 19.88 days (34.11 days estimated for the purchase card method).

(706)

Cataloging Copy—General Issues

Academic

■ A study reported in 1965 at 3 state college libraries and 1 campus of the state university concerning use made of the Library of Congress classification decisions (survey size: a total of 588 catalog cards from all 4 institutions) *showed that* the 3 state colleges together had an average of 84% of their catalog cards based on LC cards received (with the remaining average of 16% resulting from original cataloging), while the state university had 71% of its cards based on LC cards (with an average of 29% resulting from original cataloging). The state college figures were accurate ±3.5% at the 95% confidence level while the state university figure was accurate ±8% at the 95% confidence level.

(583)

■ A 1977 study at Cornell Law Library of 157 OCLC member records and 424 LC records in the OCLC data base *showed that* the average cataloging time per record for records with OCLC member cataloging copy was 9.076 minutes compared to 8.148 minutes cataloging time per record for records with LC cataloging copy. **(367)**

Ibid. . . . *showed that* the average inputting time per record for records with OCLC member cataloging copy was 5.966 minutes compared to 4.498 minutes average inputting time per record for records with LC cataloging copy. **(367)**

■ A 1977 study at Cornell Law Library of 301 cataloging records found in the OCLC data base (151 input by LC; 150 input by OCLC member libraries) *showed that* to make usable cataloging the LC records required an average of 1.13 modifications per record, while the OCLC member cataloging required an average of 2.97 modifications per record. When call number problems were ignored (which may pose unique problems to law cataloging in the LC schedules) the average number of LC modifications per record dropped to .78, while the average number of modifications per record for OCLC member cataloging dropped to 2.53. **(367)**

■ A 1977 survey of academic libraries with collections of 300,000 volumes or more that were also OCLC members concerning cataloging practices (survey size: 147 libraries; responding: 121 or 82.3%) *showed that* in large libraries (900,000 volumes or more) cataloging staff were used as follows:

adapting LC records for the same edition: 1.6% libraries used professional catalogers only, 58.3% used support staff only, and 40% used both professional and support staff;

adapting LC records for different editions: 23.3% libraries used professional catalogers only, 31.6% used support staff only, and 45% used both professional and support staff;

completing CIP records: 5% libraries used professional catalogers only, 66.6% used support staff only, and 28.3% used both professional and support staff;

verifying member cataloging records: 23.3% libraries used professionals only, 11.5% used professionals with support staff assisting in verification, 13.3% used support staff only, and 46.6% used both professional and support staff [remaining percentage unaccounted for];

cataloging without copy: 56.6% libraries used professionals only, 16.6% used professionals with support staff assisting with verification, 1.6% used support staff only, and 15% used both professionals and support staff. **(760)**

Ibid. . . . *showed that* in small (under 900,000 volumes) libraries, cataloging staff were used as follows:

adapting LC records for the same edition: 10% libraries used professionals only, 28% used support staff only, and 62% used both professional and support staff;

adapting LC records for different editions: 33% libraries used professionals only, 9% used support staff only, and 59% used both professional and support staff;

completing CIP records: 7% libraries used professionals only, 43% used support staff only, and 50% used both professional and support staff;

verifying member cataloging records: 21% libraries used professionals only, 29% used professionals with assistance from support staff, 7% used support staff only, and 43% used both professional and support staff;

cataloging without copy: 59% libraries used professionals only, 29% used professionals assisted by support staff for verification, none used support staff only, and 12% used both professional and support staff. **(760)**

Ibid. . . . *showed that* the following sources of cataloging copy were used in addition to OCLC (large libraries = 900,000 volumes or more; small libraries = less than 900,000 volumes):

National Union Catalog	100.0% large;	100.0% small libraries
Mansell	95.0% large;	97.0% small libraries
MCRS	13.2% large;	5.0% small libraries
MARCFICHE	8.5% large;	2.0% small libraries
other	0.0% large;	4.0% small libraries

(760)

Ibid. . . . *showed that* for OCLC member records the following items were verified (large libraries = 900,000 volumes or more; small libraries = under 900,000 volumes):

call number	79.0% large; 73.0% small libraries
choice and form of entry	71.6% large; 74.0% small libraries
added entries	73.2% large; 68.0% small libraries

continued

all of the above	70.0% large; 61.0% small libraries
none of the above	18.3% large; 20.0% small libraries

Further, the following treatment of subject headings in member records was reported by the following libraries:

subject headings verified as valid LC headings	70.0% large; 81.7% small libraries
subject headings checked for appropriateness	61.6% large; 67.0% small libraries
subject headings assigned if lacking	88.3% large; 90.0% small libraries
all of the above	56.6% large; 61.7% small libraries
none of the above	8.3% large; 1.0% small libraries

                                                                    (760)

■ A 1979-81 study at the University of Louisville (Ekstrom Library) involving pre-cataloging searching on the OCLC data base for monographic titles that had member input copy (090) or no copy at all (0) with several searches conducted over a period of 20.4 weeks [no N given for total number of items searched] *showed that* items for which LCIII copy (LC record input by member library) or 090E copy (2 records available, a record input by a member library and a DLC/DLC record for an edition of the work) was found during the first search were seldom upgraded by the time the second search was made. Of 773 books classified as LCIII's at the end of the first search, 92% (711) were still so classified when a second search was undertaken, while 94% of the 090E's remained unchanged at the time a second search was undertaken.   **(314)**

Ibid. . . . *showed that* over the 3-year study period a weekly first searching of an average of 62.5 books in the 090 category (member input copy) revealed that 10% of the books had LC copy, 8% had LCIII copy, and 13% had 090E copy, while 69% of the books were still designated 090; that a second search of these remaining 090 books (an average of 56.1 books per week) revealed that an additional 7% had LC copy, 1% had LCIII copy, and 2% had 090E copy, while 90% of the books were still designated 090; and that a third search of the remaining 090 books (an average of 55.3 books per week) revealed that an additional 14% of the books had LC copy and 1% had 090E copy, while 85% were still designated 090. All 3 searches were conducted within an average time period of 20.4 weeks.
                                                                    (314)

Ibid. . . . *showed that* over the 3-year study period a weekly first searching of an average of 42.6 books in the 0 category (no record available) revealed that 10% of the books had LC copy, 1% had LCIII copy, 5% had OE copy, while 48% of the books were still designated 0; that a second search of these remaining 0 books (an average of 20.4 books per week) revealed that an additional 5% had LC copy, 22% had 090 copy, 1% had OE copy, while 72% of the books were still designated 0; and that a third search of the remaining 0 books (an average of 14.9 books per week) revealed that an additional 5% had LC copy, 1% had LCIII copy, 2.5% had 090 copy, 1% had OE copy, while 75% were still designated 0. All 3 searches were conducted within an average time period of 20.4 weeks. **(314)**

Ibid. . . . *showed that* regardless of whether the first search was conducted 1 week after the book was received or 4 weeks after the book was received at least 85% of the books still had not received LC copy; that there was no real improvement in cataloging copy when the second search was conducted 7-8 weeks after the first search rather than 4-6 weeks after the first search; and that of 3 time differences between the second and third searches, 4-7 weeks, 8-14 weeks, or 14-17 weeks, the 8-14 week difference was the best. **(314)**

■ A study reported in 1983 of the cataloging records for music, music scores, and musical sound recordings over a 2-month period in 1980 from the Indiana University Music Library and the music cataloging unit of the University of Illinois-Urbana Library (996 cataloging records) *showed that* 213 different institutions were responsible for inputting the 996 cataloging records in the sample. LC MARC records accounted for 16% of the total, LC records input by OCLC member libraries accounted for 12%, public libraries accounted for 8%, ARL members (excluding Library of Congress) accounted for 34%, and other academic libraries accounted for 30%. **(757)**

Ibid. . . . *showed that* the Library of Congress played a much larger role in the cataloging of music books than in the cataloging of music materials or scores. For example, 58% of the book records were LC MARC records, while 11% of the book records were LC records input by OCLC members. In contrast, only 30% of the records for music materials were generated by LC, while 70% of the records were generated by OCLC member libraries. **(757)**

Special

■ A 1975 survey of North American medical school libraries concerning subject cataloging practices (survey size: 134 libraries; responding: 114 or 85%) *showed that*, of 78 respondents who used MeSH as the primary authority for subject headings and who also had divided catalogs, the following practices were followed when National Library of Medicine subject cataloging copy was available:

follow NLM with minor
   variations   55 (70%) libraries
follow NLM without exception   14 (18%) libraries
follow NLM with many changes   3 (4%) libraries
other   4 (5%) libraries
no response   2 (3%) libraries   **(712)**

■ A 1977 study at Cornell Law Library of 157 OCLC member records and 424 LC records in the OCLC data base *showed that* the average cataloging time per record for records with OCLC member cataloging copy was 9.076 minutes compared to 8.148 minutes cataloging time per record for records with LC cataloging copy.   **(367)**

Ibid. . . . *showed that* the average inputting time per record for records with OCLC member cataloging copy was 5.966 minutes compared to 4.498 minutes average inputting time per record for records with LC cataloging copy.   **(367)**

■ A 1977 study at Cornell Law Library of 301 cataloging records found in the OCLC data base (151 input by LC; 150 input by OCLC member libraries) *showed that* to make usable cataloging the LC records required an average of 1.13 modifications per record, while the OCLC member cataloging required an average of 2.97 modifications per record. When call number problems were ignored (which may pose unique problems to law cataloging in the LC schedules) the average number of LC modifications per record dropped to .78, while the average number of modifications per record for OCLC member cataloging dropped to 2.53.   **(367)**

■ A study reported in 1983 of the cataloging records for music, music scores, and musical sound recordings over a 2-month period in 1980 from the Indiana University Music Library and the music cataloging unit of the University of Illinois-Urbana Library (996 cataloging records) *showed that* 213 different institutions were responsible for inputting the 996 cataloging records in the sample. LC MARC records accounted for 16% of the total, LC records input by OCLC member libraries accounted for 12%, public libraries accounted for 8%, ARL members (excluding Library of Congress) accounted for 34%, and other academic libraries accounted for 30%.   **(757)**

Ibid. . . . *showed that* the Library of Congress played a much larger role in the cataloging of music books than in the cataloging of music materials or scores. For example, 58% of the book records were LC MARC records, while 11% of the book records were LC records input by OCLC members. In contrast, only 30% of the records for music materials were generated by LC, while 70% of the records were generated by OCLC member libraries.

(757)

Cataloging Copy—Additions and Corrections

Academic

■ A study reported in 1965 at 3 state college libraries and 1 campus of the state university concerning use made of the Library of Congress classification decisions (survey size: a total of 588 catalog cards from all 4 institutions) *showed that* for the 3 state colleges, the following changes were made in the 377 LC cards they received (only LC class numbers considered):

no change	65% of cards	
shelf number changed	16% of cards	
date or volume number changed or added	11% of cards	
class letters or number changed	6% of cards	
no number furnished on LC card	2% of cards	(583)

■ A 1975 survey of North American medical school libraries concerning subject cataloging practices (survey size: 134 libraries; responding: 114 or 85%) *showed that*, of 78 respondents who used MeSH as the primary authority for subject headings and who also had divided catalogs, the following practices were followed when National Library of Medicine subject cataloging copy was available:

follow NLM with minor variations	55 (70%) libraries	
follow NLM without exception	14 (18%) libraries	
follow NLM with many changes	3 (4%) libraries	
other	4 (5%) libraries	
no response	2 (3%) libraries	(712)

■ A 1977 study at Cornell Law Library of 301 cataloging records found in the OCLC data base (151 input by LC; 150 input by OCLC member libraries) *showed that* to make usable cataloging the LC records required an average of 1.13 modifications per record, while the OCLC member cataloging required an average of 2.97 modifications per record. When call number problems were ignored (which may pose unique problems to law cataloging in the LC schedules) the average number of LC modifications per record dropped to .78, while the average number of modifications per record for OCLC member cataloging dropped to 2.53.   **(367)**

■ A 1979 survey of academic libraries listed in the 1979 edition of *OCLC Participating Libraries Arranged by Network and Institution* (survey size: 200 libraries; responding: 166 or 83%) *showed that*, of 109 respondents, 137 (86.2%) reported that they always made substantial checks (i.e., checking "for more than typographical and tagging errors and completing the fixed field") in at least some types of non-LC records in the OCLC data base. Only 22 (13.8%) libraries reported that they never substantially checked non-LC records. The 3 most frequently checked types of non-LC records were:

all types	75 (68.8%) libraries
records from certain cataloging libraries	21 (19.3%) libraries
audiovisual materials	11 (10.1%) libraries **(764)**

Ibid. . . . *showed that*, of 158 respondents, the number of non-LC records that libraries reported changing, excluding Cataloging-in-Print copy, changes in the 049 field (local holdings), 590 field (local note), 910 field (user option data), and the 082/092 fields (Dewey call number), were as follows:

no records changed	2 (1.3%) libraries
1-9% records changed	28 (17.7%) libraries
10-24% records changed	38 (24.1%) libraries
25-49% records changed	30 (19.0%) libraries
50-74% records changed	35 (22.2%) libraries
75-99% records changed	22 (13.9%) libraries
100% records changed	3 (1.9%) libraries **(764)**

Ibid. . . . *showed that*, of 158 respondents, the number of LC records that libraries reported changing, excluding Cataloging-in-Print copy, changes in the 049 field (local holdings), 590 field (local note), 910 field (user option data), and the 082/092 fields (Dewey call number), were as follows:

no records changed	14 (8.9%) libraries
1-9% records changed	99 (62.7%) libraries

continued

10-24% records changed	32 (20.3%) libraries	
25-49% records changed	7 (4.4%) libraries	
50% or more records changed	6 (3.8%) libraries	**(764)**

■ A 1979 study at Memphis State University concerning errors in the OCLC data base and based on all error reports generated at Memphis State over a 2-month period (175 error reports) *showed that*, of the 993 member library records used for cataloging during the test period, 136 (13.7%) contained errors, while of the 2,435 MARC records used for cataloging during this same period, only 39 (1.6%) contained errors.

(765)

Ibid. . . . *showed that*, of 93 indexing errors found in OCLC member records, the 4 most frequently reported were: ISBN for monographs (31 errors), LCCN for monographs (22 errors), uniform title for [music] scores (17 errors), and title for [music] scores (10 errors). Of 20 indexing errors found in OCLC MARC records, the most common was ISBN for monographs (19 errors).

(765)

Ibid. . . . *showed that* the cost (labor only) of reporting the 175 OCLC data base errors was $184.07 for 175 error reports.

(765)

■ A study reported in 1983 of the cataloging records for music, music scores, and musical sound recordings over a 2-month period in 1980 from the Indiana University Music Library and the music cataloging unit of the University of Illinois-Urbana Library (996 cataloging records) *showed that* the number of corrections and changes that had to be made in the OCLC record showed wide variation by format. The average book required 6.1 changes per record, the average score required 10.5 changes per record, and the average sound recording required 15.9 changes per record.

(757)

Ibid. . . . *showed that* most of the changes required were in the control data of the OCLC records (control data elements are represented in the MARC record by the 0XX fields and are generally more important for use in an online catalog than in card production). Specifically, 79% of the changes required in book records, 71% of the changes required by scores, and 54% of the changes required by sound recordings were control data elements.   **(757)**

Ibid. . . . *showed that* fewer changes were required for cataloging records generated by the Library of Congress than for cataloging records generated by OCLC members. For example, books required an average of 5.5 changes per record for LC cataloging compared to an average of 11.8 changes per record for OCLC members' cataloging.   **(757)**

Special

■ A 1975 survey of North American medical school libraries concerning subject cataloging practices (survey size: 134 libraries; responding: 114 or 85%) *showed that*, of 78 respondents who used MeSH as the primary authority for subject headings and who also had divided catalogs, the following practices were followed when National Library of Medicine subject cataloging copy was available:

follow NLM with minor variations	55 (70%) libraries
follow NLM without exception	14 (18%) libraries
follow NLM with many changes	3 (4%) libraries
other	4 (5%) libraries
no response	2 (3%) libraries **(712)**

■ A 1977 study at Cornell Law Library of 301 cataloging records found in the OCLC data base (151 input by LC; 150 input by OCLC member libraries) *showed that* to make usable cataloging the LC records required an average of 1.13 modifications per record, while the OCLC member cataloging required an average of 2.97 modifications per record. When call number problems were ignored (which may pose unique problems to law cataloging in the LC schedules) the average number of LC modifications per record dropped to .78, while the average number of modifications per record for OCLC member cataloging dropped to 2.53.   **(367)**

■ A study reported in 1983 of the cataloging records for music, music scores, and musical sound recordings over a 2-month period in 1980 from the Indiana University Music Library and the music cataloging unit of the University of Illinois-Urbana Library (996 cataloging records) *showed that* the number of corrections and changes that had to be made in the OCLC record showed wide variation by format. The average book required 6.1 changes per record, the average score required 10.5 changes per record,

and the average sound recording required 15.9 changes per record.
                                                                    (757)

Ibid. . . . *showed that* most of the changes required were in the control
data of the OCLC records (control data elements are represented in the
MARC record by the 0XX fields and are generally more important for use
in an online catalog than in card production). Specifically, 79% of the
changes required in book records, 71% of the changes required by scores,
and 54% of the changes required by sound recordings were control data
elements.   **(757)**

Ibid. . . . *showed that* fewer changes were required for cataloging records
generated by the Library of Congress than for cataloging records generated by OCLC members. For example, books required an average of 5.5
changes per record for LC cataloging compared to an average of 11.8
changes per record for OCLC members' cataloging.   **(757)**

Cataloging Copy—Hit Rate

General

■ A 1977 study comparing the use of the Blackwell North America and
OCLC data bases as sources of cataloging copy for 344 English-language
imprints received on the B/NA approval program during a 3-month period
[library not reported] *showed that*, after 2 searches about 2 months apart,
247 (72%) of the items were found in the B/NA data base and 315 (92%)
were found in the OCLC data base. Further, 232 (67%) were located in
both data bases, while 14 (4.1%) were located in neither data base. Neither
place nor date of publication affected the hit rate.   **(448)**

■ A study reported in 1981, of 45 monographs in microform format
(randomly selected from the 1979 *Microforms in Print*) searched in RLIN,
OCLC, and the *National Union Catalog*, *showed that*:

> exact copy was found for 17.7% of the microform items
> searched of which 4.4% was Library of Congress cataloging
> and 13.3% was shared cataloging;

> variant copy was found for 22.3% of the microform items
> searched of which 6.7% was Library of Congress cataloging
> and 15.6% was shared cataloging;

> exact copy was found for 55.5% of the hard copy editions of

the items of which 31.1% was Library of Congress cataloging and 24.4% was shared cataloging;

variant copy was found for 17.7% of the hard copy editions of the 45 items of which 13.3% was Library of Congress cataloging and 4.4% was shared cataloging.   **(768)**

Ibid. . . . *showed that*, of the exact copy that was found for 17.7% of the microforms, RLIN provided no exact matches, OCLC provided 11.1% of the matches (all shared cataloging), and the *National Union Catalog* provided 8.8% of the matches (evenly divided between LC and shared cataloging).   **(768)**

■   A study reported in 1981 of OCLC's online union catalog to investigate the scope of its music holdings by checking 4 major lists of materials ("Books Recently Published" column of *Notes*; "Music Received" column of *Notes*; "New Listings" column of the *Schwann-1 Record and Tape Guide*; and *A Basic Music Library: Essential Scores and Books*) in the catalog, *showed that*, of the 317 books listed in the December 1979 "Books Recently Published" column and searched 1 year later, 312 (98.42%) were found in the OCLC union catalog, while, of the 287 books listed in the September 1980 "Books Recently Published" column and searched 7 months later, 272 (94.78%) were found in the OCLC union catalog.
                                                                                                                        (757)

Ibid. . . . *showed that*, of the 420 items listed in the December 1979 "Music Received" column and searched 1 year later, 255 (60.71%) were found in the OCLC union catalog, while, of the 351 items listed in the September 1980 "Music Received" column and searched 1-2 months later, 109 (31.05%) were found in the OCLC union catalog.   **(757)**

Ibid. . . . *showed that*, of the 276 items listed in the December 1979 "New Listings" column and searched 14 months later, 162 (58.7%) were found in the OCLC union catalog, while, of the 282 items listed in the September 1980 "New Listings" column and searched 1-2 months later, 64 (22.7%) were found in the OCLC union catalog.   **(757)**

Ibid. . . . *showed that*, of the 941 items listed in *A Basic Music Library*, 861 (91.5%) were found, including 231 (94.29%) of the study scores, 195 (96.53%) of the performing editions, and 114 (82.01%) of the instrumental methods and studies. Further, "a large number of specific editions not found in the search" were represented in the OCLC union catalog by other editions.   **(757)**

CIP

Academic

■ A 1976 study of CIP entries (those found on the verso of the title page, not those appearing on MARC tapes) for every title acquired by Perkins Library at Duke University for a period of just over a month (sample size: 620 titles; usable: 610 titles) *showed that* 417 titles (68.36%) had at least 1 item that differed when CIP was compared to final LC copy. Statistically one could generalize to the population with a 95% probability that the actual difference between CIP entry and LC final copy lay between 64.67% and 72.05%.   **(233)**

Ibid. . . . *showed that* 193 (31.64%) titles had no difference between CIP and LC final copy; 225 (36.89%) had one difference; and 192 (31.47%) had 2 or more differences.   **(233)**

Ibid. . . . *showed that* materials with a 1973 imprint had 53.33% of their titles with differences between CIP and LC final copy; 1974 imprints had 67.65% of their titles with differences; 1975 had 69.14% of their titles with differences; 1976 had 68.47% of their titles with differences.   **(233)**

Ibid. . . . *showed that* 3 areas accounted for almost half (49.19%) of the total differences (744) noted between CIP and LC final copy. Bibliography notes had 173 (23.25%) differences involving 38.36% of the titles; index notes had 114 (15.32%) differences involving 18.69% of the titles; and LC call numbers had 79 (10.62%) differences involving 12.95% of the titles.   **(233)**

Ibid. . . . *showed that* 207 (27.8%) of the 744 differences noted between CIP and final LC copy (involving 147 or 24.1% of the titles) were considered to be substantial, i.e., form of personal name different, wording of title different, wording of subject tracings different, etc. **(233)**

Classification—General Issues

General

■ A 1969 study of professionals in various kinds of North American libraries as well as instructors of technical and reader services in accredited library schools (survey size: 244; responding: 152 or 62.3%) concerning the role and importance of classifying library materials *showed that* library professionals generally rejected the following propositions:

> effective library classification reflected the "true" order of science and nature (66.2% did not agree);
>
> evidence of classification enhanced librarians' professional status among patrons (67.1% did not agree);
>
> close shelf classification had a pedagogical rationale (88.5% did not agree).   **(597)**

Ibid. . . . *showed that* there was relatively strong support for the general idea of open-shelf access and browsing as evidenced by support for the following ideas:

> all readers should be encouraged to browse (77.7% agreed);
>
> browsing provided a valuable learning experience (81.2% agreed);
>
> shelf classification was necessary for browsing (78.4% agreed).

Further, there was strong rejection (89.2%) of the idea of "exclusively bibliographical" access to the collection.   **(597)**

Ibid. . . . *showed that* there was strong agreement with the idea that "serendipity" ("making desirable but unsought for discoveries") was a major value of browsing (89.9% agreed). Further, "almost three-fourths" of the respondents agreed that shelf classification made serendipitous discoveries more likely.   **(597)**

Ibid. . . . *showed that* there was some ambivalence concerning the role of shelf classification in subject searching:

> 58.8% agreed that shelf classification was "more important as a locational device than as a means of systematic subject approach";
>
> 58.0% agreed that subject headings in the catalog were more useful to the patron than shelf classification;
>
> 42.7% agreed that the average patron could not "follow" close classification notation on the shelves.   **(597)**

■ A study reported in 1982 comparing the 780 section (music schedule) of the 19th edition of Dewey to a proposed revision of that section "originating with the Library Association (United Kingdom) in 1973 and prepared in Great Britain under the supervision of Russell Sweeney and

John Clews at the Leeds Polytechnic Institute," based on how each organized a random sample of 400 ensemble music scores selected from the 1973-78 editions of the *British Catalogue of Music, showed that* when each system of classification was compared to an ideal performance-oriented arrangement of materials the proposed revision was a better arrangement than the arrangement given by Dewey 19 although the difference was not statistically significant. Specifically, the number of matches between the ideal arrangement and Dewey 19 was 152 out of 400, while the number of matches between the proposed revision and the ideal arrangement was 164 out of 400. **(771)**

Classification—Cutter

Public

■ A survey reported in 1976 of 67 American, Canadian, and British libraries that had been identified at some point as using the Cutter classification scheme *showed that* only 12 libraries still continued to use the Cutter scheme to classify the majority of their new acquisitions. These libraries were all located in North America and included 4 tax-supported public libraries, 4 subscription or proprietary libraries, and 4 governmental or special libraries. None of the libraries contained over 100,000 volumes. **(638)**

Special

■ A survey reported in 1976 of 67 American, Canadian, and British libraries that had been identified at some point as using the Cutter classification scheme *showed that* only 12 libraries still continued to use the Cutter scheme to classify the majority of their new acquisitions. These libraries were all located in North America and included 4 tax-supported public libraries, 4 subscription or proprietary libraries, and 4 governmental or special libraries. None of the libraries contained over 100,000 volumes. **(638)**

Classification—Dewey

General

■ A study reported in 1970 of the "Summaries of Annual Reports, Processing Department, Decimal Classification Division" in the *Library of Congress Information Bulletin showed that* during the period 1931-39 the number of Library of Congress cards with Dewey Decimal numbers on them was 88%. This number declined in subsequent years to a low of 24%

in 1965-66 and returned to 49% in 1967-68.   **(591)**

■ A study reported in 1979 of MARC tapes for the years 1969-70, 1974-75, 1975-76, 1976-77, and 1977-78 *showed that* beginning with 1974-75 Dewey numbers appeared in 96.6% of the records for that year, in 90.4% of the records for the next year, in 83.4% of the records for the following year, and in 69.3% of the records for the last year.   **(347)**

Ibid. . . . *showed that* if the Dewey numbers were divided into groups of 10 (e.g., 300-309, 310-319, etc.) the 8 groups with the consistently highest percentage of Dewey class numbers during the period 1974 through 1978 were: 300, 330, 340, 370, 610, 620, 810, and 820.   **(347)**

■ A survey reported in 1981 of chief administrators of U.S. theater collections concerning methods of cataloging nonbook theatrical memorabilia (survey size: 40 libraries; responding: 26; usable: 25 or 62.5%) *showed that*, whereas an earlier study had reported that 92% of the libraries surveyed in 1939 classified their materials with a specially designed system, only 8 (33%) did so in the present survey. Specifically, the classification schemes used by 24 libraries were as follows:

own original system	5 (20.8%) libraries
own original system in conjunction with LC system	3 (12.5%) libraries
LC classification system	5 (20.8%) libraries
modified LC	3 (12.5%) libraries
Dewey	3 (12.5%) libraries
modified Dewey	1 (4.2%) libraries
LC and Dewey or modified Dewey	4 (16.7%) libraries **(769)**

■ A study reported in 1982 comparing the 780 section (music schedule) of the 19th edition of Dewey to a proposed revision of that section "originating with the Library Association (United Kingdom) in 1973 and prepared in Great Britain under the supervision of Russell Sweeney and John Clews at the Leeds Polytechnic Institute," based on how each organized a random sample of 400 ensemble music scores selected from the 1973-78 editions of the *British Catalogue of Music, showed that* when each system of classification was compared to an ideal performance-oriented arrangement of materials the proposed revision was a better arrangement than the arrangement given by Dewey 19 although the difference was not statistically significant. Specifically, the number of matches between the ideal arrangement and Dewey 19 was 152 out of 400, while the number of matches between the proposed revision and the ideal arrangement was 164 out of 400. **(771)**

Academic

■ A survey reported in 1968 of all junior colleges (sample: 837; responding: 690 or 82%) concerning their use of classification systems *showed that* 532 (77.1%) used Dewey, 92 (13.3%) used LC, 58 (8.4%) were changing from Dewey to LC, 4 (0.6%) were planning on changing from Dewey to LC, and 4 (0.6%) used other classification schemes. **(185)**

■ A 1972 survey of U.S. academic and special law libraries (sample size: 46; responding: 32 or 69.6%) concerning their foreign and international law collections *showed that* the following classification systems were used for foreign law collections:

own system, alphabetical arrangment, or unclassified	16 (50.0%) respondents
Hicks (or modified Hicks)	5 (15.6%) respondents
Los Angeles County	3 (9.4%) respondents
Schiller	3 (9.4%) respondents
Stanford	2 (6.3%) respondents
Elizabeth Benyon Class K	2 (6.3%) respondents
Dewey	1 (3.1%) respondents

(532)

■ A study reported in 1972 of college and university libraries that reported "other" when asked if they used Library of Congress or Dewey classification in an earlier survey (Bronson Price's *Library Statistics of Colleges and Universities: Data for Individual Institutions*, Fall 1967) (survey size: 174 libraries that reported "other"; responding: 149 or 85.6%) *showed that* the breakdown of the "other" category was as follows:

a combination of LC and Dewey	54 (36%) libraries
another system	44 (30%) libraries
LC and another system	18 (12%) libraries
erroneous listings (7 used LC; 9 Dewey)	16 (11%) libraries

continued

Dewey and another system   11 (7%) libraries
LC, Dewey, and another system   6 (4%) libraries

This amended the original survey (based on 2,167 academic institutions) by increasing the number of libraries using LC only or in part from 508 (23.4%) to at least 593 (27.4%). The original survey reported classification systems as follows:

use of LC	508 (23.4%)	libraries
use of Dewey	1,480 (68.4%)	libraries
other	174 (8.0%)	libraries
no response	5 (0.2%)	libraries **(598)**

■ A 1972 survey of chief library administrators in public comprehensive community colleges (population: 586; usable responses: 75.9% [no raw number given]) *showed that* 56.4% of the respondents reported their holdings organized according to Library of Congress classification and 42.9% reported Dewey Decimal. Audiovisual materials were often reported as organized by many different local schemes, although 22.5% of the respondents reported using LC classification and 21.5% reported using Dewey Decimal.   **(452)**

■ A survey reported in 1977 concerning university libraries' handling of doctoral and master's theses generated locally, based on a stratified sample of universities offering the doctoral degree (survey size: 100; responding: 90 or 90%), *showed that* of 85 respondents the classification schemes used were as follows: Library of Congress (43 or 50.6% libraries), local scheme (38 or 44.7% libraries), and Dewey Decimal (4 or 4.7% libraries).   **(639)**

■ A 1977 survey of academic libraries with collections of 300,000 volumes or more that were also OCLC members concerning cataloging practices (survey size: 147 libraries; responding: 121 or 82.3%) *showed that*, of the libraries with 900,000 volumes or more, 96% used LC classification, while 4% used Dewey classification; of the libraries with less than 900,000 volumes, 85% used LC classification, while 13% used Dewey classification [the remaining libraries may be accounted for by a combination of Dewey and LC].   **(760)**

■ A 1979 survey of U.S. community college libraries selected from the 1978 *Community, Junior and Technical College Directory* (sample size: 98; responding: 52; usable: 48 or 48.98%) *showed that* 23 (47.92%) libraries used Dewey Decimal classification for monographs, while 25 (52.08%)

libraries used Library of Congress classification. **(498)**

Ibid. . . . *showed that*, for audiovisual materials (multiple systems used in some cases), 13 (25.00%) libraries used Dewey Decimal classification, 11 (21.15%) libraries used Library of Congress classification, 10 (19.23%) libraries used accession number schemes, 14 (26.92%) libraries used format and accession number schemes, and 4 (7.69%) used some other scheme. **(498)**

■ A study reported in 1981 at Purdue University of the degree to which books in 5 different subject areas, as determined by reviews and bibliographies in the disciplines, were actually classed in those areas by Dewey and LC cataloging [source of cataloging not given] (anthropology: 254 books; history: 352 books; political science: 534 books; sociology: 602 books; and philosophy: 265 books) *showed that* a shelflist count [based on class numbers] would have missed between 30-80% of the titles in the 5 disciplines. **(574)**

Ibid. . . . *showed that* the number of titles in each of the disciplines not reflected by an appropriate Dewey class number was as follows:

anthropology	204 (80.3%)	not in class
history	241 (68.5%)	not in class
sociology	390 (64.7%)	not in class
philosophy	58 (35.2%)	not in class
political science	167 (31.3%)	not in class	**(574)**

Special

■ A 1972 survey of U.S. academic and special law libraries (sample size: 46; responding: 32 or 69.6%) concerning their foreign and international law collections *showed that* the following classification systems were used for foreign law collections:

own system, alphabetical arrangment, or unclassified	16 (50.0%)	respondents
Hicks (or modified Hicks)	5 (15.6%)	respondents
Los Angeles County	3 (9.4%)	respondents
Schiller	3 (9.4%)	respondents
Stanford	2 (6.3%)	respondents
Elizabeth Benyon Class K	2 (6.3%)	respondents
Dewey	1 (3.1%)	respondents

(532)

Classification—Library of Congress

General

■ A survey reported in 1981 of chief administrators of U.S. theater collections concerning methods of cataloging nonbook theatrical memorabilia (survey size: 40 libraries; responding: 26; usable: 25 or 62.5%) *showed that*, whereas an earlier study had reported that 92% of the libraries surveyed in 1939 classified their materials with a specially designed system, only 8 (33%) did so in the present survey. Specifically, the classification schemes used by 24 libraries were as follows:

own original system	5 (20.8%) libraries	
own original system in conjunction with LC system	3 (12.5%) libraries	
LC classification system	5 (20.8%) libraries	
modified LC	3 (12.5%) libraries	
Dewey	3 (12.5%) libraries	
modified Dewey	1 (4.2%) libraries	
LC and Dewey or modified Dewey	4 (16.7%) libraries	**(769)**

Academic

■ A study reported in 1965 at 3 state college libraries and 1 campus of the state university concerning use made of the Library of Congress classification decisions (survey size: a total of 588 catalog cards from all 4 institutions) *showed that* the 3 state colleges together had an average of 84% of their catalog cards based on LC cards received (with the remaining average of 16% resulting from original cataloging), while the state university had 71% of its cards based on LC cards (with the remaining average of 29% resulting from original cataloging). The state college figures were accurate ±3.5% at the 95% confidence level while the state university figure was accurate ±8% at the 95% confidence level.   **(583)**

Ibid. . . . *showed that*, for the 3 state colleges, the following changes were made in the 377 LC cards they received (only LC class numbers considered):

no change	65% of cards	
shelf number changed	16% of cards	
date or volume number changed or added	11% of cards	
class letters or number changed	6% of cards	
no number furnished on LC card	2% of cards	**(583)**

■ A 1967 survey by the Institute of Higher Education at Teachers College, Columbia University of innovative programs in libraries in academic institutions with liberal arts programs (sample size: 1,193; responding: 781 or 65%) *showed that* the main innovative change in administrative practices was adoption of LC classification. 336 libraries (43%) used LC classification with 243 (31%) having used it since 1961. A further 79 libraries (10%) were planning to adopt it at the time of the study.   **(190)**

■ A survey reported in 1968 of all junior colleges (sample: 837; responding: 690 or 82%) concerning their use of classification systems *showed that* 532 (77.1%) used Dewey, 92 (13.3%) used LC, 58 (8.4%) were changing from Dewey to LC, 4 (0.6%) were planning on changing from Dewey to LC, and 4 (0.6%) used other classification schemes.   **(185)**

■ A 1972 survey of U.S. academic and special law libraries (sample size: 46; responding: 32 or 69.6%) concerning their foreign and international law collections *showed that* the following classification systems were used for international law collections:

Library of Congress Class JX	14 (43.8%) respondents
own system, alphabetical arrangement, or unclassified	9 (28.1%) respondents
Schwerin	3 (9.4%) respondents
Los Angeles County	2 (6.3%) respondents
Stanford	2 (6.3%) respondents
modified Hicks	2 (6.3%) respondents

                                                                          (532)

■ A study reported in 1972 of college and university libraries that reported "other" when asked if they used Library of Congress or Dewey classification in an earlier survey (Bronson Price's *Library Statistics of Colleges and Universities: Data for Individual Institutions*, Fall 1967) (survey size: 174 libraries that reported "other"; responding: 149 or 85.6%) *showed that* the breakdown of the "other" category was as follows:

a combination of LC and Dewey	54 (36%) libraries
another system	44 (30%) libraries
LC and another system	18 (12%) libraries
erroneous listings (7 used LC; 9 Dewey)	16 (11%) libraries
Dewey and another system	11 (7%) libraries
LC, Dewey, and another system	6 (4%) libraries

This amended the original survey (based on 2,167 academic institutions) by increasing the number of libraries using LC only or in part from 508 (23.4%) to at least 593 (27.4%). The original survey reported classification systems as follows:

use of LC	508 (23.4%)	libraries
use of Dewey	1,480 (68.4%)	libraries
other	174 (8.0%)	libraries
no response	5 (0.2%)	libraries **(598)**

■ A 1972 survey of chief library administrators in public comprehensive community colleges (population: 586; usable responses: 75.9% [no raw number given]) *showed that* 56.4% of the respondents reported their holdings organized according to Library of Congress classification and 42.9% reported Dewey Decimal. Audiovisual materials were often reported as organized by many different local schemes, although 22.5% of the respondents reported using LC classification and 21.5% reported using Dewey Decimal. **(452)**

■ A survey reported in 1977 concerning university libraries' handling of doctoral and master's theses generated locally, based on a stratified sample of universities offering the doctoral degree (survey size: 100; responding: 90 or 90%), *showed that* of 85 respondents the classification schemes used were as follows: Library of Congress (43 or 50.6% libraries), local scheme (38 or 44.7% libraries), and Dewey Decimal (4 or 4.7% libraries). **(639)**

■ A 1977 survey of U.S. law libraries over 10,000 volumes taken from the 1976 *Directory of Law Libraries* (sample size: 1,080; responding: 373 or 35%) *showed that* of 123 academic law libraries and 250 other law libraries use of Library of Congress classification was highest among academic law libraries (84% compared to 34% in all other types of law libraries combined). Of the law libraries that use LC classification 72% of the academic law libraries used it without substantial modification compared to 25% of the remaining law libraries. **(366)**

■ A 1977 survey of academic libraries with collections of 300,000 volumes or more that were also OCLC members concerning cataloging practices (survey size: 147 libraries; responding: 121 or 82.3%) *showed that*, of the libraries with 900,000 volumes or more, 96% used LC classification while

4% used Dewey classification; of the libraries with less than 900,000 volumes, 85% used LC classification while 13% used Dewey classification [the remaining libraries may be accounted for by a combination of Dewey and LC]. **(760)**

Ibid. . . . *showed that,* when cataloging copy was not available, 95% of the larger (900,000 volumes or more) libraries and 84% of the smaller (under 900,000 volumes) libraries followed LC practice when assigning call numbers and establishing the form of name headings, subject headings, and series entries. However, "one-third" of the larger libraries and "one-half" of the smaller libraries that followed LC practice used a local call number system for some materials. These were generally microforms, juvenile literature, and theses. **(760)**

■ A 1979 survey of U.S. community college libraries selected from the 1978 *Community, Junior and Technical College Directory* (sample size: 98; responding: 52; usable: 48 or 48.98%) *showed that* 23 (47.92%) libraries used Dewey Decimal classification for monographs, while 25 (52.08%) libraries used Library of Congress classification. **(498)**

Ibid. . . . *showed that,* for audiovisual materials (multiple systems used in some cases), 13 (25.00%) libraries used Dewey Decimal classification, 11 (21.15%) libraries used Library of Congress classification, 10 (19.23%) libraries used accession number schemes, 14 (26.92%) libraries used format and accession number schemes, and 4 (7.69%) used some other scheme. **(498)**

■ A 1980 survey of law school libraries with collections in excess of 175,000 volumes (sample size: 50; responding: 37 or 70%) *showed that* 17 libraries reported using LC classification schedules; 12 libraries reported using LC along with some other system such as SuDocs, UN, Yale, or Bassett; and 8 libraries reported making no use of LC ("most of these [using] some variation of a local system"). 79% of the responding libraries use LC exclusively or in part as their classification scheme. **(369)**

■ A study reported in 1981 at Purdue University of the degree to which books in 5 different subject areas, as determined by reviews and bibliographies in the disciplines, were actually classed in those areas by Dewey and LC cataloging [source of cataloging not given] (anthropology: 254 books; history: 352 books; political science: 534 books; sociology: 602 books; and philosophy: 265 books) *showed that* a shelflist count [based on class numbers] would have missed between 30-80% of the titles in the 5 disciplines.   **(574)**

Special

■ A 1972 survey of U.S. academic and special law libraries (sample size: 46; responding: 32 or 69.6%) concerning their foreign and international law collections *showed that* the following classification systems were used for international law collections:

Library of Congress Class JX	14 (43.8%) respondents
own system, alphabetical arrangement, or unclassified	9 (28.1%) respondents
Schwerin	3 (9.4%) respondents
Los Angeles County	2 (6.3%) respondents
Stanford	2 (6.3%) respondents
modified Hicks	2 (6.3%) respondents

(532)

■ A 1977 survey of U.S. law libraries over 10,000 volumes taken from the 1976 *Directory of Law Libraries* (sample size: 1,080; responding: 373 or 35%) *showed that* of 123 academic law libraries and 250 other law libraries use of Library of Congress classification was highest among academic law libraries (84% compared to 34% in all other types of law libraries combined). Of the law libraries that use LC classification 72% of the academic law libraries used it without substantial modification compared to 25% of the remaining law libraries.   **(366)**

■ A 1980 survey of law school libraries with collections in excess of 175,000 volumes (sample size: 50; responding: 37 or 70%) *showed that* 17 libraries reported using LC classification schedules; 12 libraries reported using LC along with some other system such as SuDocs, UN, Yale, or Bassett; and 8 libraries reported making no use of LC ("most of these [using] some variation of a local system"). 79% of the responding libraries use LC exclusively or in part as their classification scheme.   **(369)**

Classification—Multiple Schemes

General

■ A study reported in 1974 of classification systems used in 941 libraries as reported in a series of U.S. national and regional medical publications as well as an international survey conducted by Dave Remington of 470 health science libraries *showed that*, while 239 British medical libraries used 82 different classification systems in 1969, 447 [U.S.] Medical Library Association libraries used only 26 classification systems in 1973.   **(701)**

Ibid. . . . *showed that* the 7 most frequently used classification systems in Medical Library Association libraries (excluding VA Hospital libraries) were as follows:

National Library of Medicine	158 (35.3%)	libraries
Library of Congress	85 (19.0%)	libraries
Boston Medical	79 (17.7%)	libraries
Dewey Decimal	69 (15.4%)	libraries
Cunningham	35 (7.8%)	libraries
own or "special" system	12 (2.7%)	libraries
Black's Classification for		
Dental Literature	9 (2.0%)	libraries **(701)**

■ A survey reported in 1981 of chief administrators of U.S. theater collections concerning methods of cataloging nonbook theatrical memorabilia (survey size: 40 libraries; responding: 26; usable: 25 or 62.5%) *showed that*, whereas an earlier study had reported that 92% of the libraries surveyed in 1939 classified their materials with a specially designed system, only 8 (33%) did so in the present survey. Specifically, the classification schemes used by 24 libraries were as follows:

own original system	5 (20.8%)	libraries
own original system in conjunction with LC system	3 (12.5%)	libraries
LC classification system	5 (20.8%)	libraries
modified LC	3 (12.5%)	libraries
Dewey	3 (12.5%)	libraries
modified Dewey	1 (4.2%)	libraries
LC and Dewey or modified Dewey	4 (16.7%)	libraries **(769)**

Academic

■ A survey reported in 1968 of all junior colleges (sample: 837; responding: 690 or 82%) concerning their use of classification systems *showed that* 532 (77.1%) used Dewey, 92 (13.3%) used LC, 58 (8.4%) were changing from Dewey to LC, 4 (0.6%) were planning on changing from Dewey to LC, and 4 (0.6%) used other classification schemes.   **(185)**

■ A study reported in 1972 of college and university libraries that reported "other" when asked if they used Library of Congress or Dewey classification in an earlier survey (Bronson Price's *Library Statistics of Colleges and Universities: Data for Individual Institutions*, Fall 1967) (survey size: 174 libraries that reported "other"; responding: 149 or 85.6%) *showed that* the breakdown of the "other" category was as follows:

a combination of LC and Dewey	54 (36%) libraries
another system	44 (30%) libraries
LC and another system	18 (12%) libraries
erroneous listings (7 used LC; 9 Dewey)	16 (11%) libraries
Dewey and another system	11 (7%) libraries
LC, Dewey and another system	6 (4%) libraries

This amended the original survey (based on 2,167 academic institutions) by increasing the number of libraries using LC only or in part from 508 (23.4%) to at least 593 (27.4%). The original survey reported classification systems as follows:

use of LC	508 (23.4%)	libraries
use of Dewey	1,480 (68.4%)	libraries
other	174 (8.0%)	libraries
no response	5 (0.2%)	libraries **(598)**

■ A 1972 survey of U.S. academic and special law libraries (sample size: 46; responding: 32 or 69.6%) concerning their foreign and international law collections *showed that* the following classification systems were used for foreign law collections:

own system, alphabetical arrangment, or unclassified	16 (50.0%) respondents
Hicks (or modified Hicks)	5 (15.6%) respondents
Los Angeles County	3 (9.4%) respondents
Schiller	3 (9.4%) respondents
Stanford	2 (6.3%) respondents
Elizabeth Benyon Class K	2 (6.3%) respondents
Dewey	1 (3.1%) respondents **(532)**

Ibid. . . . *showed that* the following classification systems were used for international law collections:

Library of Congress Class JX	14 (43.8%) respondents
own system, alphabetical arrangement, or unclassified	9 (28.1%) respondents

continued

Schwerin	3 (9.4%) respondents
Los Angeles County	2 (6.3%) respondents
Stanford	2 (6.3%) respondents
modified Hicks	2 (6.3%) respondents

(532)

■ A 1972 survey of chief library administrators in public comprehensive community colleges (population: 586; usable responses: 75.9% [no raw number given]) *showed that* 56.4% of the respondents reported their holdings organized according to Library of Congress classification and 42.9% reported Dewey Decimal. Audiovisual materials were often reported as organized by many different local schemes, although 22.5% of the respondents reported using LC classification and 21.5% reported using Dewey Decimal. **(452)**

■ A survey reported in 1977 concerning university libraries' handling of doctoral and master's theses generated locally, based on a stratified sample of universities offering the doctoral degree (survey size: 100; responding: 90 or 90%), *showed that* of 85 respondents the classification schemes used were as follows: Library of Congress (43 or 50.6% libraries), local scheme (38 or 44.7% libraries), and Dewey Decimal (4 or 4.7% libraries). **(639)**

■ A 1977 survey of academic libraries with collections of 300,000 volumes or more that were also OCLC members concerning cataloging practices (survey size: 147 libraries; responding: 121 or 82.3%) *showed that*, of the libraries with 900,000 volumes or more, 96% used LC classification while 4% used Dewey classification; of the libraries with less than 900,000 volumes, 85% used LC classification while 13% used Dewey classification [the remaining libraries may be accounted for by a combination of Dewey and LC]. **(760)**

■ A 1979 survey of U.S. community college libraries selected from the 1978 *Community, Junior and Technical College Directory* (sample size: 98; responding: 52; usable: 48 or 48.98%) *showed that* 23 (47.92%) libraries used Dewey Decimal classification for monographs, while 25 (52.08%) libraries used Library of Congress classification. **(498)**

Ibid. . . . *showed that*, for audiovisual materials (multiple systems used in some cases), 13 (25.00%) libraries used Dewey Decimal classification, 11 (21.15%) libraries used Library of Congress classification, 10 (19.23%)

libraries used accession number schemes, 14 (26.92%) libraries used format and accession number schemes, and 4 (7.69%) used some other scheme.   **(498)**

■ A 1980 survey of law school libraries with collections in excess of 175,000 volumes (sample size: 50; responding: 37 or 70%) *showed that* 17 libraries reported using LC classification schedules; 12 libraries reported using LC along with some other system such as SuDocs, UN, Yale, or Bassett; and 8 libraries reported making no use of LC ("most of these [using] some variation of a local system"). 79% of the responding libraries use LC exclusively or in part as their classification scheme.   **(369)**

■ A study reported in 1981 at Purdue University of the degree to which books in 5 different subject areas, as determined by reviews and bibliographies in the disciplines, were actually classed in those areas by Dewey and LC cataloging [source of cataloging not given] (anthropology: 254 books; history: 352 books; political science: 534 books; sociology: 602 books; and philosophy: 265 books) *showed that* a shelflist count [based on class numbers] would have missed between 30-80% of the titles in the 5 disciplines.   **(574)**

Ibid. . . . *showed that* the number of titles in each of the disciplines not reflected by an appropriate Dewey class number was as follows:

anthropology	204 (80.3%) not in class
history	241 (68.5%) not in class
sociology	390 (64.7%) not in class
philosophy	58 (35.2%) not in class
political science	167 (31.3%) not in class **(574)**

Special

■ A 1972 survey of U.S. academic and special law libraries (sample size: 46; responding: 32 or 69.6%) concerning their foreign and international law collections *showed that* the following classification systems were used for foreign law collections:

own system, alphabetical arrangment, or unclassified	16 (50.0%) respondents
Hicks (or modified Hicks)	5 (15.6%) respondents
Los Angeles County	3 (9.4%) respondents
Schiller	3 (9.4%) respondents
Stanford	2 (6.3%) respondents
Elizabeth Benyon Class K	2 (6.3%) respondents
Dewey	1 (3.1%) respondents

                                                                              (532)

Ibid. . . . *showed that* the following classification systems were used for international law collections:

Library of Congress Class JX	14 (43.8%) respondents
own system, alphabetical arrangement, or unclassified	9 (28.1%) respondents
Schwerin	3 (9.4%) respondents
Los Angeles County	2 (6.3%) respondents
Stanford	2 (6.3%) respondents
modified Hicks	2 (6.3%) respondents

(532)

■ A 1980 survey of law school libraries with collections in excess of 175,000 volumes (sample size: 50; responding: 37 or 70%) *showed that* 17 libraries reported using LC classification schedules; 12 libraries reported using LC along with some other system such as SuDocs, UN, Yale, or Bassett; and 8 libraries reported making no use of LC ("most of these [using] some variation of a local system"). 79% of the responding libraries use LC exclusively or in part as their classification scheme. **(369)**

Classification—National Library of Medicine

General

■ A study reported in 1974 of classification systems used in 941 libraries as reported in a series of U.S. national and regional medical publications as well as an international survey conducted by Dave Remington of 470 health science libraries *showed that* in 23 years a substantial shift toward use of the National Library of Medicine classification scheme had taken place in Medical Library Association libraries. Between 1950 and 1959, 15 libraries had switched to NLM classification, while between 1959 and 1973, 69 libraries had switched to NLM classification. **(701)**

Ibid. . . . *showed that* the 7 most frequently used classification systems in Medical Library Association libraries (excluding VA Hospital libraries) were as follows:

National Library of Medicine	158 (35.3%) libraries
Library of Congress	85 (19.0%) libraries
Boston Medical	79 (17.7%) libraries
Dewey Decimal	69 (15.4%) libraries
Cunningham	35 (7.8%) libraries

continued

own or "special" system	12 (2.7%) libraries
Black's Classification for Dental Literature	9 (2.0%) libraries **(701)**

Ibid. . . . *showed that* the total number of libraries using the National Library of Medicine classification system worldwide was 589, of which 556 (94.4%) libraries were in the U.S., 13 (2.2%) were in Canada, 11 (1.9%) in Great Britain, and a scattering elsewhere. **(701)**

Ibid. . . . *showed that* the 3 main reasons given for switching were (multiple responses allowed): to take advantage of the NLM cataloging service (13 or 52%), to provide better shelf arrangement for the library's books (11 or 44%), and found classification easier with the NLM system (10 or 40%). **(701)**

Ibid. . . . *showed that* 24 (96%) libraries used the Library of Congress classification system for subjects outside the scope of the NLM classification while 1 (4%) did not. Of those 24, 9 reported use of selected broad LC class numbers while 16 reported use of specific LC class numbers. **(701)**

Ibid. . . . *showed that* the effects of switching to NLM classification were minimal. For example, of 23 libraries, 8 (34.8%) libraries reported patrons had expressed a preference for the NLM classification system, none had expressed a preference for the previous system, and 15 (65.2%) libraries reported patrons had not expressed a preference. **(701)**

Costs

General

■ A 1974 survey of the 47 charter members of the OCLC network, including site visits and interviews (148) with all levels of library personnel in member libraries, *showed that* 63% of the charter member libraries had reduced cataloging staff since beginning online cataloging, dropping a total of 76.83 net positions. However, the degree to which online cataloging contributed to this saving is unclear since other factors such as reorganization, decreased workload, and the like were also involved. **(112)**

Ibid. . . . *showed that*, of the 10 library directors who indicated that their principal goal for joining the OCLC network was cost savings, 80% reported this goal successfully met, while only 41% of the directors of the remaining libraries reported that this goal had been successfully met.

(112)

Ibid. . . . *showed that*, of the charter members, 12 libraries reported no particular objectives for joining the OCLC network, 15 were principally interested in faster cataloging, 10 were principally interested in reducing cataloging costs, 7 in improved ILL, and 3 in miscellaneous objectives. The directors of 80% of the libraries reported their primary objectives had been met.

(112)

Academic

■ A 1973 study at the University of Colorado Medical Center of cataloging and card production costs of English-language monographs with 1972-73 imprints that required complete cataloging (sample size: 319 items) *showed that* unit costs of in-library processing were as follows (estimated unit cost of purchased card method in parentheses):

bibliographic searching	$ .26 (.31) per item
cataloging	$1.33 (.66) per item
card production	$ .62 (1.08) per item
book preparation	$ .63 (.63) per item
TOTAL UNIT COST	$2.84 (2.68) per item **(706)**

Ibid. . . . *showed that* the unit cost for in-library cataloging in different situations was as follows:

original cataloging	$1.47 per item
NLM copy available	$1.09 per item
LC cataloging in publication available	$1.29 per item **(706)**

■ A 1979 study at Memphis State University concerning errors in the OCLC data base and based on all error reports generated at Memphis State over a 2-month period (175 error reports) *showed that* the cost (labor only) of reporting the 175 OCLC data base errors was $184.07 for 175 error reports.

(765)

■ A study reported in 1981 at Washington State University comparing the costs of an automated network system (Washington Library Network) and a local manual system of cataloging and book processing *showed that* the automated system was "almost 20%" less expensive than the manual system based on derived monthly costs. The higher costs of the manual system were "essentially staff costs." Even in the automated system the nonstaff costs of cataloging and book processing only accounted for 27% of the total. **(335)**

Public

■ An analysis of cataloging costs at the Washington State Library *showed that* there was an increase from $3.40 per title in 1962 to $10.40 per title in 1970. **(058)**

Special

■ A 1973 study at the University of Colorado Medical Center of cataloging and card production costs of English-language monographs with 1972-73 imprints that required complete cataloging (sample size: 319 items) *showed that* unit costs of in-library processing were as follows (estimated unit cost of purchased card method in parentheses):

bibliographic searching	$ .26 (.31) per item
cataloging	$1.33 (.66) per item
card production	$ .62 (1.08) per item
book preparation	$ .63 (.63) per item
TOTAL UNIT COST	$2.84 (2.68) per item **(706)**

Ibid. . . . *showed that* the unit cost for in-library cataloging in different situations was as follows:

original cataloging	$1.47 per item
NLM copy available	$1.09 per item
LC cataloging in publication available	$1.29 per item **(706)**

Documents

General

■ A survey of 50 depository libraries selected at random from the 1970 issue of the *Monthly Catalog* and reported in 1972 (36 or 72% responding) concerning subject access to government documents *showed that* 92% of responding libraries reported that "some" rather than "most," "all," or "none" of their government documents received full subject cataloging.

(214)

Academic

■ A survey of 31 members of the Association for Research Libraries in 1958 (23 or 75% responding) dealing with the treatment of government documents collections *showed that* out of the 12 libraries that reported housing their documents collections either completely or mostly separately, 8 reported that they did not fully catalog nonfederal documents. However, all 12 reported that in their experience the necessity of patrons to access these collections through a variety of special printed catalogs posed no serious problem.

(108)

■ A 1979 survey of U.S. community college libraries selected from the 1978 *Community, Junior and Technical College Directory* (sample size: 98; responding: 52; usable: 48 or 48.98%) *showed that* 41 (85.4%) libraries classed and cataloged their government documents the same as books and periodicals; 5 (10.4%) libraries used Superintendent of Documents classification, while 1 (2.1%) library used both methods, and 2 (4.2%) libraries did not respond.

(498)

Entries, Added

General

■ An analysis of the number of added entries assigned cataloged material listed in the *National Union Catalog* during the period 1950-73 *showed that* there was an increase in the average number of added entries per item, rising consistently from 1 added entry in 1950 to 1.5 added entries in 1973. Over this period there was a drop in the number of titles receiving no added entries from 22.6% to 8.6%.

(055)

Ibid. . . . *showed that* the average number of added entries per main entry increased from 1 to 1.5, a statistically significant increase.

(055)

Entries, Form of

General

■ A study reported in 1971 of 3,905 Indonesian authors listed in 5 different Indonesian bibliographies over varying time periods *showed that* most names were entered under the last element of the name, while only 648 (18%) were entered under the first element of the name. Of these 648 names, 90% are Indonesian names of Chinese origin, where the first element of the name is the surname. **(596)**

Academic

■ A 1977 survey of academic libraries with collections of 300,000 volumes or more that were also OCLC members concerning cataloging practices (survey size: 147 libraries; responding: 121 or 82.3%) *showed that* when cataloging copy was not available, 95% of the larger (900,000 volumes or more) libraries and 84% of the smaller (under 900,000 volumes) libraries followed LC practice when assigning call numbers and establishing the form of name headings, subject headings, and series entries. However, "one-third" of the larger libraries and "one-half" of the smaller libraries that follow LC practice used a local call number system for some materials. These were generally microforms, juvenile literature, and theses. **(760)**

■ A study reported in 1982 concerning the impact of AACR 2 on the card catalog in a medium-sized (740,000 volumes) academic library, based on a random sample of 909 catalog records (1,714 headings) taken from a year's pre-AACR 2, OCLC archival tapes and searched in the post-AACR 2, OCLC LC name authority file, *showed that* 217 (12.7%) different headings required changes under AACR 2 rules. 43% of these "unique" headings were verified in the online name authority file as of January 1981. **(770)**

Ibid. . . . *showed that* the distribution of changes to be made by type of heading was as follows:

personal (1,246 headings)	98 (7.9%) changes
corporate (125 headings)	53 (42.4%) changes
geographical (153 headings)	20 (13.1%) changes
uniform title (34 headings)	1 (2.9%) changes
series (156 headings)	45 (28.8%) changes

However, since not every heading that required a change under AACR 2 was already represented in the catalog, the number of conflicts was less than the number of changes. The number of conflicts by type of heading was as follows:

personal (1,246 headings)	85 (6.8%) conflicts	
corporate (125 headings)	27 (21.6%) conflicts	
geographical (153 headings)	15 (9.8%) conflicts	
uniform title (34 headings)	1 (2.9%) conflicts	
series (156 headings)	42 (26.9%) conflicts	**(770)**

Ibid. . . . *showed that* a summary review of the literature came up with the following rates of difference ("headings which would be constructed differently under AACR 2") and rates of conflict ("AACR 2 headings for names already entered in the catalog under a different form"):

of 295 records and 541 headings studied at Johns Hopkins University, the rate of difference was 17.3% and the rate of conflict was 11%;

of 484 records studied at Duke University the rate of conflict was 15.5%;

of 330 titles and 577 headings at Emory University the rate of difference was 15%;

of 300 titles and 447 headings at the University of Minnesota the rate of difference was 3%;

of 258 headings at the University of Washington the rate of difference was 30%;

of 325 titles and 644 entries at Southern Illinois University, Carbondale, the rate of difference was 20.3%. **(770)**

Job Satisfaction

General

■ A 1974 survey of the 47 charter members of the OCLC network, including site visits and interviews (148) with all levels of library personnel in member libraries concerning the implications of OCLC online cataloging, *showed that* 74% of the interviewees stated that the non-professional work had been made more demanding, while only 3 interviewees reported that professional cataloging had been made more demanding. **(112)**

Academic

■ A comparison reported in 1978 of catalogers and reference librarians in 91 university libraries (sample size: 444 full-time librarians; responding: 349 or 78.6%) *showed that* there were statistically significant differences in 3 out of 20 areas of job satisfaction. Reference librarians were more satisfied in terms of creativity, social service, and variety than catalogers (significant at the .05 level or better). **(009)**

Ibid. . . . *showed that* in terms of overall job satisfaction there was no statistically significant difference between the 2 groups (significant at the .05 level). **(009)**

MARC

General

■ A comparison reported in 1976 of MARC records for 1969-70 and 1974-75 at the Information Retrieval Research Laboratory at the University of Illinois *showed that* the number of records distributed in 1969-70 was 52,294, while the number for 1974-75 was 124,355. The average record length for 1969-70 was 636 characters, while the average for 1974-75 was 666.418 characters, indicating a 5% increase in average record size over the 4 years. **(325)**

Ibid. . . . *showed that* the average number of data elements (fields) in the MARC records increased from 10.7 in 1969-70 to 11.45 in 1974-75. Furthermore, of the 47 elements that appeared in both time periods, 44 increased in length while 3 decreased. **(325)**

■ A study reported in 1979 of MARC tapes for the years 1969-70, 1974-75, 1975-76, 1976-77, and 1977-78 *showed that* the average MARC record length (and range) for each of those years beginning with 1969-70 was: 636.00 characters (280 to 1,987), 666.42 (263 to 2,032), 681.93 (248 to 2,030), 689.67 (251 to 2,047) and 685.21 (247 to 2,050). This represented annual changes (generally increases) beginning with 1969-70 and running to 1974-75 of 4.8%, 2.3%, 1.1%, and −.6%, respectively. **(347)**

Ibid. . . . *showed that* the average number of records (1 bibliographic unit) per issue (generally weekly) for each of those years beginning with 1974-75 was: 2,391, 2,758, 3,387, and 3,346. **(347)**

Ibid. . . . *showed that* beginning with 1974-75 Dewey numbers appeared in 96.6% of the records for that year, in 90.4% of the records for the next year, in 83.4% of the records for the following year, and in 69.3% of the records for the last year. **(347)**

Ibid. . . . *showed that* if the Dewey numbers were divided into groups of 10 (e.g., 300-309, 310-319, etc.) the 8 groups with the consistently highest percentage of Dewey class numbers during the period 1974 through 1978 were: 300, 330, 340, 370, 610, 620, 810, and 820. **(347)**

Ibid. . . . *showed that* a special look at the MARC records for the last 3 years of the study revealed that the average record length for scientific monographs (Q, R, S, and T) was longer than the overall average and beginning with 1975-76 averaged 713, 719, and 727 characters, respectively (compared to the overall average 681.9, 689.7, and 685.2 characters, respectively). However, language and literature records (P) were shorter than the overall average and beginning with 1975-76 ran, respectively, 585, 595, and 588 characters in length. **(347)**

Academic

■ A study reported in 1970 at the University of Chicago of the arrival dates of 5,020 Library of Congress proofslips and corresponding MARC II magnetic tape records over a 7-week period *showed that* generally the MARC II tapes were more timely than the proofslips. Specifically, 4,004 (79.8%) of the proofslips matched MARC records received the same week or earlier. Further, the number of proofslips arriving the same week as the MARC tapes or later ranged from 48.9% to 91.6%. **(646)**

■ A 1977 survey of academic libraries with collections of 300,000 volumes or more that were also OCLC members concerning cataloging practices (survey size: 147 libraries; responding: 121 or 82.3%) *showed that* the following sources of cataloging copy were used in addition to OCLC (large libraries = 900,000 volumes or more; small libraries = less than 900,000 volumes):

National Union Catalog	100.0% large;	100.0% small libraries
Mansell	95.0% large;	97.0% small libraries
MCRS	13.2% large;	5.0% small libraries
MARCFICHE	8.5% large;	2.0% small libraries
other	0.0% large;	4.0% small libraries

(760)

■ A 1977 study at Cornell Law Library of 157 OCLC member records and 424 LC records in the OCLC data base *showed that* the average cataloging time per record for records with OCLC member cataloging copy was 9.076 minutes compared to 8.148 minutes cataloging time per record for records with LC cataloging copy.   **(367)**

Ibid. . . . *showed that* the average inputting time per record for records with OCLC member cataloging copy was 5.966 minutes compared to 4.498 minutes average inputting time per record for records with LC cataloging copy.   **(367)**

■ A 1978 study of RLIN cataloging at the Law School Library, UC Berkeley over a 6-month period *showed that*, of 2,748 titles for which no MARC or RLIN copy cataloging was found, 1,099 (40%) were published in or after 1970.   **(368)**

Ibid. . . . *showed that*, of 781 full MARC records in the RLIN data base, 51% required no modification, while of 91 standard Contributed Data File records 55% required no modification.   **(368)**

■ A 1979 survey of academic libraries listed in the 1979 edition of *OCLC Participating Libraries Arranged by Network and Institution* (survey size: 200 libraries; responding: 166 or 83%) *showed that*, of 109 respondents, 137 (86.2%) reported that they always made substantial checks (i.e., checking "for more than typographical and tagging errors and completing the fixed field") in at least some types of non-LC records in the OCLC data base. Only 22 (13.8%) libraries reported that they never substantially checked non-LC records. The 3 most frequently checked types of non-LC records were:

<table>
<tr><td>all types</td><td>75 (68.8%) libraries</td><td></td></tr>
<tr><td>records from certain
cataloging libraries</td><td>21 (19.3%) libraries</td><td></td></tr>
<tr><td>audiovisual materials</td><td>11 (10.1%) libraries</td><td>**(764)**</td></tr>
</table>

Ibid. . . . *showed that*, of 158 respondents, the number of non-LC records that libraries reported changing, excluding Cataloging-in-Print copy, changes in the 049 field (local holdings), 590 field (local note), 910 field (user option data), and the 082/092 fields (Dewey call number), were as follows:

no records changed	2 (1.3%) libraries	
1-9% records changed	28 (17.7%) libraries	
10-24% records changed	38 (24.1%) libraries	
25-49% records changed	30 (19.0%) libraries	
50-74% records changed	35 (22.2%) libraries	
75-99% records changed	22 (13.9%) libraries	
100% records changed	3 (1.9%) libraries	**(764)**

Ibid. . . . *showed that*, of 158 respondents, the number of LC records that libraries reported changing, excluding Cataloging-in-Print copy, changes in the 049 field (local holdings), 590 field (local note), 910 field (user option data), and the 082/092 fields (Dewey call number), were as follows:

no records changed	14 (8.9%) libraries	
1-9% records changed	99 (62.7%) libraries	
10-24% records changed	32 (20.3%) libraries	
25-49% records changed	7 (4.4%) libraries	
50% or more records changed	6 (3.8%) libraries	**(764)**

■ A 1979 study at Memphis State University concerning errors in the OCLC data base and based on all error reports generated at Memphis State over a 2-month period (175 error reports) *showed that*, of the 993 member library records used for cataloging during the test period, 136 (13.7%) contained errors, while of the 2,435 MARC records used for cataloging during this same period, only 39 (1.6%) contained errors.

(765)

Ibid. . . . *showed that*, of 93 indexing errors found in OCLC member records, the 4 most frequently reported were: ISBN for monographs (31 errors), LCCN for monographs (22 errors), uniform title for [music] scores (17 errors), and title for [music] scores (10 errors). Of 20 indexing errors found in OCLC MARC records, the most common was ISBN for monographs (19 errors).   **(765)**

■ A 1980 survey of North American medical school libraries concerning automation of internal library operations (population: 139; responding: 93 or 69%) *showed that* 50 (53.8%) respondents had some MARC or MARC-compatible records, while 7 (7.5%) had machine-readable records in other formats. Further, only 26 (28.0%) respondents had been receiving OCLC's MARC subscription tapes for 3 years or more. And only 2 (2.2%) respondents reported all catalog records in MARC format.   **(741)**

■ A study reported in 1983 of the cataloging records for music, music scores, and musical sound recordings over a 2-month period in 1980 from the Indiana University Music Library and the music cataloging unit of the University of Illinois-Urbana Library (996 cataloging records) *showed that* fewer changes were required for cataloging records generated by the Library of Congress than for cataloging records generated by OCLC members. For example, books required an average of 5.5 changes per record for LC cataloging compared to an average of 11.8 changes per record for OCLC members' cataloging.   **(757)**

Ibid. . . . *showed that* 213 different institutions were responsible for inputting the 996 cataloging records in the sample. LC MARC records accounted for 16% of the total, LC records input by OCLC member libraries accounted for 12%, public libraries accounted for 8%, ARL members (excluding Library of Congress) accounted for 34%, and other academic libraries accounted for 30%.   **(757)**

Ibid. . . . *showed that* the Library of Congress played a much larger role in the cataloging of music books than in the cataloging of music materials or scores. For example, 58% of the book records were LC MARC records, while 11% of the book records were LC records input by OCLC members. In contrast, only 30% of the records for music materials were generated by LC, while 70% of the records were generated by OCLC member libraries.
                                                                                    (757)

Special

■ A 1977 study at Cornell Law Library of 301 cataloging records found in the OCLC data base (151 input by LC; 150 input by OCLC member libraries) *showed that* to make usable cataloging the LC records required an average of 1.13 modifications per record, while the OCLC member cataloging required an average of 2.97 modifications per record. When call number problems were ignored (which may pose unique problems to law cataloging in the LC schedules) the average number of LC modifications per record dropped to .78, while the average number of modifications per record for OCLC member cataloging dropped to 2.53.   **(367)**

■ A 1977 study at Cornell Law Library of 157 OCLC member records and 424 LC records in the OCLC data base *showed that* the average cataloging time per record for records with OCLC member cataloging copy was 9.076 minutes compared to 8.148 minutes cataloging time per record for records with LC cataloging copy.   **(367)**

Ibid. . . . *showed that* the average inputting time per record for records with OCLC member cataloging copy was 5.966 minutes compared to 4.498 minutes average inputting time per record for records with LC cataloging copy.   **(367)**

■ A 1978 study of RLIN cataloging at the Law School Library, UC Berkeley over a 6-month period *showed that*, of 2,748 titles for which no MARC or RLIN copy cataloging was found, 1,099 (40%) were published in or after 1970.   **(368)**

Ibid. . . . *showed that*, of 781 full MARC records in the RLIN data base, 51% required no modification, while of 91 standard Contributed Data File records 55% required no modification.   **(368)**

■ A 1980 survey of North American medical school libraries concerning automation of internal library operations (population: 139; responding: 93 or 69%) *showed that* 50 (53.8%) respondents had some MARC or MARC-compatible records, while 7 (7.5%) had machine-readable records in other formats. Further, only 26 (28.0%) respondents had been receiving OCLC's MARC subscription tapes for 3 years or more. And only 2 (2.2%) respondents reported all catalog records in MARC format.   **(741)**

■ A study reported in 1983 of the cataloging records for music, music scores, and musical sound recordings over a 2-month period in 1980 from the Indiana University Music Library and the music cataloging unit of the

University of Illinois-Urbana Library (996 cataloging records) *showed that* fewer changes were required for cataloging records generated by the Library of Congress than for cataloging records generated by OCLC members. For example, books required an average of 5.5 changes per record for LC cataloging compared to an average of 11.8 changes per record for OCLC members' cataloging.   **(757)**

Ibid. . . . *showed that* 213 different institutions were responsible for inputting the 996 cataloging records in the sample. LC MARC records accounted for 16% of the total, LC records input by OCLC member libraries accounted for 12%, public libraries accounted for 8%, ARL members (excluding Library of Congress) accounted for 34%, and other academic libraries accounted for 30%.   **(757)**

Ibid. . . . *showed that* the Library of Congress played a much larger role in the cataloging of music books than in the cataloging of music materials or scores. For example, 58% of the book records were LC MARC records, while 11% of the book records were LC records input by OCLC members. In contrast, only 30% of the records for music materials were generated by LC, while 70% of the records were generated by OCLC member libraries.   **(757)**

Media

Academic

■ A 1972 survey of chief library administrators in public comprehensive community colleges (population: 586; unusableresponses: 75.9% [no raw number given]) *showed that* 56.4% of the respondents reported their holdings organized according to Library of Congress classification and 42.9% reported Dewey Decimal. Audiovisual materials were often reported as organized by many different local schemes, although 22.5% of the respondents reported using LC classification and 21.5% reported using Dewey Decimal.   **(452)**

■ A 1979 survey of U.S. community college libraries selected from the 1978 *Community, Junior and Technical College Directory* (sample size: 98; responding: 52; usable: 48 or 48.98%) *showed that* for audiovisual materials (multiple systems used in some cases) 13 (25.00%) libraries used Dewey Decimal classification, 11 (21.15%) libraries used Library of Congress classification, 10 (19.23%) libraries used accession number schemes, 14 (26.92%) libraries used format and accession number schemes, and 4 (7.69%) used some other scheme. **(498)**

Ibid. . . . *showed that* for monographs 6 (12.24%) libraries used Sears for their subject heading list, while 43 (87.76%) libraries used Library of Congress. For audiovisual materials, 6 (12.24%) used Sears for their subject heading list, 41 (83.67%) used LC, and 2 (4.08%) used some other subject heading authority. (One library reported using both Sears and LC, so the totals equal 49 rather than 48.) **(498)**

Ibid. . . . *showed that* for audiovisual materials:

24 (50.0%) libraries did full cataloging and interfiled entries in the central catalog;

8 (16.7%) libraries did full cataloging but filed audiovisual entires in a separate catalog;

1 (2.1%) library did full cataloging and filed audiovisual entires in separate drawers of the central catalog;

6 (12.5%) libraries did full ctaloging but filed audiovisual entries in a separate catalog in the AV center;

9 (18.8%) libraries did full cataloging and filed audiovisual entries both in the central catalog and in a separate catalog in the AV center. **(498)**

Ibid. . . . *showed that* the number of audiovisual materials added monthly to the collection was as follows:

0-100	31 (64.60%) libraries
500+	1 (2.08%) libraries
not recorded/not answered	16 (33.33%) libraries **(498)**

■ A 1979 survey of academic libraries listed in the 1979 edition of *OCLC Participating Libraries Arranged by Network and Institution* (survey size: 200 libraries; responding: 166 or 83%) *showed that* 164 (98.8%) respondents reported using OCLC to produce catalog cards. Further, of 163 respondents, 73 (44.8%) reported use of another card production system as well. The 3 most common additional methods used were (in descending order of importance): use of a photocopier (37 libraries), typing complete card sets (17 libraries), and purchasing commerically available cards, including Library of Congress cards (15 libraries). **(764)**

Ibid. . . . *showed that*, of 71 respondents, non-OCLC card production systems were used to produce cards for the following 3 most frequently mentioned types of materials (multiple responses allowed):

audiovisual	22 (31.0%) libraries
non-Roman alphabet texts	17 (23.9%) libraries
local ephemera (including student theses and papers)	15 (21.1%) libraries

Further, the number of titles per year for which cards were produced using an alternate (to OCLC) system, based on responses from 67 libraries, ranged from 10 titles to 31,200 titles with a median of 450 titles per year. **(764)**

Public

■ A 1981-82 study of media cataloging practices in 932 public libraries (responding: 466 or 50%; usable: 488 or 48%) across the U.S. serving communities of all sizes *showed that* 83% catalog their nonprint holdings. A further 21 (4.7%) reported that they cataloged part of their nonprint holdings. **(161)**

Ibid. . . . *showed that* 46% of responding libraries were using AACR 2 for nonprint cataloging (compared to 57% using AACR 2 for print materials). Of those not using AACR 2 for cataloging, 54% reported no plans for adopting it for printed materials, and 71% reported no plans for adopting it for nonprint use. **(161)**

Ibid. . . . *showed that* although 96+% of respondents used Dewey classification for print materials, only about one-third used it for nonprint materials. **(161)**

Special

■ A survey reported in 1983 of Medical Library Association institutional members concerning their use of audiovisual materials (survey size: 300; responding: 201; usable: 198 or 66%) *showed that*, of 143 respondents (91 hospital, 29 medical school, and 13 "other" libraries) that did provide AV services, 90% of the hospital libraries, 88% of the medical school libraries, and 55% of the other libraries reported using MeSH subject headings.

(750)

OCLC—General Issues

General

■ A survey in 1974 of the 47 charter members of the OCLC network, including site visits and interviews (148) with all levels of library personnel in member libraries, *showed that* 49% of surveyed libraries held books in the cataloging department until cards were received, while 51% sent books on for final processing and shelving directly after cataloging at the terminal.

(112)

Ibid. . . . *showed that* 6 libraries continue to check the complete shipment of catalog cards to determine if every card for every title was received, although they reported finding very few errors.

(112)

Ibid. . . . *showed that*, in most of the libraries using LC classification, clericals and paraprofessionals did a major part of the cataloging involving records in the OCLC data base, while in all except 1 of the 14 libraries using Dewey, professional catalogers were used to catalog records in the online file.

(112)

■ A 1978 study of OCLC's online union catalog preparatory to converting to AACR 2 form of name headings and uniform titles, involving a 1% test file (41,212 records) and a thorough review of AACR 2 rules, *showed that* AACR 2 contained 454 "significant" rule changes or new rules, of which 56% would benefit neither librarian nor patron, 23% of which would benefit librarians, and 21% of which would benefit patrons.

(337)

Ibid. . . . *showed that* 39% of the total records in the online union catalog were ultimately converted to AACR 2 form.

(337)

■ A 1982 study of the OCLC union catalog to investigate the extent of record duplication, based on 100 records randomly selected from the OCLC data base and subsequently searched in the OCLC data base for duplicates by using the alphabetic and numeric search keys generated from the selected record, *showed that* 17 (17%) records had duplicate entries, some more than 1 duplicate, for a total of 40 duplicate records (an average of 2.4 duplicate entries for each of the 17 duplicated records).   **(772)**

Ibid. . . . *showed that*, based on an average of 3.6 alphabetic searches per record, 23% of the search keys evoked the response "[search key] produces more than 50 entries."   **(772)**

Academic

■ A 1977 survey investigating cataloging practices among academic libraries with collections of 300,000 volumes or more that were also OCLC members (survey size: 147 libraries; responding: 121 or 82.3%) *showed that*:

> for libraries with 900,000 volumes or more, the average OCLC production (on a first-time use basis) was 2,175 titles per month and ranged from 500 to 5,455 titles per month;
>
> for libraries with less than 900,000 volumes, the average OCLC production (on a first-time use basis) was 1,256 titles per month and ranged from 300 to 3,800 titles per month.   **(760)**

Ibid. . . . *showed that* for OCLC member records the following items were verified (large libraries = 900,000 volumes or more; small libraries = under 900,000 volumes):

call number	79.0% large; 73.0% small libraries
choice and form of	
entry	71.6% large; 74.0% small libraries
added entries	73.2% large; 68.0% small libraries
all of the above	70.0% large; 61.0% small libraries
none of the above	18.3% large; 20.0% small libraries

Further, the following treatment of subject headings in member records was reported by the following libraries:

subject headings verified	
as valid LC headings	70.0% large; 81.7% small libraries
subject headings checked	
for appropriateness	61.6% large; 67.0% small libraries
subject headings	
assigned if lacking	88.3% large; 90.0% small libraries
all of the above	56.6% large; 61.7% small libraries
none of the above	8.3% large; 1.0% small libraries

(760)

OCLC **59**

■ A 1979 survey of U.S. community college libraries selected from the 1978 *Community, Junior and Technical College Directory* (sample size: 98; responding: 52; usable: 48 or 48.98%) *showed that*, of 46 respondents, 39 (84.8%) reported that they did not participate in computerized cataloging networks. Of the 39, 23 (59.0%) reported they did not plan to join such a network, while 7 (17.9%) said they did, 8 (20.5%) said they were undecided, and 3 (7.7%) did not respond. Of the 7 libraries that did participate in such networks, 6 (85.7%) used OCLC, while 1 (14.3%) used the Washington Library Network. **(498)**

■ A 1979 survey of academic libraries listed in the 1979 edition of OCLC *Participating Libraries Arranged by Network and Institution* (survey size: 200 libraries; responding: 166 or 83%) *showed that* 164 (98.8%) respondents reported using OCLC to produce catalog cards. Further, of 163 respondents, 73 (44.8%) reported use of another card production system as well. The 3 most common additional methods used were (in descending order of importance): use of a photocopier (37 libraries), typing complete card sets (17 libraries), and purchasing commercially available cards, including Library of Congress cards (15 libraries). **(764)**

Ibid. . . . *showed that* the length of time libraries reported being online with OCLC was as follows:

less than 1 year	7 (4.2%)	libraries
1 to less than 3 years	70 (42.4%)	libraries
3 to less than 5 years	69 (41.8%)	libraries
5 to less than 7 years	11 (6.7%)	libraries
7 years or more	8 (4.8%)	libraries **(764)**

Ibid. . . . *showed that* of 166 respondents the number of titles cataloged per year via OCLC was as follows:

less than 5,000 titles	69 (41.6%)	libraries
5,000-9,999 titles	39 (23.5%)	libraries
10,000-14,999 titles	31 (18.7%)	libraries
15,000 or more titles	27 (16.2%)	libraries **(764)**

Ibid. . . . *showed that* of 163 respondents the number of backlogged titles awaiting cataloging was as follows:

less than 1,000 titles	125 (76.7%)	libraries
1,000-4,999 titles	22 (13.5%)	libraries

continued

5,000-9,999 titles   5 (3.1%) libraries
10,000 or more titles   11 (6.7%) libraries   **(764)**

Ibid. . . . *showed that* of 163 respondents the number of OCLC terminals used for cataloging per library was as follows:

1 terminal   104 (63.8%) libraries
2 terminals   36 (22.1%) libraries
3 terminals   8 (4.9%) libraries
4 terminals   9 (5.5%) libraries
5-17 terminals   6 (3.7%) libraries   **(764)**

Ibid. . . . *showed that*, of 160 respondents, 13 (8.1%) reported using the OCLC-MARC tapes, 85 (53.1%) reported that they planned to use the tapes, and 62 (38.7%) reported they "do not use" the tapes.   **(764)**

■ A 1979 study at Memphis State University concerning errors in the OCLC data base and based on all error reports generated at Memphis State over a 2-month period (175 error reports) *showed that* the cost (labor only) of reporting the 175 OCLC data base errors was $184.07 for 175 error reports.   **(765)**

■ A 1979-81 study at the University of Louisville (Ekstrom Library) involving pre-cataloging searching on the OCLC data base for monographic titles that had member input copy (090) or no copy at all (0) with several searches conducted over a period of 20.4 weeks (no N given for total number of items searched) *showed that* items for which LCIII copy (LC record input by member library) or 090E copy (2 records available, a record input by a member library and a DLC/DLC record for an edition of the work) was found during the first search were seldom upgraded by the time the second search was made. Of 773 books classified as LCIII's at the end of the first search, 92% (711) were still so classified when a second search was undertaken, while 94% of the 090E's remained unchanged at the time a second search was undertaken.   **(314)**

Ibid. . . . *showed that* over the 3-year study period a weekly first searching of an average of 62.5 books in the 090 category (member input copy) revealed that 10% of the books had LC copy, 8% had LCIII copy, and 13% had 090E copy, while 69% of the books were still designated 090; that a second search of these remaining 090 books (an average of 56.1 books per week) revealed that an additional 7% had LC copy, 1% had LCIII copy, and 2% had 090E copy, while 90% of the books were still designated 090; and that a third search of the remaining 090 books (an average of 55.3 books per week) revealed that an additional 14% of the books had LC copy and 1% had 090E copy, while 85% were still designated 090. All 3 searches were conducted within an average time period of 20.4 weeks.

(314)

Ibid. . . . *showed that* over the 3-year study period a weekly first searching of an average of 42.6 books in the 0 category (no record available) revealed that 10% of the books had LC copy, 1% had LCIII copy, 5% had OE copy, while 48% of the books were still designated 0; that a second search of these remaining 0 books (an average of 20.4 books per week) revealed that an additional 5% had LC copy, 22% had 090 copy, 1% had OE copy, while 72% of the books were still designated 0; and that a third search of the remaining 0 books (an average of 14.9 books per week) revealed that an additional 5% had LC copy, 1% had LCIII copy, 2.5% had 090 copy, 1% had OE copy, while 75% were still designated 0. All 3 searches were conducted within an average time period of 20.4 weeks. **(314)**

Ibid. . . . *showed that* regardless of whether the first search was conducted 1 week after the book was received or 4 weeks after the book was received at least 85% of the books still had not received LC copy; that there was no real improvement in cataloging copy when the second search was conducted 7-8 weeks after the first search rather than 4-6 weeks after the first search; and that of 3 time differences between the second and third searches, 4-7 weeks, 8-14 weeks, or 14-17 weeks, the 8-14 week difference was the best. **(314)**

■ A 1980 survey of Catholic colleges with collections containing less than 300,000 bibliographic items (survey size: 105 libraries; responding: 62; usable: 60 or 57.1%) *showed that*, of 36 libraries with some form of automation, 33 (91.7%) had automated the cataloging process (and are members of OCLC). Of these, the cataloging process was the only automated process in the library for 21 libraries. **(754)**

■ A 1980 survey of North American medical school libraries concerning automation of internal library operations (population: 139; responding: 93 or 69%) *showed that* 81 (87.1%) libraries participated in 1 or more of the major bibliographic utilities (OCLC, RLIN, or UTLAS) for shared cataloging. **(741)**

■ A study reported in 1982 concerning the impact of AACR 2 on the card catalog in a medium-sized (740,000 volumes) academic library, based on a random sample of 909 catalog records (1,714 headings) taken from a year's pre-AACR 2 OCLC archival tapes and searched in the post AACR 2 OCLC LC name authority file, *showed that* 217 (12.7%) different headings required changes under AACR 2 rules. 43% of these "unique" headings were verified in the online name authority file as of January 1981.   **(770)**

Ibid. . . . *showed that* the distribution of changes to be made by type of heading was as follows:

personal (1,246 headings)	98 (7.9%) changes
corporate (125 headings)	53 (42.4%) changes
geographical (153 headings)	20 (13.1%) changes
uniform title (34 headings)	1 (2.9%) changes
series (156 headings)	45 (28.8%) changes

However, since not every heading that required a change under AACR 2 was already represented in the catalog, the number of conflicts was less than the number of changes. The number of conflicts by type of heading was as follows:

personal (1,246 headings)	85 (6.8%) conflicts
corporate (125 headings)	27 (21.6%) conflicts
geographical (153 headings)	15 (9.8%) conflicts
uniform title (34 headings)	1 (2.9%) conflicts
series (156 headings)	42 (26.9%) conflicts **(770)**

Ibid. . . . *showed that* a summary review of the literature came up with the following rates of difference ("headings which would be constructed differently under AACR 2") and rates of conflict ("AACR 2 headings for names already entered in the catalog under a different form"):

of 295 records and 541 headings studied at Johns Hopkins University, the rate of difference was 17.3% and the rate of conflict was 11%;

of 484 records studied at Duke University the rate of conflict was 15.5%;

of 330 titles and 577 headings at Emory University the rate of difference was 15%;

of 300 titles and 447 headings at the University of Minnesota the rate of difference was 3%;

of 258 headings at the University of Washington the rate of difference was 30%;

of 325 titles and 644 entries at Southern Illinois University, Carbondale, the rate of difference was 20.3%. **(770)**

■ A study reported in 1983 of the cataloging records for music, music scores, and musical sound recordings over a 2-month period in 1980 from the Indiana University Music Library and the music cataloging unit of the University of Illinois-Urbana Library (996 cataloging records) *showed that* 213 different institutions were responsible for inputting the 996 cataloging records in the sample. LC MARC records accounted for 16% of the total, LC records input by OCLC member libraries accounted for 12%, public libraries accounted for 8%, ARL members (excluding Library of Congress) accounted for 34%, and other academic libraries accounted for 30%. **(757)**

Ibid. . . . *showed that* the Library of Congress played a much larger role in the cataloging of music books than in the cataloging of music materials or scores. For example, 58% of the book records were LC MARC records, while 11% of the book records were LC records input by OCLC members. In contrast, only 30% of the records for music materials were generated by LC, while 70% of the records were generated by OCLC member libraries. **(757)**

Special

■ A 1980 survey of North American medical school libraries concerning automation of internal library operations (population: 139; responding: 93 or 69%) *showed that* 81 (87.1%) libraries participated in 1 or more of the major bibliographic utilities (OCLC, RLIN, or UTLAS) for shared cataloging. **(741)**

■ A study reported in 1983 of the cataloging records for music, music scores, and musical sound recordings over a 2-month period in 1980 from the Indiana University Music Library and the music cataloging unit of the University of Illinois-Urbana Library (996 cataloging records) *showed that* 213 different institutions were responsible for inputting the 996 cataloging records in the sample. LC MARC records accounted for 16% of the total, LC records input by OCLC member libraries accounted for 12%, public libraries accounted for 8%, ARL members (excluding Library of Congress) accounted for 34%, and other academic libraries accounted for 30%. **(757)**

Ibid. . . . *showed that* the Library of Congress played a much larger role in the cataloging of music books than in the cataloging of music materials or scores. For example, 58% of the book records were LC MARC records, while 11% of the book records were LC records input by OCLC members. In contrast, only 30% of the records for music materials were generated by LC, while 70% of the records were generated by OCLC member libraries.

(757)

OCLC—Data Base Accuracy

General

■ A survey in 1978 of 612 serial records in the OCLC data base *showed that* 23% were found to have at least 1 substantial error. 12.6% had only 1 error, 4.4% had 2 errors, 2.6% had 3 errors, and 3.4% had more than 3 errors. **(027)**

Ibid. . . . *showed that* there were errors in the following fields (total is over 100% due to multiple errors):

title field (field 245, 246, 247)	6.3% errors
subject heading field	12.0% errors
imprint field (260)	19.1% errors
dates of publication and volume designation (field 362)	45.0% errors
dates	26.0% errors
succeeding title (field 785)	19.1% errors
publication status	20.5% errors **(027)**

Ibid. . . . *showed that* the percentage of times data was omitted in the 6 basic fields was as follows:

imprint (field 260)	1.5%
collation (field 300)	11.7%
subject heading field	24.5%
dates of publication and volume designation (field 362)	28.9%
ISSN (field 022)	33.5%
call number (field 050)	35.1%

Only 62.7% had both a call number and subject headings in LC form. Overall, 68% of the records lacked 1 of the basic elements, 14% lacked 2, and 20.4% lacked 3 or more of the basic elements. **(027)**

Ibid. . . . *showed that* the percentage of errors in the following fields was negligible, less than 1%:

LC call number (050)
main entry—corporate name (110)
collation (300)
key title (222)
current frequency (310)
former frequency (321)
added entry—corporate name (710)
added entry—conference or meeting (711).   **(027)**

Ibid. . . . *showed that*, of the records with errors, 22% were LC cataloging, 57.4% were non-LC cataloging, and 20% were of "unknown" origin.
                                                          (027)

Ibid. . . . *showed that* 32.5% of the records lacking at least 1 of 6 basic elements (call number in LC form, subject heading in LC form, imprint, collation, ISSN, and date of publication and volume designation) had been authenticated by LC.   **(027)**

■ A survey in 1978 of 93 serial titles (which had been recently changed), taken from *New Serial Titles* and compared to title listings in the OCLC data base, *showed that* OCLC listed 59.1% correctly and up to date, 17.2% were listed incorrectly, and 23.6% were listed incompletely.   **(027)**

■ A study reported in 1978 of selected fields of 700 non-MARC (i.e., member cataloging) records from the OCLC data base (input after September 1, 1975) *showed that* 417 or 60% were correct while 283 records contained a total of 393 errors.   **(334)**

Ibid. . . . *showed that* the 5 most error-prone fields were: collation (111 or 39% of the total errors), subject headings (88 or 31% of total errors), series (55 or 19% of total errors), added entries (44 or 16% of total errors), and main entry (44 or 16% of the total errors).   **(334)**

■ A survey reported in 1982 of 144 libraries contracting for OCLC services through the Bibliographic Center for Research (126 or 87.5%

responding) *showed that* when 2 or more copies of a work were acquired at 1 time 44.4% of the respondents reported they would not indicate multiple copy ownership in the OCLC record if all copies went into the same collection, while 30.2% reported they would not indicate multiple copy ownership even if copies went into different collections. **(342)**

Ibid. . . . *showed that* when a subsequent copy of a title cataloged earlier on OCLC was purchased 70.6% of the respondents reported they would not enter information on the subsequent copy into the OCLC record if the copy were going into the same collection as the earlier copy, while 30.2% reported they would not enter information on the subsequent copy even if it were going into a different collection from the earlier copy. **(342)**

Ibid. . . . *showed that* when the only copy of a work in the library was withdrawn 70.6% of the respondents reported canceling the holdings recorded in the OCLC data base, while 19.8% reported they did not, 6.4% reported varying practices, and 3.2% did not reply to the question.

(342)

Ibid. . . . *showed that* when 1 of several copies of a work in the library that were previously cataloged on OCLC was withdrawn 21.4% of the respondents reported that the OCLC holdings were updated, while 65.9% of the respondents reported that the holdings were not, 4.8% reported that their practice varied, and 7.9% did not answer. **(342)**

Academic

■ A survey in 1978 of 612 serial records in the OCLC data base *showed that* 32.5% of the records lacking at least 1 of the 6 basic elements (call number in LC form, imprint, collation, ISSN, dates of publication and volume designation) had been authenticated by LC. **(027)**

Ibid. . . . *showed that* the percentage of times data was omitted in the 6 basic fields was as follows:

imprint (field 260)	1.5%
collation (field 300)	11.7%
subject heading field	24.5%
dates of publication and volume designation (field 362)	28.9%

continued

ISSN (field 022)	33.5%
call number (field 050)	35.1%

Only 62.7% had both a call number and subject headings in LC form. Overall, 68% of the records lacked 1 of the basic elements, 14% lacked 2, and 20.4% lacked 3 or more of the basic elements.   **(027)**

Ibid. . . . *showed that* 29% of the records with errors in them had been authenticated by the Library of Congress.   **(027)**

Ibid. . . . *showed that* there were errors in the following fields (total is over 100% due to multiple errors):

title field (field 245, 246, 247)	6.3%	errors
subject heading field	12.0%	errors
imprint field (260)	19.1%	errors
dates of publication and volume designation (field 362)	45.0%	errors
dates	26.0%	errors
succeeding title (field 785)	19.1%	errors
publication status	20.5%	errors **(027)**

Ibid. . . . *showed that* the percentage of errors in the following fields was negligible (i.e., less than 1%):

LC call number (field 050)
main entry—corporate name (110)
collation (field 300)
key title (field 222)
current frequency (field 310)
former frequency (field 321)
added entry—corporate name (field 710)
added entry—conference or meeting (field 711)   **(027)**

Ibid. . . . *showed that*, of the records with errors, 22% were LC cataloging, 57.4% were non-LC cataloging, and 20% were of "unknown origin."   **(027)**

Ibid. . . . *showed that* 23% were found to have at least 1 substantial error. 12.5% had only 1 error, 4.4% had 2 errors, 2.6% had 3 errors, and 3.5% had more than 3 errors.   **(027)**

■ A survey of 93 recently changed serial titles taken from *New Serials
Titles* and compared to title listings in the OCLC data base in 1978 *showed
that* OCLC listed 59.1% correctly and up to date, 17.2% were listed
incorrectly, and 23.6% were listed incompletely.   **(027)**

■ A 1979 survey of academic libraries listed in the 1979 edition of *OCLC
Participating Libraries Arranged by Network and Institution* (survey size:
200 libraries; responding: 166 or 83%) *showed that*, of 109 respondents,
137 (86.2%) reported that they always made substantial checks (i.e.,
checking "for more than typographical and tagging errors and completing
the fixed field") in at least some types of non-LC records in the OCLC data
base. Only 22 (13.8%) libraries reported that they never substantially
checked non-LC records. The 3 most frequently checked types of non-LC
records were:

all types	75 (68.8%) libraries	
records from certain		
cataloging libraries	21 (19.3%) libraries	
audiovisual materials	11 (10.1%) libraries	**(764)**

■ A 1979 study at Memphis State University concerning errors in the
OCLC data base and based on all error reports generated at Memphis
State over a 2-month period (175 error reports) *showed that*, of the 993
member library records used for cataloging during the test period, 136
(13.7%) contained errors, while of the 2,435 MARC records used for
cataloging during this same period, only 39 (1.6%) contained errors.
                                                                        (765)

Ibid. . . . *showed that*, of 175 errors in the OCLC data base that were
reported, 28 (16%) were corrected by OCLC within 2 months, and a total
of 92 (52.6%) were corrected by OCLC within 4 months.   **(765)**

Ibid. . . . *showed that*, of 93 indexing errors found in OCLC member
records, the 4 most frequently reported were: ISBN for monographs (31
errors), LCCN for monographs (22 errors), uniform title for [music] scores
(17 errors), and title for [music] scores (10 errors). Of 20 indexing errors
found in OCLC MARC records, the most common was ISBN for monographs (19 errors).   **(765)**

Ibid. . . . *showed that* the number of duplicate records found (201 records
for 94 titles) was greater than the number of records containing errors (175
records). Specifically, 84 titles had 2 records each, 8 titles had 3 records

each, 1 title had 4 records, and 1 title had 5 records.   **(765)**

Ibid. . . . *showed that* the cost (labor only) of reporting the 175 OCLC data base errors was $184.07 for 175 error reports.   **(765)**

Special

■ A study reported in 1983 of the cataloging records for music, music scores, and musical sound recordings over a 2-month period in 1980 from the Indiana University Music Library and the music cataloging unit of the University of Illinois-Urbana Library (996 cataloging records) *showed that* the number of corrections and changes that had to be made in the OCLC record showed wide variation by format. The average book required 6.1 changes per record, the average score required 10.5 changes per record, and the average sound recording required 15.9 changes per record.

    (757)

Ibid. . . . *showed that* most of the changes required were in the control data of the OCLC records (control data elements are represented in the MARC record by the 0XX fields and are generally more important for use in an online catalog than in card production). Specifically, 79% of the changes required in book records, 71% of the changes required by scores, and 54% of the changes required by sound recordings were control data elements.   **(757)**

Ibid. . . . *showed that* fewer changes were required for cataloging records generated by the Library of Congress than for cataloging records generated by OCLC members. For example, books required an average of 5.5 changes per record for LC cataloging compared to an average of 11.8 changes per record for OCLC members' cataloging.   **(757)**

OCLC—Data Base Currency

General

■ A study reported in 1981 of OCLC's online union catalog to investigate the scope of its music holdings by checking 4 major lists of materials ("Books Recently Published" column of *Notes*; "Music Received" column of *Notes*; "New Listings" column of the *Schwann-1 Record and Tape Guide*; and *A Basic Music Library: Essential Scores and Books*) in the catalog *showed that*, of the 317 books listed in the December 1979 "Books

Recently Published" column and searched 1 year later, 312 (98.42%) were found in the OCLC union catalog, while of the 287 books listed in the September 1980 "Books Recently Published" column and searched 7 months later, 272 (94.78%) were found in the OCLC union catalog.

(757)

Ibid. . . . *showed that*, of the 420 items listed in the December 1979 "Music Received" column and searched 1 year later, 255 (60.71%) were found in the OCLC union catalog, while of the 351 items listed in the September 1980 "Music Received" column and searched 1-2 months later, 109 (31.05%) were found in the OCLC union catalog. **(757)**

Ibid. . . . *showed that*, of the 276 items listed in the December 1979 "New Listings" column and searched 14 months later, 162 (58.7%) were found in the OCLC union catalog, while of the 282 items listed in the September 1980 "New Listings" column and searched 1-2 months later, 64 (22.7%) were found in the OCLC union catalog. **(757)**

OCLC—Data Entry

General

■ A survey in 1974 of the 47 charter members of the OCLC network, including site visits and interviews (148) with all levels of library personnel in member libraries, *showed that* estimates from 40 libraries for the rate of inputting bibliographic records from pre-tagged input forms averaged 8.7 records/hour excluding time for revision. Revision rates, based on reports from several libraries, suggested a revision rate in the range of 4 minutes/ title, indicating an overall input rate of 6 titles/hour. **(112)**

■ A survey reported in 1982 of 144 libraries contracting for OCLC services through the Bibliographic Center for Research (126 or 87.5% responding) *showed that* the top 3 ways of establishing location for an item entered in the OCLC data base were: automatic stamp in the 049 field (49 or 38.9% respondents), automatic stamp in the 049 field for some locations with input stamp in the 049 field for other locations (34 or 27.0% respondents), and input stamp in the 049 field (20 or 15.9% respondents).

(342)

Ibid. . . . *showed that* in addition to location information the 3 most common elements of local information entered on the OCLC record were: copy number (52 or 41.3% respondents consistently entered this data), accession number (49 or 38.9% respondents consistently entered this data), and extent of holdings of a multipart publication (72 or 57.1% respondents reported that they would enter this data if only part of a multivolume set were purchased). **(342)**

Ibid. . . . *showed that* when 2 or more copies of a work were acquired at 1 time 44.4% of the respondents reported they would not indicate multiple copy ownership in the OCLC record if all copies went into the same collection, while 30.2% reported they would not indicate multiple copy ownership even if copies went into different collections. **(342)**

Ibid. . . . *showed that* when a subsequent copy of a title cataloged earlier on OCLC was purchased 70.6% of the respondents reported they would not enter information on the subsequent copy into the OCLC record if the copy were going into the same collection as the earlier copy, while 30.2% reported they would not enter information on the subsequent copy even if it were going into a different collection from the earlier copy. **(342)**

Ibid. . . . *showed that* when the only copy of a work in the library was withdrawn 70.6% of the respondents reported canceling the holdings recorded in the OCLC data base, while 19.8% reported they did not, 6.4% reported varying practices, and 3.2% did not reply to the question.
(342)

Ibid. . . . *showed that* when 1 of several copies of a work in the library that were previously cataloged on OCLC was withdrawn 21.4% of the respondents reported that the OCLC holdings were updated, while 65.9% of the respondents reported that the holdings were not, 4.8% reported that their practice varied, and 7.9% did not answer. **(342)**

Ibid. . . . *showed that* 23 respondents (18.3%) reported editing all fixed fields so that they are complete, 14 (11.1%) respondents reported editing selected fixed fields, 73 (57.9%) respondents reported generally not editing fixed fields, and 16 (12.7%) reported that the practice varies. **(342)**

Academic

■ A 1977 study at Cornell Law Library of 157 OCLC member records and 424 LC records in the OCLC data base *showed that* the average inputting time per record for records with OCLC member cataloging copy was 5.966 minutes compared to 4.498 minutes average inputting time per record for records with LC cataloging copy. **(367)**

■ A 1979 survey of academic libraries listed in the 1979 edition of *OCLC Participating Libraries Arranged by Network and Institution* (survey size: 200 libraries; responding: 166 or 83%) *showed that*, of 158 respondents, the number of non-LC records that libraries reported changing, excluding Cataloging-in-Print copy, changes in the 049 field (local holdings), 590 field (local note), 910 field (user option data), and the 082/092 fields (Dewey call number), were as follows:

no records changed	2 (1.3%)	libraries
1-9% records changed	28 (17.7%)	libraries
10-24% records changed	38 (24.1%)	libraries
25-49% records changed	30 (19.0%)	libraries
50-74% records changed	35 (22.2%)	libraries
75-99% records changed	22 (13.9%)	libraries
100% records changed	3 (1.9%)	libraries **(764)**

Ibid. . . . *showed that*, of 158 respondents, the number of LC records that libraries reported changing, excluding Cataloging-in-Print copy, changes in the 049 field (local holdings), 590 field (local note), 910 field (user option data), and the 082/092 fields (Dewey call number), were as follows:

no records changed	14 (8.9%)	libraries
1-9% records changed	99 (62.7%)	libraries
10-24% records changed	32 (20.3%)	libraries
25-49% records changed	7 (4.4%)	libraries
50% or more records changed	6 (3.8%)	libraries **(764)**

■ A study reported in 1983 of the cataloging records for music, music scores, and musical sound recordings over a 2-month period in 1980 from the Indiana University Music Library and the music cataloging unit of the University of Illinois-Urbana Library (996 cataloging records) *showed that* the number of corrections and changes that had to be made in the OCLC record showed wide variation by format. The average book required 6.1 changes per record, the average score required 10.5 changes per record, and the average sound recording required 15.9 changes per record.

(757)

Ibid. . . . *showed that* most of the changes required were in the control data of the OCLC records (control data elements were represented in the MARC record by the 0XX fields and are generally more important for use in an online catalog than in card production). Specifically, 79% of the changes required in book records, 71% of the changes required by scores, and 54% of the changes required by sound recordings were control data elements. **(757)**

Ibid. . . . *showed that* fewer changes were required for cataloging records generated by the Library of Congress than for cataloging records generated by OCLC members. For example, books required an average of 5.5 changes per record for LC cataloging compared to an average of 11.8 changes per record for OCLC members' cataloging. **(757)**

Ibid. . . . *showed that* 213 different institutions were responsible for inputting the 996 cataloging records in the sample. LC MARC records accounted for 16% of the total, LC records input by OCLC member libraries accounted for 12%, public libraries accounted for 8%, ARL members (excluding Library of Congress) accounted for 34%, and other academic libraries accounted for 30%. **(757)**

Ibid. . . . *showed that* the Library of Congress played a much larger role in the cataloging of music books than in the cataloging of music materials or scores. For example, 58% of the book records were LC MARC records, while 11% of the book records were LC records input by OCLC members. In contrast, only 30% of the records for music materials were generated by LC, while 70% of the records were generated by OCLC member libraries. **(757)**

Special

■ A 1977 study at Cornell Law Library of 157 OCLC member records and 424 LC records in the OCLC data base *showed that* the average inputting time per record for records with OCLC member cataloging copy was 5.966 minutes compared to 4.498 minutes average inputting time per record for records with LC cataloging copy. **(367)**

■ A study reported in 1983 of the cataloging records for music, music scores, and musical sound recordings over a 2-month period in 1980 from the Indiana University Music Library and the music cataloging unit of the University of Illinois-Urbana Library (996 cataloging records) *showed that* the number of corrections and changes that had to be made in the OCLC record showed wide variation by format. The average book required 6.1 changes per record, the average score required 10.5 changes per record, and the average sound recording required 15.9 changes per record. **(757)**

Ibid. . . . *showed that* most of the changes required were in the control data of the OCLC records (control data elements were represented in the MARC record by the 0XX fields and are generally more important for use in an online catalog than in card production). Specifically, 79% of the changes required in book records, 71% of the changes required by scores, and 54% of the changes required by sound recordings were control data elements. **(757)**

Ibid. . . . *showed that* fewer changes were required for cataloging records generated by the Library of Congress than for cataloging records generated by OCLC members. For example, books required an average of 5.5 changes per record for LC cataloging compared to an average of 11.8 changes per record for OCLC members' cataloging. **(757)**

Ibid. . . . *showed that* 213 different institutions were responsible for inputting the 996 cataloging records in the sample. LC MARC records accounted for 16% of the total, LC records input by OCLC member libraries accounted for 12%, public libraries accounted for 8%, ARL members (excluding Library of Congress) accounted for 34%, and other academic libraries accounted for 30%. **(757)**

Ibid. . . . *showed that* the Library of Congress played a much larger role in the cataloging of music books than in the cataloging of music materials or scores. For example, 58% of the book records were LC MARC records, while 11% of the book records were LC records input by OCLC members. In contrast, only 30% of the records for music materials were generated by LC, while 70% of the records were generated by OCLC member libraries. **(757)**

OCLC—Hit Rate

General

■ A survey in 1974 of the 47 charter members of the OCLC network, including site visits and interviews (148) with all levels of library personnel in member libraries, *showed that* when cataloging all except 5 libraries searched all Roman alphabet titles in the data base regardless of publication data or language. An average of 74% of the books in hand were found on the first search, with the range running from 67% for the largest libraries to 80% for the smallest. **(112)**

■ A 1977 study comparing the use of the Blackwell North America and OCLC data bases as sources of cataloging copy for 344 English-language imprints received on the B/NA approval program during a 3-month period [library not reported] *showed that*, after 2 searches about 2 months apart, 247 (72%) of the items were found in the B/NA data base and 315 (92%) were found in the OCLC data base. Further, 232 (67%) were located in both data bases, while 14 (4.1%) were located in neither data base. Neither place nor date of publication affected the hit rate.   **(448)**

■ A study reported in 1981 of OCLC's online union catalog to investigate the scope of its music holdings by checking 4 major lists of materials ("Books Recently Published" column of *Notes*; "Music Received" column of *Notes*; "New Listings" column of the *Schwann-1 Record and Tape Guide*; and *A Basic Music Library: Essential Scores and Books*) in the catalog *showed that*, of the 941 items listed in *A Basic Music Library*, 861 (91.5%) were found, including 231 (94.29%) of the study scores, 195 (96.53%) of the performing editions, and 114 (82.01%) of the instrumental methods and studies. Further, "a large number of specific editions not found in the search" were represented in the OCLC union catalog by other editions.   **(757)**

Ibid. . . . *showed that*, of the 420 items listed in the December 1979 "Music Received" column and searched 1 year later, 255 (60.71%) were found in the OCLC union catalog, while of the 351 items listed in the September 1980 "Music Received" column and searched 1-2 months later, 109 (31.05%) were found in the OCLC union catalog.   **(757)**

Ibid. . . . *showed that*, of the 276 items listed in the December 1979 "New Listings" column and searched 14 months later, 162 (58.7%) were found in the OCLC union catalog, while of the 282 items listed in the September 1980 "New Listings" column and searched 1-2 months later, 64 (22.7%) were found in the OCLC union catalog.   **(757)**

■ A study reported in 1981, of 45 monographs in microform format (randomly selected from the 1979 *Microforms in Print*) searched in RLIN, OCLC, and the *National Union Catalog*, *showed that*:

   exact copy was found for 17.7% of the microform items searched of which 4.4% was Library of Congress cataloging and 13.3% was shared cataloging;

   variant copy was found for 22.3% of the microform items searched of which 6.7% was Library of Congress cataloging and 15.6% was shared cataloging;

exact copy was found for 55.5% of the hard copy editions of the items of which 31.1% was Library of Congress cataloging and 24.4% was shared cataloging;

variant copy was found for 17.7% of the hard copy editions of the 45 items of which 13.3% was Library of Congress cataloging and 4.4% was shared cataloging.   **(768)**

Ibid. . . . *showed that* of the exact copy that was found for 17.7% of the microforms, RLIN provided no exact matches, OCLC provided 11.1% of the matches (all shared cataloging), and the *National Union Catalog* provided 8.8% of the matches (evenly divided between LC and shared cataloging).   **(768)**

Academic

■ A 1978 study at Ohio State University Library involving 2 full days' transactions in the OCLC data base for each of the OSU terminals (1,153 searches of the data base) *showed that* of 605 monographic cataloging searches the 2 most frequent types of searches were by name/title (313 or 51.7% of the monographic cataloging searches of which 180 or 57.5% were successful) and by LCCN (201 or 33.2% of the monographic cataloging searches of which 158 or 78.6% were successful).   **(336)**

Ibid. . . . *showed that*, of 94 serials cataloging searches, the 2 most frequent types of searches were by title (72 or 76.6% of the serials searches of which 32 or 44.4% of the serials cataloging searches were successful) and by name/title (15 or 15.9% of the serials cataloging searches of which 3 or 20.0% were successful).   **(336)**

■ A study reported in 1982 of retrospective conversion of 3 library collections at the University of South Carolina, involving a main collection (Thomas Cooper Library, 47,514 records), a rare book collection (1,985 records), and a historical collection (the South Caroliniana Library, 16,281 records), *showed that* the hit rate for finding records in the data base (OCLC) was 92.7% for the main collection, 78.0% for the rare book collection, and 48.5% for the historical collection.   **(344)**

Special

■ A 1978 study at the General Electric Research and Development Center (Schenectady, New York) comparing the availability of cataloging copy in OCLC vs. Inforonics, which involved searching 3 months of monograph acquisitions (183 titles) in both data bases, *showed that* cataloging copy was found for 153 titles in the OCLC data base compared to 101 titles found in the Inforonics data base. Further, the hit rate in OCLC was better than in Inforonics regardless of country of publication, date of publication, or availability of LC card number. **(433)**

■ A 1977-78 study of acquisitions in 3 Canadian addictions libraries (Alberta Alcoholism and Drug Abuse Commission, British Columbia Alcohol and Drug Commission, Addiction Research Foundation of Ontario) over a 10-month period that were then searched in the OCLC data base (601 titles) *showed that* overall 422 (70.2%) were found in OCLC. Hit rates for the individual libraries were 67%, 68%, and 74%. **(643)**

Ibid. . . . *showed that* 76% of the items were U.S. materials while 19.5% were Canadian titles. The hit rate in OCLC for U.S. materials only was 78.9%, while the hit rate in OCLC for Canadian materials only (117 items) was 40 or 34.2%. **(643)**

OCLC—Impact

General

■ A survey in 1974 of the 47 charter members of the OCLC network, including site visits and interviews (148) with all levels of library personnel in member libraries, *showed that* original cataloging had all but been eliminated in the small libraries (those with printed materials budgets under $100,000) and appeared to be below 20% in the remaining medium to large libraries. **(112)**

Ibid. . . . *showed that* responses from 35 of the libraries regarding production rates for cataloging with records in the OCLC data base ran at an overall average of 14.3 titles/hour. The rate for the 25 libraries using LC classification ran an average of 14.9 titles/hour, while the rate for the 10 libraries using Dewey classification ran 12.9 titles/hour. **(112)**

Ibid. . . . *showed that*, of the libraries using the LC classification system, the cataloging production rate for 5 libraries using restrictive procedures (exact match) was 17.4 titles/hour, for 10 libraries using semirestrictive procedures (close match) 14.9 titles/hour, and for 10 libraries using nonrestrictive procedures the rate was 12.1 titles/hour.   **(112)**

Ibid. . . . *showed that* estimates from 40 libraries for the rate of inputting bibliographic records from pre-tagged input forms averaged 8.7 records/ hour excluding time for revision. Revision rates, based on reports from several libraries, suggested a revision rate in the range of 4 minutes/title, indicating an overall input rate of 6 titles/hour.   **(112)**

Ibid. . . . *showed that* 85% of the interviewees reported that use of the OCLC online data base had not made problems of catalog integration (matching new cataloging with old in terms of series authority, subject authority, names, and corporate bodies) more severe.   **(112)**

Ibid. . . . *showed that* 74% of the interviewees stated that the nonprofessional work had been made more demanding, while only 3 interviewers reported that professional cataloging had been made more demanding.
(112)

Ibid. . . . *showed that*, of the 10 library directors who indicated that their principal goal for joining the OCLC network was cost savings, 80% reported this goal successfully met, while only 41% of the directors of the remaining libraries reported that this goal had been successfully met.
(112)

Ibid. . . . *showed that* reorganization did not necessarily follow from the implementation of online cataloging. After 3 years only 9 libraries (20%) had reorganized the departmental structure of technical services, although the tendency was strongest in the larger libraries.   **(112)**

Ibid. . . . *showed that*, of the charter members, 12 libraries reported no particular objectives for joining the OCLC network, 15 were principally interested in faster cataloging, 10 were principally interested in reducing cataloging costs, 7 in improved ILL, and 3 in miscellaneous objectives. The directors of 80% of the libraries reported their primary objectives had been met.   **(112)**

Ibid. . . . *showed that* 91% of the libraries reported that the time required to catalog books and produce sets of catalog cards had been reduced by online cataloging, while estimates from 28 (59.6%) libraries suggested that the decrease in cataloging and card production turnaround time averaged 2.8 months.   **(112)**

Ibid. . . . *showed that* 63% of the charter member libraries had reduced cataloging staff since beginning online cataloging, dropping a total of 76.83 net positions. However, the degree to which online cataloging contributed to this saving is unclear since other factors such as reorganization, decreased workload, and the like were also involved. **(112)**

Procedures—General Issues

General

■ A study reported in 1971 of 3,905 Indonesian authors listed in 5 different Indonesian bibliographies over varying time periods *showed that* most names were entered under the last element of the name, while only 648 (18%) were entered under the first element of the name. Of these 648 names, 90% are Indonesian names of Chinese origin, where the first element of the name is the surname. **(596)**

■ A survey in 1974 of the 47 charter members of the OCLC network, including site visits and interviews (148) with all levels of library personnel in member libraries, *showed that* 49% of surveyed libraries held books in the cataloging department until cards were received, while 51% sent books on for final processing and shelving directly after cataloging at the terminal. **(112)**

Ibid. . . . *showed that* 6 libraries continued to check the complete shipment of catalog cards to determine if every card for every title was received, although they reported finding very few errors. **(112)**

Ibid. . . . *showed that* reorganization did not necessarily follow from the implementation of online cataloging. After 3 years only 9 libraries (20%) had reorganized the departmental structure of technical services, although the tendency was strongest in the larger libraries. **(112)**

■ A survey reported in 1981 of chief administrators of U.S. theater collections concerning methods of cataloging nonbook theatrical memorabilia (survey size: 40 libraries; responding: 26; usable: 25 or 62.5%) *showed that*:

22 (88%) libraries reported having no complete accessing tools to the nonbook items in the collection;

22 (88%) libraries reported that their cataloging system was

designed by the library staff for their particular collection (however, 6 or 24% libraries reported that they had adopted a preestablished system for the collection). **(769)**

Academic

■   A survey reported in 1966 of 68 libraries in colleges related to a church and having church historical materials in their collection (57 or 83.8% responding; usable replies: 48 or 70.6%) *showed that* 22 libraries reported cataloging all church historical materials, 19 cataloged part of them, and 7 did not catalog any of them. **(176)**

■   A 1970 study at the Washington University School of Medicine Library, investigating the correlation between National Library of Medicine classification numbers and medical subject headings based on cataloging records of 8,137 books cataloged at Washington University during the period 1965-70, *showed that* annotating the subject list with classification numbers might be a helpful procedure. Specifically, out of 8,449 unique subject heading terms, 6,013 (71.2%) terms were associated with a classification number used more than once. **(691)**

■   A 1975 survey of North American medical school libraries concerning subject cataloging practices (survey size: 134 libraries; responding: 114 or 85%) *showed that* the form of the local subject authority file was as follows:

separate card file	55 (48%) libraries	
checking off terms used in the authority	26 (23%) libraries	
public catalog	25 (22%) libraries	
book catalog compiled by library	3 (3%) libraries	
no response	5 (4%) libraries	**(712)**

Ibid. . . . *showed that*, of 78 respondents who used MeSH as the primary authority for subject headings and who also had divided catalogs, 69 (89%) reported using the National Library of Medicine authority for language and geographic subheadings, 5 (7%) reported using "other," and 4 (5%) reported using no authority. **(712)**

Ibid. . . . *showed that*, of 78 respondents who used MeSH as the primary authority for subject headings and who also had divided catalogs, the following practices were followed when National Library of Medicine subject cataloging copy was available:

follow NLM with minor variations	55 (70%) libraries
follow NLM without exception	14 (18%) libraries
follow NLM with many changes	3 (4%) libraries
other	4 (5%) libraries
no response	2 (3%) libraries **(712)**

■ A 1977 survey of U.S. law libraries over 10,000 volumes taken from the 1976 *Directory of Law Libraries* (sample size: 1,080; responding: 373 or 35%) *showed that*, of 123 academic law libraries and 250 remaining law libraries, 98% of the academic law libraries and 66% of the remaining law libraries reported using the Anglo-American Cataloging rules, while 78% of the academic law libraries and 61% of the remaining law libraries reported using the ALA filing rules. **(366)**

■ A survey reported in 1977 concerning university libraries' handling of doctoral and master's theses generated locally, based on a stratified sample of universities offering the doctoral degree (survey size: 100; responding: 90 or 90%), *showed that*, of 89 respondents, 67 (75.3%) reported receiving the theses in an unbound state, 19 (21.3%) received bound theses, 2 (2.2%) received master's theses bound and the doctoral theses unbound, and 1 (1.1%) received microfilm copy only. **(639)**

Ibid. . . . *showed that*, of the 88 respondents that reported formal thesis format regulations, the library alone was responsible for establishing the format standards in 1 (1.1%) case, while the library cooperated in establishing standards with other unviersity bodies in 13 (14.8%) cases. As far as checking the format was concerned, of the 90 respondents the library alone was responsible for such checking in 3 (3.3%) cases, while the library shared responsibility for format checking in 17 (18.9%) cases. **(639)**

■ A 1977 survey of academic libraries with collections of 300,000 volumes or more that were also OCLC members concerning cataloging practices (survey size: 147 libraries; responding: 121 or 82.3%) *showed that* the following local authority files were used by libraries (large libraries = 900,000 volumes or more; small libraries = less than 900,000 volumes):

name authority file	78.1% large; 59% small libraries
subject authority file	64.9% large; 50% small libraries
series authority file	88.1% large; 97% small libraries
other (usually geographic names)	5.9% large; 2% small libraries **(760)**

■ A 1978 survey of law school libraries listed in the 1977 *AALS Directory of Law Teachers* (population: 167; responding: 158 or 95%) *showed that* 19 (12%) of the law school libraries had their materials cataloged in the university library. This compares to 15% reported in a 1973 survey and 24% reported in a 1937 survey. **(362)**

■ A 1979 survey of U.S. community college libraries selected from the 1978 *Community, Junior and Technical College Directory* (sample size: 98; responding: 52; usable: 48 or 48.98%) *showed that*, of 46 respondents, 39 (84.8%) reported that they did not participate in computerized cataloging networks. Of the 39, 23 (59.0%) reported they did not plan to join such a network, while 7 (17.9%) said they did, 8 (20.5%) said they were undecided, and 3 (7.7%) did not respond. Of the 7 libraries that did participate in such networks, 6 (85.7%) used OCLC, while 1 (14.3%) used the Washington Library Network. **(498)**

■ A 1979 study at Memphis State University concerning errors in the OCLC data base and based on all error reports generated at Memphis State over a 2-month period (175 error reports) *showed that* the cost (labor only) of reporting the 175 OCLC data base errors was $184.07 for 175 error reports. **(765)**

■ A survey in 1979 of 119 major academic business libraries (responding: 89 or 75%; usable: 86) *showed that*, out of 85 responses, 45% of the libraries indicated that they catalog working papers. Of those that did catalog the papers, 17 cataloged them as monographs, 19 as serials, and 10 as either. **(120)**

Ibid. . . . *showed that*, of the faculty responding, 38 of the Illinois faculty (48.7%) and 33 of the Purdue faculty (80.5%) felt that the library should catalog all working papers. **(120)**

Ibid. . . . *showed that* of 82 respondents the treatment of imperfect copies was as follows:

collate and correct	40 (48.8%) libraries
return to student, department, or school	15 (18.3%) libraries
not dealt with by catalogers	12 (14.6%) libraries
describe as received	9 (11.0%) libraries
do not collate but try to correct flaws	6 (7.3%) libraries **(639)**

■ A study reported in 1981 at Washington State University comparing the costs of an automated network system (Washington Library Network) and a local manual system of cataloging and book processing *showed that* the automated system was "almost 20%" less expensive than the manual system based on derived monthly costs. The higher costs of the manual system were "essentially staff costs." Even in the automated system the nonstaff costs of cataloging and book processing only accounted for 27% of the total. **(335)**

Public

■ A 1969 survey of Canadian public libraries serving populations of more than 10,000 people as well as all county and regional libraries belonging to the Canadian Library Association concerning holdings and use of non-English collections (survey size: 203; responding: 83 or 41%) *showed that*, of 74 respondents, 56 (75.7%) libraries reported they fully cataloged books in non-English languages. In 52 (70.3%) libraries the cataloging was handled by library staff. **(534)**

■ A 1981-82 study of media cataloging practices in 932 public libraries (responding: 466 or 50%; usable: 488 or 48%) across the U.S. serving communities of all sizes *showed that* 83% catalog their nonprint holdings. A further 21 (4.7%) reported that they cataloged part of their nonprint holdings. **(161)**

Ibid. . . . *showed that* 46% of responding libraries were using AACR 2 for nonprint cataloging (compared to 57% using AACR 2 for print materials). Of those not using AACR 2 for cataloging, 54% reported no plans for adopting it for printed materials, and 71% reported no plans for adopting it for nonprint use. **(161)**

Ibid. . . . *showed that*, although 96+% of respondents used Dewey classification for print materials, only about one-third used it for nonprint materials. **(161)**

Special

■ A 1970 study at the Washington University School of Medicine Library, investigating the correlation between National Library of Medicine classification numbers and medical subject headings based on cataloging records of 8,137 books cataloged at Washington University during the period 1965-70, *showed that* annotating the subject list with classification numbers might be a helpful procedure. Specifically, out of 8,449 unique subject heading terms, 6,013 (71.2%) terms were associated with a classification number used more than once.   **(691)**

■ A study reported in 1974 of U.S. libraries that had switched to the National Library of Medicine classification system between 1959 and 1973 (survey size: 25 libraries; responding: 25 or 100%) *showed that* the 3 main reasons given for switching were (multiple responses allowed): to take advantage of the NLM cataloging service (13 or 52%), to provide better shelf arrangement for the library's books (11 or 44%), and found classification easier with the NLM system (10 or 40%).   **(701)**

Ibid. . . . *showed that* 24 (96%) libraries used the Library of Congress classification system for subjects outside the scope of the NLM classification, while 1 (4%) did not. Of those 24, 9 reported use of selected broad LC class numbers, while 16 reported use of specific LC class numbers.
                                                                                    (701)

■ A 1975 survey of North American medical school libraries concerning subject cataloging practices (survey size: 134 libraries; responding: 114 or 85%) *showed that* the form of the local subject authority file was as follows:

separate card file	55 (48%) libraries	
checking off terms used in the authority	26 (23%) libraries	
public catalog	25 (22%) libraries	
book catalog compiled by library	3 (3%) libraries	
no response	5 (4%) libraries	**(712)**

Ibid. . . . *showed that*, of 78 respondents who used MeSH as the primary authority for subject headings and who also had divided catalogs, 69 (89%) reported using the National Library of Medicine authority for language and geographic subheadings, 5 (7%) reported using "other," and 4 (5%) reported using no authority.   **(712)**

Ibid. . . . *showed that*, of 78 respondents who used MeSH as the primary authority for subject headings and who also had divided catalogs, the following practices were followed when National Library of Medicine subject cataloging copy was available:

follow NLM with minor variations	55 (70%) libraries
follow NLM without exception	14 (18%) libraries
follow NLM with many changes	3 (4%) libraries

continued

other   4 (5%) libraries
no response   2 (3%) libraries   **(712)**

■ A survey reported in 1975 of subject heading use in a wide range of law libraries selected from the 1972 edition of the American Association of Law Libraries *Directory of Law Libraries* (sample size: 256; responding: 204; usable: 200 or 78.1%) *showed that* respondents used the following subject heading lists:

Library of Congress list (with
    modification)   46 (23.0%) respondents
Library of Congress list (with no
    modification)   33 (16.5%) respondents
responding library's own list   27 (13.5%) respondents
Ellinger list (with modification)   16 (8.0%) respondents
Ellinger list (with no modification)   5 (2.5%) respondents
Columbia list   5 (2.5%) respondents
some other published list   2 (1.0%) respondents
combination of above lists
    (including Northwestern list)   66 (33.0%) respondents
                                                              (393)

Ibid. . . . *showed that*, of 129 respondents using modified lists, the 2 main changes were: changes in the subject headings starting with the word "law" including subdivisions, such as "law and legislation" (87 or 67.4% respondents) and establishment of new subject headings at the responding library (e.g., when LC is slow in establishing them) (73 or 56.6% respondents).
                                                              (393)

Ibid. . . . *showed that* 79 (39.5%) respondents kept their subject heading list as a "marked copy of a published list," 50 (25%) kept their subject heading list as a card file, 30 (15%) used more than 1 way of keeping their subject heading list, 28 (14%) used looseleaf format, and 2 (1%) used miscellaneous other formats. 8 (4%) respondents reported they had no subject authority file, and 3 (1.5%) did not respond.   **(393)**

Ibid. . . . *showed that* 148 (74%) respondents reported they did not keep auxiliary subject heading records, while (multiple responses allowed) 25 (12.5%) reported keeping subject subdivision files, and 17 (8.5%) kept geographic name files. 15 (7.5%) other responses were not considered appropriate for the purposes of this question.   **(393)**

Ibid. . . . *showed that* the following cross-reference structure was kept in the public card catalog:

full structure (see and see also references)	97 (48.5%) respondents
see references and selected see also references	71 (35.5%) respondents
see references only	20 (10.0%) respondents
none	12 (6.0%) respondents **(393)**

Ibid. . . . *showed that* 50 (25%) respondents were satisfied with the subject heading list they were using, 80 (40%) were somewhat satisfied, 7 (3.5%) were dissatisfied, and 63 (31.5%) had no opinion. **(393)**

■ A 1977 survey of U.S. law libraries over 10,000 volumes taken from the 1976 *Directory of Law Libraries* (sample size: 1,080; responding: 373 or 35%) *showed that*, of 123 academic law libraries and 250 remaining law libraries, 65% of the academic law libraries and 57% of the remaining law libraries reported using authority files for subject headings, 39% of the academic law libraries and 20% of the remaining law libraries reported using authority files for personal and corporate names, and 63% of the academic law libraries and 23% of the remaining law libraries reported using authority files for series. **(366)**

Ibid. . . . *showed that*, of 123 academic law libraries and 250 remaining law libraries, 94% of the academic law libraries and 84% of the remaining law libraries reported using "see references," while 76% of the academic law libraries and 67% of the remaining law libraries reported using "see also references." **(366)**

Ibid. . . . *showed that*, of 123 academic law libraries and 250 remaining law libraries, 98% of the academic law libraries and 66% of the remaining law libraries reported using the Anglo-American Cataloging rules, while 78% of the academic law libraries and 61% of the remaining law libraries reported using the ALA filing rules. **(366)**

■ A 1978 survey of law school libraries listed in the 1977 *AALS Directory of Law Teachers* (population: 167; responding: 158 or 95%) *showed that* 19 (12%) of the law school libraries had their materials cataloged in the university library. This compares to 15% reported in a 1973 survey and 24% reported in a 1937 survey. **(362)**

■ A study reported in 1983 investigating consistency of indexing in MEDLINE, based on 760 articles published between 1974 and 1980 that were indexed twice in INDEX MEDICUS, *showed that* MeSH headings and subheadings were applied with more consistency to central concepts than to peripheral points, that the addition of subheadings to main headings lowered consistency, and that "floating" subheadings were more consistent than attached subheadings. The degree of consistency for different types of headings and subheadings was as follows:

checktags	74.7%	consistency
central concept main headings	61.1%	consistency
geographics	56.6%	consistency
descriptors	55.4%	consistency
central concept subheadings	54.9%	consistency
subheadings	48.7%	consistency
main headings	48.2%	consistency
central concept main headings/ subheadings combinations	43.1%	consistency
main heading/subheading combinations	33.8%	consistency **(748)**

Ibid. . . . *showed that* inconsistency in the use of geographic terms was not caused by different geographic terms applied to the same item but whether a geographic term was used at all. In other words, some indexers would use a geographic heading for an article and some would not. In order to retrive all relevant articles, therefore, care should be taken when using a geographic heading. **(748)**

Ibid. . . . *showed that* length of article, language of article, and journal indexing priority had no statistically significant effect on consistency. Further, in all 9 categories of index terms the average number of terms used (depth of indexing) showed no statistically significant differences. **(748)**

Procedures—Bibliographic Elements, MeSH

General

■ A study reported in 1983 investigating consistency of indexing in MEDLINE, based on 760 articles published between 1974 and 1980 that were indexed twice in INDEX MEDICUS, *showed that* MeSH headings and subheadings were applied with more consistency to central concepts than to peripheral points, that the addition of subheadings to main headings lowered consistency, and that "floating" subheadings were more consistent than attached subheadings. The degree of consistency for different types of headings and subheadings was as follows:

checktags	74.7% consistency
central concept main headings	61.1% consistency
geographics	56.6% consistency
descriptors	55.4% consistency
central concept subheadings	54.9% consistency
subheadings	48.7% consistency
main headings	48.2% consistency
central concept main headings/ subheadings combinations	43.1% consistency
main heading/subheading combinations	33.8% consistency **(748)**

Ibid. . . . *showed that* inconsistency in the use of geographic terms was not caused by different geographic terms applied to the same item but whether a geographic term was used at all. In other words, some indexers would use a geographic heading for an article and some would not. In order to retrive all relevant articles, therefore, care should be taken when using a geographic heading.   **(748)**

Ibid. . . . *showed that* length of article, language of article, and journal indexing priority had no statistically significant effect on consistency. Further, in all 9 categories of index terms the average number of terms used (depth of indexing) showed no statistically significant differences.
(748)

Procedures—MeSH

Academic

■ A 1970 study at the Washington University School of Medicine Library, investigating the correlation between National Library of Medicine classification numbers and medical subject headings based on cataloging records of 8,137 books cataloged at Washington University during the period 1965-70, *showed that* annotating the subject list with classification numbers might be a helpful procedure. Specifically, out of 8,449 unique subject heading terms, 6,013 (71.2%) terms were associated with a classification number used more than once. **(691)**

■ A 1975 survey of North American medical school libraries concerning subject cataloging practices (survey size: 134 libraries; responding: 114 or 85%) *showed that*, of 78 respondents who used MeSH as the primary authority for subject headings and who also had divided catalogs, 69 (89%) reported using the National Library of Medicine authority for language and geographic subheadings, 5 (7%) reported using "other," and 4 (5%) reported using no authority. **(712)**

Ibid. . . . *showed that*, of 78 respondents who used MeSH as the primary authority for subject headings and who also had divided catalogs, the following practices were followed when National Library of Medicine subject cataloging copy was available:

follow NLM with minor variations	55 (70%) libraries
follow NLM without exception	14 (18%) libraries
follow NLM with many changes	3 (4%) libraries
other	4 (5%) libraries
no response	2 (3%) libraries **(712)**

Special

■ A 1970 study at the Washington University School of Medicine Library, investigating the correlation between National Library of Medicine classification numbers and medical subject headings based on cataloging records of 8,137 books cataloged at Washington University during the period 1965-70, *showed that* annotating the subject list with classification numbers might be a helpful procedure. Specifically, out of 8,449 unique subject heading terms, 6,013 (71.2%) terms were associated with a classification number used more than once. **(691)**

■ A 1975 survey of North American medical school libraries concerning subject cataloging practices (survey size: 134 libraries; responding: 114 or 85%) *showed that*, of 78 respondents who used MeSH as the primary authority for subject headings and who also had divided catalogs, 69 (89%) reported using the National Library of Medicine authority for language and geographic subheadings, 5 (7%) reported using "other," and 4 (5%) reported using no authority. **(712)**

Ibid. . . . *showed that*, of 78 respondents who used MeSH as the primary authority for subject headings and who also had divided catalogs, the following practices were followed when National Library of Medicine subject cataloging copy was available:

follow NLM with minor variations	55 (70%)	libraries
follow NLM without exception	14 (18%)	libraries
follow NLM with many changes	3 (4%)	libraries
other	4 (5%)	libraries
no response	2 (3%)	libraries **(712)**

Procedures—OCLC

General

■ A survey reported in 1982 of 144 libraries contracting for OCLC services through the Bibliographic Center for Research (126 or 87.5% responding) *showed that* the top 3 ways of establishing location for an item entered in the OCLC data base were: automatic stamp in the 049 field (49 or 38.9% respondents), automatic stamp in the 049 field for some locations with input stamp in the 049 field for other locations (34 or 27.0% respondents), and input stamp in the 049 field (20 or 15.9% respondents).
(342)

Ibid. . . . *showed that* in addition to location information the 3 most common elements of local information entered on the OCLC record were: copy number (52 or 41.3% respondents consistently entered this data), accession number (49 or 38.9% respondents consistently entered this data), and extent of holdings of a multipart publication (72 or 57.1% respondents reported that they would enter this data if only part of a multivolume set were purchased).
(342)

Ibid. . . . *showed that* when 2 or more copies of a work were acquired at 1 time 44.4% of the respondents reported they would not indicate multiple copy ownership in the OCLC record if all copies went into the same collection, while 30.2% reported they would not indicate multiple copy ownership even if copies went into different collections.
(342)

Ibid. . . . *showed that* when a subsequent copy of a title cataloged earlier on OCLC was purchased 70.6% of the respondents reported they would not enter information on the subsequent copy into the OCLC record if the copy was going into the same collection as the earlier copy, while 30.2%

reported they would not enter information on the subsequent copy even if it was going into a different collection from the earlier copy. **(342)**

Academic

■ A 1977 survey of academic libraries with collections of 300,000 volumes or more that were also OCLC members concerning cataloging practices (survey size: 147 libraries; responding: 121 or 82.3%) *showed that* in large libraries (900,000 volumes or more) cataloging staff were used as follows:

> adapting LC records for the same edition: 1.6% libraries used professional catalogers only, 58.3% used support staff only, and 40% used both professional and support staff;

> adapting LC records for different editions: 23.3% libraries used professional catalogers only, 31.6% used support staff only, and 45% used both professional and support staff;

> completing CIP records: 5% libraries used professional catalogers only, 66.6% used support staff only, and 28.3% used both professional and support staff;

> verifying member cataloging records: 23.3% libraries used professionals only, 11.5% used professionals with support staff assisting in verification, 13.3% used support staff only, and 46.6% used both professional and support staff [remaining percentage unaccounted for];

> cataloging without copy: 56.6% libraries used professionals only, 16.6% used professionals with support staff assisting with verification, 1.6% used support staff only, and 15% used both professionals and support staff. **(760)**

Ibid. . . . *showed that*, in small (under 900,000 volumes) libraries, cataloging staff were used as follows:

> adapting LC records for the same edition: 10% libraries used professionals only, 28% used support staff only, and 62% used both professional and support staff;

> adapting LC records for different editions: 33% libraries used professionals only, 9% used support staff only, and 59% used both professional and support staff;

> completing CIP records: 7% libraries used professionals only, 43% used support staff only, and 50% used both professional and support staff;

> verifying member cataloging records: 21% libraries used professionals only, 29% used professionals with assistance from support staff, 7% used support staff only, and 43% used both professional and support staff;

cataloging without copy: 59% libraries used professionals only, 29% used professionals assisted by support staff for verification, none used support staff only, and 12% used both professional and support staff.   **(760)**

■ A 1978 study at Ohio State University Library involving 2 full days' transactions in the OCLC data base for each of the OSU terminals (1,153 searches of the data base) *showed that* of 605 monographic cataloging searches the 2 most frequent types of searches were by name/title (313 or 51.7% of the monographic cataloging searches of which 180 or 57.5% were successful) and by LCCN (201 or 33.2% of the monographic cataloging searches of which 158 or 78.6% were successful).   **(336)**

Ibid. . . . *showed that* of 94 serials cataloging searches the 2 most frequent types of searches were by title (72 or 76.6% of the serials searches of which 32 or 44.4% of the serials cataloging searches were successful) and by name/title (15 or 15.9% of the serials cataloging searches of which 3 or 20.0% were successful).   **(336)**

Ibid. . . . *showed that* the use of the personal author (by itself), ISBN, ISSN, and CODEN search keys "was very limited for all library functions. Corporate-author search keys were not used at all."   **(336)**

■ A 1979 survey of academic libraries listed in the 1979 edition of *OCLC Participating Libraries Arranged by Network and Institution* (survey size: 200 libraries; responding: 166 or 83%) *showed that*, of 109 respondents, 137 (86.2%) reported that they always made substantial checks (i.e., checking "for more than typographical and tagging errors and completing the fixed field") in at least some types of non-LC records in the OCLC data base. Only 22 (13.8%) libraries reported that they never substantially checked non-LC records. The 3 most frequently checked types of non-LC records were:

all types	75 (68.8%) libraries	
records from certain cataloging libraries	21 (19.3%) libraries	
audiovisual materials	11 (10.1%) libraries	**(764)**

Ibid. . . . *showed that*, of 160 respondents, 13 (8.1%) reported using the OCLC-MARC tapes, 85 (53.1%) reported that they planned to use the tapes, and 62 (38.7%) reported they "do not use" the tapes.   **(764)**

■ A study reported in 1983 of the cataloging records for music, music scores, and musical sound recordings over a 2-month period in 1980 from the Indiana University Music Library and the music cataloging unit of the University of Illinois-Urbana Library (996 cataloging records) *showed that* the number of corrections and changes that had to be made in the OCLC record showed wide variation by format. The average book required 6.1 changes per record, the average score required 10.5 changes per record, and the average sound recording required 15.9 changes per record.

(757)

Ibid. . . . *showed that* most of the changes required were in the control data of the OCLC records (control data elements are represented in the MARC record by the 0XX fields and are generally more important for use in an online catalog than in card production). Specifically, 79% of the changes required in book records, 71% of the changes required by scores, and 54% of the changes required by sound recordings were control data elements.

(757)

Ibid. . . . *showed that* fewer changes were required for cataloging records generated by the Library of Congress than for cataloging records generated by OCLC members. For example, books required an average of 5.5 changes per record for LC cataloging compared to an average of 11.8 changes per record for OCLC members' cataloging.

(757)

Ibid. . . . *showed that* when the only copy of a work in the library was withdrawn 70.6% of the respondents reported canceling the holdings recorded in the OCLC data base, while 19.8% reported they did not, 6.4% reported varying practices, and 3.2% did not reply to the question.

(342)

Ibid. . . . *showed that* when 1 of several copies of a work in the library that were previously cataloged on OCLC was withdrawn 21.4% of the respondents reported that the OCLC holdings were updated, while 65.9% of the respondents reported that the holdings were not, 4.8% reported that their practice varied, and 7.9% did not answer.

(342)

Special

■ A study reported in 1983 of the cataloging records for music, music scores, and musical sound recordings over a 2-month period in 1980 from the Indiana University Music Library and the music cataloging unit of the University of Illinois-Urbana Library (996 cataloging records) *showed that* the number of corrections and changes that had to be made in the OCLC record showed wide variation by format. The average book required 6.1 changes per record, the average score required 10.5 changes per record, and the average sound recording required 15.9 changes per record.

(757)

Ibid. . . . *showed that* most of the changes required were in the control data of the OCLC records (control data elements are represented in the MARC record by the 0XX fields and are generally more important for use in an online catalog than in card production). Specifically, 79% of the changes required in book records, 71% of the changes required by scores, and 54% of the changes required by sound recordings were control data elements.   **(757)**

Ibid. . . . *showed that* fewer changes were required for cataloging records generated by the Library of Congress than for cataloging records generated by OCLC members. For example, books required an average of 5.5 changes per record for LC cataloging compared to an average of 11.8 changes per record for OCLC members' cataloging.   **(757)**

Ibid. . . . *showed that* when the only copy of a work in the library was withdrawn 70.6% of the respondents reported canceling the holdings recorded in the OCLC data base, while 19.8% reported they did not, 6.4% reported varying practices, and 3.2% did not reply to the question.

(342)

Ibid. . . . *showed that* when 1 of several copies of a work in the library that were previously cataloged on OCLC was withdrawn 21.4% of the respondents reported that the OCLC holdings were updated, while 65.9% of the respondents reported that the holdings were not, 4.8% reported that their practice varied, and 7.9% did not answer.   **(342)**

Procedures—Romanization

General

■ A 1974 survey of libraries world-wide concerning scripts used and script conversion practices employed in their catalogs (sample size: 231; responding: 146 or 63%) *showed that* the Cyrillic romanization schemes used by 90 respondents were as follows:

Library of Congress or adaptions thereof	33 (36.7%)
International Organization for Standardization or adaptions thereof	28 (31.1%)
Preussische Instruktionen	13 (14.4%)
own	7 (7.8%)
British Standards Institution	5 (5.6%)
British Museum	2 (2.2%)
other published schemes	2 (2.2%) **(356)**

Ibid. . . . *showed that* the romanization schemes used for Japanese by 56 respondents were as follows: Hepburn (51 or 91.1%), own (4 or [7.1%]), and Kunrei-shiki (1 or [1.8%]). **(356)**

Ibid. . . . *showed that* the romanization schemes used for Devanagari (India) by 44 respondents were as follows:

Library of Congress or adaptions thereof	19 (43.2%)
own	10 (22.7%)
other published schemes	7 (16.0%)
Preussische Instruktionen	6 (13.6%)
British Museum	2 (4.5%) **(356)**

Ibid. . . . *showed that* the romanization schemes used for Arabic by 76 respondents were as follows:

Library of Congress or adaptions thereof	29 (37.7%)
own	13 (16.9%)
International Organization for Standardization	12 (15.6%)
Preussische Instruktionen	11 (14.2%)
other published	7 (9.1%)
British Museum	4 (5.2%)
British Standards Institution	1 (1.3%) **(356)**

Ibid. . . . *showed that* the romanization schemes used for Chinese by 69 respondents were:

Wade-Giles	57 (82.6%)
own	7 (10.1%)
Pin-Yin	2 (2.9%)
Kunrei-shiki	2 (2.9%)
other published	1 (1.5%) **(356)**

Ibid. . . . *showed that* the romanization schemes used for Korean by 45 respondents were:

McCune-Reischauer	37 (82.3%)	
own	4 (8.9%)	
Kunrei-shiki	2 (4.4%)	
other published	2 (4.4%)	**(356)**

Ibid. . . . *showed that* the romanization schemes used for Greek by 67 respondents were:

Library of Congress or adaptions thereof	30 (44.8%)	
own	13 (19.4%)	
International Organization for Standardization or adaptions thereof	12 (17.9%)	
Preussische Instruktionen	9 (13.4%)	
British Museum	1 (1.5%)	
British Standards Institution	1 (1.5%)	
other published	1 (1.5%)	**(356)**

Ibid. . . . *showed that* the romanization schemes used for Hebrew by 67 respondents were:

Library of Congress or adaptions thereof	27 (40.3%)	
Preussische Instruktionen	13 (19.4%)	
own	12 (17.9%)	
International Organization for Standardization	9 (13.4%)	
other published	4 (6.0%)	
British Museum	1 (1.5%)	**(356)**

Ibid. . . . *showed that* 98 (67.1%) libraries reported romanizing all their scripts, 20 (13.7%) libraries reported that Cyrillic and/or Greek were romanized but that separate catalogs were used for other scripts, and 28 (19.2%) libraries reported that separate catalogs were used for each script. **(356)**

Ibid. . . . *showed that*, of 134 respondents, 76 (56%) romanized the whole entry, 44 (32%) romanized both the author and the title, and 24 (18%) romanized either the author's name or the title. **(356)**

Ibid. . . . *showed that* those parts of the entry that are translated by responding libraries were as follows: corporate author (11 or 8% respondents always translated, 26 or 18% sometimes translated), title (16 or 11% always translated, 15 or 10% sometimes translated), and whole entry (1 or less than 1% always translated, 6 or 4% sometimes translated). **(356)**

Ibid. . . . *showed that* 5 (3%) libraries provided cross-references from non-Roman to romanized entries, while 5 (3%) libraries provided cross-references from romanized entries to non-Roman entries. **(356)**

Ibid. . . . *showed that* 12 (8%) libraries used no kind of script conversion in their catalogs. **(356)**

■ A study reported in 1978 concerning book publishing in non-Roman scripts based on book production figures reported in the *UNESCO Statistical Yearbook* (1974) *showed that* of 566,000 titles reported published in 1973 the 10 most frequently used scripts (accounting for 99.2% of the reported publishing) were:

Roman	404,000 (71.3%)	titles
Cyrillic	81,000 (14.3%)	titles
Japanese	35,500 (6.3%)	titles
Chinese	11,200 (1.9%)	titles
Devanagari	8,800 (1.6%)	titles
Arabic	7,500 (1.3%)	titles
Korean	7,400 (1.3%)	titles
Greek	2,300 (0.4%)	titles
Thai	2,200 (0.4%)	titles
Hebrew	2,000 (0.4%)	titles **(641)**

Production Rate

General

■ A survey reported in 1974 of the 47 charter members of the OCLC network, including site visits and interviews (148) with all levels of library personnel in member libraries, *showed that* responses from 35 of the libraries regarding production rates for cataloging with records in the OCLC data base ran at an overall average of 14.3 titles/hour. The rate for the 25 libraries using LC classification ran an average of 14.9 titles/hour, while the rate for the 10 libraries using Dewey classification ran 12.9 titles/hour. **(112)**

Ibid. . . . *showed that* of the libraries using the LC classification system the production rate for 5 libraries using restrictive procedures (exact match) was 17.4 titles/hour, for 10 libraries using semirestrictive procedures (close match) 14.9 titles/hour, and for 10 libraries using nonrestrictive procedures the rate was 12.1 titles/hour. **(112)**

Ibid. . . . *showed that* estimates from 40 libraries for the rate of inputting bibliographic records from pre-tagged input forms averaged 8.7 records/hour excluding time for revision. Revision rates, based on reports from several libraries, suggested a revision rate in the range of 4 minutes/title, indicating an overall input rate of 6 titles/hour. **(112)**

Academic

■ A study during academic 1972-73 of cataloging production at Wichita State University involving 4 professional catalogers who handled original and problem cataloging and reclassification along with other duties such as catalog maintenance and editing of nonprofessional copy cataloging (a total of 15,450 titles; 24,494 volumes) *showed that* the average number of titles handled per day per professional ranged from 10 to 25, while the average number of volumes handled per day ranged from 20 to 31.
(637)

■ A 1977 study at Cornell Law Library of 157 OCLC member records and 424 LC records in the OCLC data base *showed that* the average cataloging time per record for records with OCLC member cataloging copy was 9.076 minutes compared to 8.148 minutes cataloging time per record for records with LC cataloging copy. **(367)**

Ibid. . . . *showed that* the average inputting time per record for records with OCLC member cataloging copy was 5.966 minutes compared to 4.498 minutes average inputting time per record for records with LC cataloging copy. **(367)**

■ A 1977 survey of academic libraries with collections of 300,000 volumes or more that were also OCLC members concerning cataloging practices (survey size: 147 libraries; responding: 121 or 82.3%) *showed that*:

for libraries with 900,000 volumes or more the average OCLC production (on a first-time use basis) was 2,175 titles per month and ranged from 500 to 5,455 titles per month;

for libraries with less than 900,000 volumes, the average OCLC production (on a first-time use basis) was 1,256 titles per month and ranged from 300 to 3,800 titles per month. **(760)**

■ A 1979 survey of U.S. community college libraries selected from the 1978 *Community, Junior and Technical College Directory* (sample size: 98; responding: 52; usable: 48 or 48.98%) *showed that* the number of books [cataloged] added monthly to the collection was as follows:

0-100	14 (29.20%) libraries
101-500	19 (39.60%) libraries
500+	1 (2.08%) libraries
not recorded/not answered	14 (29.20%) libraries **(498)**

Ibid. . . . *showed that* the number of audiovisual materials added monthly to the collection was as follows:

0-100	31 (64.60%) libraries
500+	1 (2.08%) libraries
not recorded/not answered	16 (33.33%) libraries **(498)**

■ A 1979 survey of academic libraries listed in the 1979 edition of *OCLC Participating Libraries Arranged by Network and Institution* (survey size: 200 libraries; responding: 166 or 83%) *showed that* of 166 respondents the number of titles cataloged per year via OCLC was as follows:

less than 5,000 titles	69 (41.6%) libraries
5,000-9,999 titles	39 (23.5%) libraries
10,000-14,999 titles	31 (18.7%) libraries
15,000 or more titles	27 (16.2%) libraries **(764)**

Special

■ A 1977 study at Cornell Law Library of 157 OCLC member records and 424 LC records in the OCLC data base *showed that* the average cataloging time per record for records with OCLC member cataloging copy was 9.076 minutes compared to 8.148 minutes cataloging time per record for records with LC cataloging copy. **(367)**

Ibid. . . . *showed that* the average inputting time per record for records with OCLC member cataloging copy was 5.966 minutes compared to 4.498 minutes average inputting time per record for records with LC cataloging copy. **(367)**

Quality

General

■ A study reported in 1983 investigating consistency of indexing in MEDLINE based on 760 articles published between 1974 and 1980 that were indexed twice in INDEX MEDICUS *showed that* MeSH headings and subheadings were applied with more consistency to central concepts than to peripheral points, that the addition of subheadings to main headings lowered consistency, and that "floating" subheadings were more consistent than attached subheadings. The degree of consistency for different types of headings and subheadings was as follows:

checktags	74.7% consistency	
central concept main headings	61.1% consistency	
geographics	56.6% consistency	
descriptors	55.4% consistency	
central concept subheadings	54.9% consistency	
subheadings	48.7% consistency	
main headings	48.2% consistency	
central concept main headings/ subheadings combinations	43.1% consistency	
main heading/subheading combinations	33.8% consistency	**(748)**

Ibid. . . . *showed that* inconsistency in the use of geographic terms was not caused by different geographic terms applied to the same item but whether a geographic term was used at all. In other words, some indexers would use a geographic heading for an article and some would not. In order to retrive all relevant articles, therefore, care should be taken when using a geographic heading. **(748)**

Ibid. . . . *showed that* length of article, language of article, and journal indexing priority had no statistically significant effect on consistency. Further, in all 9 categories of index terms the average number of terms used (depth of indexing) showed no statistically significant differences. **(748)**

Academic

■ A study during the academic year 1961-62 in the physics library of the University of California, Los Angeles comparing book titles with subject headings assigned during cataloging (study size: 410 titles acquired during a 12-month period, excluding added copies, textbooks, etc.) *showed that*:

exact or equivalent match	147 (36%)	titles
probable match	151 (37%)	titles
no match	72 (15%)	titles
special problems	19 (5%)	titles
no headings	21 (7%)	titles (582)

■ A study reported in 1965 of card catalogs in 8 libraries (7 academic and 1 other), all of which followed the *Subject Headings Used in the Dictionary Catalog of the Library of Congress, showed that* subject headings did not appear to be assigned with a great deal of consistency from 1 library to the next. Specifically, of 76 titles that had been assigned the subject term "communication" in at least 1 library but that appeared in more than 1 of the 8 libraries, only 55 (72%) of the titles had had the subject term assigned consistently in all libraries. (584)

■ A study reported in 1981 at Purdue University of the degree to which books in 5 different subject areas as determined by reviews and bibliographies in the disciplines were actually classed in those areas by Dewey and LC cataloging [source of cataloging not given] (anthropology: 254 books; history: 352 books; political science: 534 books; sociology: 602 books; and philosophy: 265 books) *showed that* a shelflist count [based on class numbers] would have missed between 30 to 80% of the titles in the 5 disciplines. (574)

Ibid. . . . *showed that* the number of titles in each of the disciplines not reflected by an appropriate Dewey class number was as follows:

anthropology	204 (80.3%)	not in class
history	241 (68.5%)	not in class
sociology	390 (64.7%)	not in class
philosophy	58 (35.2%)	not in class
political science	167 (31.3%)	not in class (574)

Special

■ A 1977 study at Cornell Law Library of 301 cataloging records found in the OCLC data base (151 input by LC; 150 input by OCLC member libraries) *showed that* to make usable cataloging the LC records required an average of 1.13 modifications per record, while the OCLC member cataloging required an average of 2.97 modifications per record. When call number problems were ignored (which may pose unique problems to law cataloging in the LC schedules) the average number of LC modifications per record dropped to .78, while the average number of modifications per record for OCLC member cataloging dropped to 2.53. (367)

Reclassification

General

■ A study reported in 1974 of U.S. libraries that had switched to the National Library of Medicine classification system between 1959 and 1973 (survey size: 25 libraries; responding: 25 or 100%) *showed that*, of 23 respondents, 18 (78.3%) reported using regular cataloging staff to reclassify, 1 (4.3%) reported they did not use regular cataloging staff to reclassify, and 4 (17.4%) reported they used regular staff "but with additional help." Further, of 24 respondents, 10 (41.7%) libraries reported they reclassified all the older material, while 14 (58.3%) reported they did not.   **(701)**

Ibid. . . . *showed that* the effects of switching to NLM classification were minimal. For example, of 23 libraries, 8 (34.8%) libraries reported patrons had expressed a preference for the NLM classification system, none had expressed a preference for the previous system, and 15 (65.2%) libraries reported patrons had not expressed a preference.   **(701)**

Ibid. . . . *showed that* the 3 main reasons given for switching were (multiple responses allowed): to take advantage of the NLM cataloging service (13 or 52%), to provide better shelf arrangement for the library's books (11 or 44%), and found classification easier with the NLM system (10 or 40%).   **(701)**

Ibid. . . . *showed that* 23 (92%) libraries reported switching to MeSH subject headings when they switched to NLM classification, while 2 (8%) reported they did not adopt the MeSH subject headings.   **(701)**

■ A study reported in 1974 of classification systems used in 941 libraries, as reported in a series of U.S. national and regional medical publications as well as an international survey conducted by Dave Remington of 470 health science libraries, *showed that* in 23 years a substantial shift toward use of the National Library of Medicine classification scheme had taken place in Medical Library Association libraries. Between 1950 and 1959, 15 libraries had switched to NLM classification, while between 1959 and 1973, 69 libraries had switched to NLM classification.   **(701)**

Academic

■ A study reported in 1962 at Stanislaus State College Library (Turlock, California) concerning reclassification of library materials (1,829 titles involving 2,032 volumes reclassified, including remarking volumes and changing catalog cards) *showed that* the amount of time required was as follows: professional staff, 446 hours; clerical staff, 269 hours; student staff, 152 hours. Together, the average number of volumes per person-hour was 2.34, while the average number of titles per person-hour was 2.11. **(580)**

■ A 1967 survey by the Institute of Higher Education at Teachers College, Columbia University of innovative programs in libraries in academic institutions with liberal arts programs (sample size: 1,193; responding: 781 or 65%) *showed that* the main innovative change in administrative practices was adoption of LC classification. 336 libraries (43%) used LC classification with 243 (31%) having used it since 1961. A further 79 libraries (10%) were planning to adopt it at the time of the study. **(190)**

■ A survey reported in 1968 of all junior colleges (sample: 837; responding: 690 or 82%) concerning their use of classification systems *showed that* 532 (77.1%) used Dewey, 92 (13.3%) used LC, 58 (8.4%) were changing from Dewey to LC, 4 (0.6%) were planning on changing from Dewey to LC, and 4 (0.6%) used other classification schemes. **(185)**

Rules

General

■ A survey reported in 1981 of chief administrators of U.S. theater collections concerning methods of cataloging nonbook theatrical memorabilia (survey size: 40 libraries; responding: 26; usable: 25 or 62.5%) *showed that*:

22 (88%) libraries reported having no complete accessing tools to the nonbook items in the collection;

22 (88%) libraries reported that their cataloging system was designed by the library staff for their particular collection (however, 6 or 24% libraries reported that they had adopted a preestablished system for the collection). **(769)**

Academic

■ A survey reported in 1977 concerning university libraries' handling of doctoral and master's theses generated locally, based on a stratified sample of universities offering the doctoral degree (survey size: 100; responding: 90 or 90%), *showed that* 89 (98.9%) respondents reported at least partial cataloging of locally produced theses and dissertations with the following breakdown of systems used:

Anglo-American Cataloging rules	73 (82.0%) libraries
local scheme	6 (6.7%) libraries
Anglo-American Cataloging rules (modified version)	3 (3.4%) libraries
AACR for doctoral theses; local system for master's theses	1 (1.1%) libraries
no response	6 (6.7%) libraries **(639)**

Special

■ A 1977 survey of U.S. law libraries over 10,000 volumes taken from the 1976 *Directory of Law Libraries* (sample size: 1,080; responding: 373 or 35%) *showed that*, of 123 academic law libraries and 250 remaining law libraries, 98% of the academic law libraries and 66% of the remaining law libraries reported using the Anglo-American Cataloging rules, while 78% of the academic law libraries and 61% of the remaining law libraries reported using the ALA filing rules.   **(366)**

Serials

General

■ A review of variant editions of periodicals listed in the *Reader's Guide to Periodical Literature* by the Special Committee to Study the Indexing of Variant Editions of Periodicals (ALA, Reference Services Division) in 1967 *showed that* there were 3 main categories of variations: (1) international editions, (2) special interest editions, and (3) U.S. regional editions. Of the 126 periodicals indexed in the *Reader's Guide*, 28 published 1 or more variant editions.   **(078)**

■ A survey in 1978 of 93 serial titles (which had been recently changed) taken from *New Serial Titles* and compared to title listings in the OCLC data base *showed that* OCLC listed 59.1% correctly and up to date, 17.2% were listed incorrectly, and 23.6% were listed incompletely.   **(027)**

■ A survey in 1978 of 612 serial records in the OCLC data base *showed that* 23% were found to have at least 1 substantial error. 12.6% had only 1 error, 4.4% had 2 errors, 2.6% had 3 errors, and 3.4% had more than 3 errors.   **(027)**

Ibid. . . . *showed that* the percentage of errors in the following fields was negligible (i.e., less than 1%):

LC call number (field 050)
main entry—corporate name (110)
collation (field 300)
key title (field 222)
current frequency (field 310)
former frequency (field 321)
added entry—corporate name (field 710)
added entry—conference or meeting (field 711)   **(027)**

Ibid. . . . *showed that*, of the records with errors, 22% were LC cataloging, 57.4% were non-LC cataloging, and 20% were of "unknown" origin.
(027)

Ibid. . . . *showed that* there were errors in the following fields (total is over 100% due to multiple errors):

title field (field 245, 246, 247)	6.3% errors
subject heading field	12.0% errors
imprint field (260)	19.1% errors
dates of publication and volume designation (field 362)	45.0% errors
dates	26.0% errors
succeeding title (field 785)	19.1% errors
publication status	20.5% errors **(027)**

Ibid. . . . *showed that* 32.5% of the records lacking at least 1 of 6 basic elements (call number in LC form, subject heading in LC form, imprint, collation, ISSN, and date of publication and volume designation) had been authenticated by LC.
(027)

Ibid. . . . *showed that* the percentage of times data was omitted in the 6 basic fields was as follows:

imprint (field 260)	1.5%
collation (field 300)	11.7%
subject heading field	24.5%
dates of publication and volume designation (field 362)	28.9%
ISSN (field 022)	33.5%
call number (field 050)	35.1%

Only 62.7% had both a call number and subject headings in LC form. Overall, 68% of the records lacked 1 of the basic elements, 14% lacked 2, and 20.4% lacked 3 or more of the basic elements.   **(027)**

Academic

■ A 1977 survey of academic libraries with collections of 300,000 volumes or more that were also OCLC members concerning cataloging practices (survey size: 147 libraries; responding: 121 or 82.3%) *showed that*, when cataloging copy was not available, 95% of the larger (900,000 volumes or more) libraries and 84% of the smaller (under 900,000 volumes) libraries followed LC practice when assigning call numbers and establishing the form of name headings, subject headings, and series entries. However, "one-third" of the larger libraries and "one-half" of the smaller libraries that follow LC practice used a local call number system for some materials. These were generally microforms, juvenile literature, and theses.   **(760)**

Ibid. . . . *showed that* 56.6% of the larger (900,000 volumes or more) libraries and 38% of the smaller libraries traced all series traced by LC. None of the larger libraries and only 2% of the smaller libraries reported that series were not traced.   **(760)**

■ A survey in 1978 of 93 recently changed serial titles taken from *New Serial Titles* and compared to title listings in the OCLC data base *showed that* OCLC listed 59.1% correctly and up to date, 17.2% were listed incorrectly, and 23.6% were listed incompletely.   **(027)**

■ A 1978 study at Ohio State University Library involving 2 full days' transactions in the OCLC data base for each of the OSU terminals (1,153 searches of the data base) *showed that* of 94 serials cataloging searches the 2 most frequent types of searches were by title (72 or 76.6% of the serials searches of which 32 or 44.4% of the serials cataloging searches were successful) and by name/title (15 or 15.9% of the serials cataloging searches of which 3 or 20.0% were successful).   **(336)**

Speed

General

■ A survey in 1974 of the 47 charter members of the OCLC network, including site visits and interviews (148) with all levels of library personnel in member libraries, *showed that* estimates from 40 libraries for the rate of inputting bibliographic records from pre-tagged input forms averaged 8.7

records/hour excluding time for revision. Revision rates, based on reports from several libraries, suggested a revision rate in the range of 4 minutes/ title indicating an overall input rate of 6 titles/hour. **(112)**

Ibid. . . . *showed that* 91% of the libraries reported that the time required to catalog books and produce sets of catalog cards had been reduced by online cataloging, while estimates from 28 (59.6%) libraries suggested that the decrease in cataloging and card production turnaround time averaged 2.8 months. **(112)**

Academic

■ A study reported in 1960 at San Franscisco State College Library concerning length of time for book ordering and processing over a 7-year period (academic 1950-51 through academic 1956-57) and involving 500 randomly selected order cards per year (excluding materials with special problems such as out of print, etc.) *showed that* (using calander days rather than working days):

the median time between order received in acquisitions to time order was placed ranged from 6.3 days in 1955-56 to 18.94 days in 1951-52;

the median time between order being placed and books received ranged from 24.47 days in 1951-52 to 32.75 days in 1954-55;

the median time between book being received and book being released [cataloged and marked] ranged from 16.24 days in 1955-56 to 46.80 days in 1950-51. **(578)**

■ A 1973 study at the University of Colorado Medical Center of cataloging and card production costs of English-language monographs with 1972-73 imprints that required complete cataloging (sample size: 319 items) *showed that* the average number of days before the books were available to users was 16.07 days (26.97 days estimated for the purchase card method), while the average number of days before the cards were filed in the catalog was 19.88 days (34.11 days estimated for the purchase card method). **(706)**

Special

■ A 1973 study at the University of Colorado Medical Center of cataloging and card production costs of English-language monographs with 1972-73 imprints that required complete cataloging (sample size: 319 items) *showed that* that the average number of days before the books were available to users was 16.07 days (26.97 days estimated for the purchase card method), while the average number of days before the cards were filed in the catalog was 19.88 days (34.11 days estimated for the purchase card method). **(706)**

Staffing—Nonprofessional

General

■ A survey in 1974 of the 47 charter members of the OCLC network, including site visits and interviews (148) with all levels of library personnel in member libraries, *showed that* in most of the libraries using LC classification clericals and paraprofessionals did a major part of the cataloging involving records in the OCLC data base, while in all except 1 of the 14 libraries using Dewey professional catalogers were used to catalog records in the online file. **(112)**

Ibid. . . . *showed that* reorganization does not necessarily follow from the implementation of online cataloging. After 3 years only 9 libraries (20%) had reorganized the departmental structure of technical services, although the tendency was strongest in the larger libraries. **(112)**

Ibid. . . . *showed that* 74% of the interviewees stated that the nonprofessional work had been made more demanding, while only 3 interviewers reported that professional cataloging had been made more demanding. **(112)**

Academic

■ A 1977 survey of academic libraries with collections of 300,000 volumes or more that were also OCLC members concerning cataloging practices (survey size: 147 libraries; responding: 121 or 82.3%) *showed that*, based on a subsample of 23 larger (900,000 volumes or more) libraries and 14 smaller (less than 900,000 volumes) libraries, the average number of staff devoted to cataloging (not catalog maintenance, marking, etc.) was as follows:

large libraries reported an average of 9.6 professional catalogers of which 1.95 were involved in administration and 7.65 in cataloging, while small libraries reported an average of 5 professional catalogers of which 1.1 were involved in administration and 3.9 in cataloging;

large libraries reported an average of 10.5 support staff involved in cataloging tasks, while small libraries reported 5.4 support staff involved in cataloging tasks. **(760)**

Ibid. . . . *showed that* in large libraries (900,000 volumes or more) cataloging staff were used as follows:

adapting LC records for the same edition: 1.6% libraries used professional catalogers only, 58.3% used support staff only, and 40% used both professional and support staff;

adapting LC records for different editions: 23.3% libraries used professional catalogers only, 31.6% used support staff only, and 45% used both professional and support staff;

completing CIP records: 5% libraries used professional catalogers only, 66.6% used support staff only, and 28.3% used both professional and support staff;

verifying member cataloging records: 23.3% libraries used professionals only, 11.5% used professionals with support staff assisting in verification, 13.3% used support staff only, and 46.6% used both professional and support staff [remaining percentage unaccounted for];

cataloging without copy: 56.6% libraries used professionals only, 16.6% used professionals with support staff assisting with verification, 1.6% used support staff only, and 15% used both professionals and support staff. **(760)**

Ibid. . . . *showed that* in small (under 900,000 volumes) libraries, cataloging staff were used as follows:

adapting LC records for the same edition: 10% libraries used professionals only, 28% used support staff only, and 62% used both professional and support staff;

adapting LC records for different editions: 33% libraries used professionals only, 9% used support staff only, and 59% used both professional and support staff;

completing CIP records: 7% libraries used professionals only, 43% used support staff only, and 50% used both professional and support staff;

verifying member cataloging records: 21% libraries used professionals only, 29% used professionals with assistance from support staff, 7% used support staff only, and 43% used both professional and support staff;

cataloging without copy: 59% libraries used professionals only,

29% used professionals assisted by support staff for
verification, none used support staff only, and 12% used both
professional and support staff.   **(760)**

■ A 1979 survey of U.S. community college libraries selected from the
1978 *Community, Junior and Technical College Directory* (sample size: 98;
responding: 52; usable: 48 or 48.98%) *showed that* the nonprofessional
cataloging staff per library was as follows:

no staff	5 (10.42%)	libraries
less than 1	11 (22.92%)	libraries
1 staff member	15 (31.25%)	libraries
more than 1	14 (29.20%)	libraries
no answer	3 (6.25%)	libraries **(498)**

Staffing—Professional

General

■ A survey in 1974 of the 47 charter members of the OCLC network,
including site visits and interviews (148) with all levels of library personnel
in member libraries, *showed that* in most of the libraries using LC
classification clericals and paraprofessionals did a major part of the
cataloging involving records in the OCLC data base, while in all except 1 of
the 14 libraries using Dewey professional catalogers were used to catalog
records in the online file.   **(112)**

Ibid. . . . *showed that* reorganization does not necessarily follow from the
implementation of online cataloging. After 3 years only 9 libraries (20%)
had reorganized the departmental structure of technical services, although
the tendency was strongest in the larger libraries.   **(112)**

Academic

■ A study during academic 1972-73 of cataloging production at Wichita
State University involving 4 professional catalogers who handled original
and problem cataloging and reclassification along with other duties such as
catalog maintenance and editing of nonprofessional copy cataloging (a
total of 15,450 titles; 24,494 volumes) *showed that* the amount of time
devoted to cataloging production after subtracting out break time, meetings, illness, professional conferences, etc., averaged overall 63.4% of the
total worktime with individual averages ranging from 53.1% to 68.4% of
total worktime.   **(637)**

■ A 1977 survey of academic libraries with collections of 300,000 volumes or more that were also OCLC members concerning cataloging practices (survey size: 147 libraries; responding: 121 or 82.3%) *showed that*, based on a subsample of 23 larger (900,000 volumes or more) libraries and 14 smaller (less than 900,000 volumes) libraries, the average number of staff devoted to cataloging (not catalog maintenance, marking, etc.) was as follows:

large libraries reported an average of 9.6 professional catalogers of which 1.95 were involved in administration and 7.65 in cataloging, while small libraries reported an average of 5 professional catalogers of which 1.1 were involved in administration and 3.9 in cataloging;

large libraries reported an average of 10.5 support staff involved in cataloging tasks, while small libraries reported 5.4 support staff involved in cataloging tasks. **(760)**

Ibid. . . . *showed that* in large libraries (900,000 volumes or more) cataloging staff were used as follows:

adapting LC records for the same edition: 1.6% libraries used professional catalogers only, 58.3% used support staff only, and 40% used both professional and support staff;

adapting LC records for different editions: 23.3% libraries used professional catalogers only, 31.6% used support staff only, and 45% used both professional and support staff;

completing CIP records: 5% libraries used professional catalogers only, 66.6% used support staff only, and 28.3% used both professional and support staff;

verifying member cataloging records: 23.3% libraries used professionals only, 11.5% used professionals with support staff assisting in verification, 13.3% used support staff only, and 46.6% used both professional and support staff [remaining percentage unaccounted for];

cataloging without copy: 56.6% libraries used professionals only, 16.6% used professionals with support staff assisting with verification, 1.6% used support staff only, and 15% used both professionals and support staff. **(760)**

Ibid. . . . *showed that* in small (under 900,000 volumes) libraries, cataloging staff were used as follows:

adapting LC records for the same edition: 10% libraries used professionals only, 28% used support staff only, and 62% used both professional and support staff;

adapting LC records for different editions: 33% libraries used professionals only, 9% used support staff only, and 59% used both professional and support staff;

completing CIP records: 7% libraries used professionals only, 43% used support staff only, and 50% used both professional and support staff;

verifying member cataloging records: 21% libraries used professionals only, 29% used professionals with assistance from support staff, 7% used support staff only, and 43% used both professional and support staff;

cataloging without copy: 59% libraries used professionals only, 29% used professionals assisted by support staff for verification, none used support staff only, and 12% used both professional and support staff. **(760)**

■ A 1979 survey of U.S. community college libraries selected from the 1978 *Community, Junior and Technical College Directory* (sample size: 98; responding: 52; usable: 48 or 48.98%) *showed that* the professional cataloging staff per library was as follows:

no professional staff	4 (8.33%) libraries
less than 1 professional staff	16 (33.33%) libraries
1 professional staff	19 (39.58%) libraries
more than 1 professional staff	5 (10.40%) libraries
no answer	4 (8.33%) libraries **(498)**

Staffing—Unspecified

General

■ A survey in 1974 of the 47 charter members of the OCLC network, including site visits and interviews (148) with all levels of library personnel in member libraries, *showed that* 63% of the charter member libraries had reduced cataloging staff since beginning online cataloging, dropping a total of 76.83 net positions. However, the degree to which online cataloging contributed to this saving is unclear since other factors such as reorganization, decreased workload, and the like were also involved. **(112)**

Ibid. . . . *showed that* 91% of the libraries reported that the time required to catalog books and produce sets of catalog cards had been reduced by online cataloging, while estimates from 28 (59.6%) libraries suggested that the decrease in cataloging and card production turnaround time averaged 2.8 months. **(112)**

Subject Headings—General Issues

General

■ An analysis of the number of added entries assigned cataloged material listed in the *National Union Catalog* during the period 1950-73 *showed that* there was little change in the average number of subject added entries per item from 1950 to 1973. The average fluctuated between 1.2 and 1.3 subject added entries per item.   **(055)**

■ A study reported in 1965 of card catalogs in 8 libraries (7 academic and 1 other), all of which followed the *Subject Headings Used in the Dictionary Catalog of the Library of Congress, showed that* subject headings did not appear to be assigned with a great deal of consistency from 1 library to the next. Specifically, of 76 titles that had been assigned the subject term "communication" in at least 1 library but that appeared in more than 1 of the 8 libraries, only 55 (72%) of the titles had had the subject term assigned consistently in all libraries.   **(584)**

■ A 1969 study of professionals in various kinds of North American libraries as well as instructors of technical and reader services in accredited library schools (survey size: 244; responding: 152 or 62.3%) concerning the role and importance of classifying library materials *showed that* there was some ambivalence concerning the role of shelf classification in subject searching:

   58.8% agreed that shelf classification was "more important as a locational device than as a means of systematic subject approach";

   58.0% agreed that subject headings in the catalog were more useful to the patron than shelf classification;

   42.7% agreed that the average patron could not "follow" close classification notation on the shelves.   **(597)**

■ A 1976-77 study over a 31-week period comparing subject retrieval in terms of both recall (probability that a relevant item will be retrieved) and precision (probability that a retrieved item will be relevant), using Library of Congress subject headings and the British Library's PRECIS terms (both found in UK MARC tapes for this period) and involving 42 users and 61 search profiles resulting in 5,326 usable citations, *showed that* use of PRECIS terms resulted in a statistically significant higher recall rate (81.9% citations) than use of LCSH terms (76.2% citations). However, use of LCSH terms resulted in a statistically significant higher precision rate (29.6% citations) than use of PRECIS terms (27.9% citations). (Both findings significant at the .05 level.) **(654)**

Ibid. . . . *showed that* searching on article titles as well as on subject terms improved the recall rate for both LCSH (from 76.2% to 90.0% citations) and PRECIS (from 81.9% to 93.0% citations). In both cases this was a statistically significant increase in percentage of citations retrieved (significant at the .05 level). However the increase eliminated any statistically significant difference between LCSH and PRECIS recall rates. Further, the use of title searching lowered the precision rate slightly, from 19.6% citations to 26.7% citations for LCSH and from 27.9% to 25.7% citations for PRECIS. In both cases this was a statistically significant decrease in percentage of citations (significant at the .05 level). However, here too the change eliminated any statistically significant difference between LCSH and PRECIS precision rates. **(654)**

Ibid. . . . *showed that*, while LCSH and PRECIS appear to work equally well in the pure/applied sciences, PRECIS had a "clear recall advantage" over LCSH for social science books. For example, recall rates in the social sciences for LCSH was 75.8% citations compared to 84.2% citations for PRECIS—a statistically significant difference (significant at the .05 level). However, recall rates in the pure/applied sciences were 75.5% citations for LCSH and 78.1% citations for PRECIS—not a statistically significant difference. **(654)**

■ A study reported in 1980 comparing the compatibility of Sears and LC subject headings (in order to see how difficult it would be for the library to switch systems), based on 1,220 LC subject heading entries selected from a 6-month run of *Publishers Weekly* and compared to the 11th edition of Sears, *showed that* 461 (37.8%) of the headings matched exactly, 618 (50.7%) of the headings did not conflict (e.g., broader, narrower, etc.), and 141 (11.6%) of the headings did conflict. At a 95% confidence level, between 10 and 14% of the Sears and LC headings could be expected to conflict. **(762)**

Academic

■ A study during the academic year 1961-62 in the Physics library of the University of California, Los Angeles comparing book titles with subject headings assigned during cataloging (study size: 410 titles acquired during a 12-month period, excluding added copies, textbooks, etc.) *showed that:*

exact or equivalent match	147 (36%)	titles
probable match	151 (37%)	titles
no match	72 (15%)	titles
special problems	19 (5%)	titles
no headings	21 (7%)	titles

(582)

■ A study reported in 1965 of card catalogs in 8 libraries (7 academic and 1 other), all of which followed the *Subject Headings Used in the Dictionary Catalog of the Library of Congress*, *showed that* subject headings did not appear to be assigned with a great deal of consistency from 1 library to the next. Specifically, of 76 titles that had been assigned the subject term "communication" in at least 1 library but that appeared in more than 1 of the 8 libraries, only 55 (72%) of the titles had had the subject term assigned consistently in all libraries. **(584)**

■ A survey reported in 1969 of medical school and selected medical research libraries (survey size: 102 libraries; responding: 92 or 90%) *showed that* the subject heading authority used by the 54 libraries with divided catalogs was as follows: MeSH, exclusively or in combination with LC subject headings (41 or 75.9% libraries); LC subject headings exclusively (9 or 16.7% libraries); and other (2 or 3.7% libraries). **(679)**

■ A 1975 survey of North American medical school libraries concerning subject cataloging practices (survey size: 134 libraries; responding: 114 or 85%) *showed that* the type of subject authority used was as follows:

MeSH exclusively	30 (26%)	libraries
MeSH supplemented by LC	57 (50%)	libraries
LC exclusively	23 (20%)	libraries
LC supplemented by MeSH	2 (2%)	libraries
no response	2 (2%)	libraries

(712)

Ibid. . . . *showed that* the form of the local subject authority file was as follows:

separate card file	55 (48%)	libraries
checking off terms used in the authority	26 (23%)	libraries
public catalog	25 (22%)	libraries

continued

book catalog compiled by library   3 (3%) libraries
no response   5 (4%) libraries   **(712)**

Ibid. . . . *showed that*, of 78 respondents who used MeSH as the primary authority for subject headings and who also had divided catalogs, 63 (81%) respondents reported they modified subject headings by combining several subheadings, while 15 (19%) reported they did not. Of those that did combine subheadings, the maximum number combined was as follows:

2 subheadings	8 respondents
3 subheadings	33 respondents
4 subheadings	15 respondents
5 subheadings	2 respondents
no policy or no limit	5 respondents **(712)**

Ibid. . . . *showed that*, of 78 respondents who used MeSH as the primary authority for subject headings and who also had divided catalogs, language and geographic subheadings were considered by respondents to be the following:

form subheadings	11 (14%) libraries
topical subheadings	4 (5%) libraries
do not distinguish	60 (77%) libraries
no response	3 (4%) libraries **(712)**

Ibid. . . . *showed that*, of 78 respondents who used MeSH as the primary authority for subject headings and who also had divided catalogs, 69 (89%) reported using the National Library of Medicine authority for language and geographic subheadings, 5 (7%) reported using "other," and 4 (5%) reported using no authority.   **(712)**

Ibid. . . . *showed that*, of 78 respondents who used MeSH as the primary authority for subject headings and who also had divided catalogs, the following practices were followed when National Library of Medicine subject cataloging copy was available:

follow NLM with minor variations	55 (70%) libraries
follow NLM without exception	14 (18%) libraries
follow NLM with many changes	3 (4%) libraries

continued

other   4 (5%) libraries
no response   2 (3%) libraries   **(712)**

■ A 1977 survey of U.S. law libraries over 10,000 volumes taken from the 1976 *Directory of Law Libraries* (sample size: 1,080; responding: 373 or 35%) *showed that*, of 123 academic law libraries and 250 other law libraries, use of Library of Congress subject headings was highest in academic libraries (96% compared to 61% in all other types of law libraries combined). Of the law libraries that use LC subject headings, 55% of the academic libraries use them without change compared to 16% of the remaining libraries who use them without change. An earlier study of selected academic law libraries found 85.5% using LC subject headings with 19% using them without modification.   **(366)**

■ A 1979 survey of U.S. community college libraries selected from the 1978 *Community, Junior and Technical College Directory* (sample size: 98; responding: 52; usable: 48 or 48.98%) *showed that* for monographs 6 (12.24%) libraries used Sears for their subject heading list, while 43 (87.76%) libraries used Library of Congress. For audiovisual materials, 6 (12.24%) used Sears for their subject heading list, 41 (83.67%) used LC, and 2 (4.08%) used some other subject heading authority. (1 library reported using both Sears and LC, so the totals equal 49 rather than 48.)   **(498)**

Special

■ A survey reported in 1969 of medical school and selected medical research libraries (survey size: 102 libraries; responding: 92 or 90%) *showed that* the subject heading authority used by the 54 libraries with divided catalogs was as follows: MeSH, exclusively or in combination with LC subject headings (41 or 75.9% libraries); LC subject headings exclusively (9 or 16.7% libraries); and other (2 or 3.7% libraries).   **(679)**

■ A survey reported in 1975 of subject heading use in a wide range of law libraries selected from the 1972 edition of the American Association of Law Libraries *Directory of Law Libraries* (sample size: 256; responding: 204; usable: 200 or 78.1%) *showed that* respondents used the following subject heading lists:

Library of Congress list (with
    modification)   46 (23.0%) respondents

continued

Library of Congress list (with no modification)	33 (16.5%) respondents
responding library's own list	27 (13.5%) respondents
Ellinger list (with modification)	16 (8.0%) respondents
Ellinger list (with no modification)	5 (2.5%) respondents
Columbia list	5 (2.5%) respondents
some other published list	2 (1.0%) respondents
combination of above lists (including Northwestern list)	66 (33.0%) respondents

(393)

Ibid. . . . *showed that*, of 129 respondents using modified lists, the 2 main changes were: changes in the subject headings starting with the word "law" including subdivisions, such as "law and legislation" (87 or 67.4% respondents) and establishment of new subject headings at the responding library (e.g., when LC is slow in establishing them) (73 or 56.6% respondents).
(393)

Ibid. . . . *showed that* 79 (39.5%) respondents kept their subject heading list as a "marked copy of a published list," 50 (25%) kept their subject heading list as a card file, 30 (15%) use more than 1 way of keeping their subject heading list, 28 (14%) use looseleaf format, and 2 (1%) use miscellaneous other formats. 8 (4%) respondents reported they had no subject authority file, and 3 (1.5%) did not respond. **(393)**

Ibid. . . . *showed that* 148 (74%) respondents reported they did not keep auxiliary subject heading records, while (multiple responses allowed) 25 (12.5%) reported keeping subject subdivision files and 17 (8.5%) kept geographic name files. 15 (7.5%) other responses were not considered appropriate for the purposes of this question. **(393)**

Ibid. . . . *showed that* 50 (25%) respondents were satisfied with the subject heading list they were using, 80 (40%) were somewhat satisfied, 7 (3.5%) were dissatisfied, and 63 (31.5%) had no opinion. **(393)**

■ A 1975 survey of North American medical school libraries concerning subject cataloging practices (survey size: 134 libraries; responding: 114 or 85%) *showed that* the type of subject authority used was as follows:

MeSH exclusively	30 (26%) libraries
MeSH supplemented by LC	57 (50%) libraries
LC exclusively	23 (20%) libraries

continued

LC supplemented by MeSH   2 (2%) libraries
no response   2 (2%) libraries   **(712)**

Ibid. . . . *showed that* the form of the local subject authority file was as follows:

separate card file	55 (48%) libraries
checking off terms used in the authority	26 (23%) libraries
public catalog	25 (22%) libraries
book catalog compiled by library	3 (3%) libraries
no response	5 (4%) libraries **(712)**

Ibid. . . . *showed that*, of 78 respondents who used MeSH as the primary authority for subject headings and who also had divided catalogs, 63 (81%) respondents reported they modified subject headings by combining several subheadings, while 15 (19%) reported they did not. Of those that did combine subheadings, the maximum number combined was as follows:

2 subheadings	8 respondents
3 subheadings	33 respondents
4 subheadings	15 respondents
5 subheadings	2 respondents
no policy or no limit	5 respondents **(712)**

Ibid. . . . *showed that*, of 78 respondents who used MeSH as the primary authority for subject headings and who also had divided catalogs, language and geographic subheadings were considered by respondents to be the following:

form subheadings	11 (14%) libraries
topical subheadings	4 (5%) libraries
do not distinguish	60 (77%) libraries
no response	3 (4%) libraries **(712)**

Ibid. . . . *showed that*, of 78 respondents who used MeSH as the primary authority for subject headings and who also had divided catalogs, 69 (89%) reported using the National Library of Medicine authority for language and geographic subheadings, 5 (7%) reported using "other," and 4 (5%) reported using no authority.   **(712)**

Ibid. . . . *showed that*, of 78 respondents who used MeSH as the primary authority for subject headings and who also had divided catalogs, the following practices were followed when National Library of Medicine subject cataloging copy was available:

follow NLM with minor variations	55 (70%) libraries
follow NLM without exception	14 (18%) libraries
follow NLM with many changes	3 (4%) libraries
other	4 (5%) libraries
no response	2 (3%) libraries **(712)**

■   A 1977 survey of U.S. law libraries over 10,000 volumes taken from the 1976 *Directory of Law Libraries* (sample size: 1,080; responding: 373 or 35%) *showed that*, of 123 academic law libraries and 250 other law libraries, use of Library of Congress subject headings was highest in academic libraries (96% compared to 61% in all other types of law libraries combined). Of the law libraries that use LC subject headings, 55% of the academic libraries use them without change compared to 16% of the remaining libraries who use them without change. An earlier study of selected academic law libraries found 85.5% using LC subject headings with 19% using them without modification.   **(366)**

■   A survey reported in 1983 of Medical Library Association institutional members concerning their use of audiovisual materials (survey size: 300; responding: 201; usable: 198 or 66%) *showed that*, of 143 respondents (91 hospital, 29 medical school, and 13 "other" libraries) that did provide AV services, 90% of the hospital libraries, 88% of the medical school libraries, and 55% of the other libraries reported using MeSH subject headings.
                                                                    (750)

Subject Headings—OCLC

Academic

■   A 1977 survey of academic libraries with collections of 300,000 volumes or more that were also OCLC members concerning cataloging practices (survey size: 147 libraries; responding: 121 or 82.3%) *showed that*, when cataloging copy was not available, 95% of the larger (900,000 volumes or more) libraries and 84% of the smaller (under 900,000 volumes) libraries followed LC practice when assigning call numbers and establishing the form of name headings, subject headings, and series entries. However, "one-third" of the larger libraries and "one-half" of the smaller libraries that followed LC practice used a local call number system for some materials. These are generally microforms, juvenile literature, and theses.

(760)

Ibid. . . . *showed that* for OCLC member records the following items were verified (large libraries = 900,000 volumes or more; small libraries = under 900,000 volumes):

call number	79.0% large; 73.0% small libraries
choice and form of	
entry	71.6% large; 74.0% small libraries
added entries	73.2% large; 68.0% small libraries
all of the above	70.0% large; 61.0% small libraries
none of the above	18.3% large; 20.0% small libraries

Further, the following treatment of subject headings in member records was reported by the following libraries:

subject headings verified	
as valid LC headings	70.0% large; 81.7% small libraries
subject headings checked	
for appropriateness	61.6% large; 67.0% small libraries
subject headings	
assigned if lacking	88.3% large; 90.0% small libraries
all of the above	56.6% large; 61.7% small libraries
none of the above	8.3% large; 1.0% small libraries

(760)

■ A 1978 study of LC subject headings assigned to monographic records in the OCLC data base (survey size: 33,455 catalog records with a total of 50,213 subject headings of which 47,036 or 93.7% were LC subject headings) *showed that* the average number of LC subject headings per record was 1.41. The number of subject headings per record was as follows:

no LC subject headings	18.6% records	
1 LC subject heading per record	40.8% records	
2 LC subject heading per record	26.8% records	
3 or more LC subject headings		
per record	13.8% records	**(766)**

Ibid. . . . *showed that*, of the 47,036 LC subject headings, 33,597 (71.4%) were topical headings. However, topical headings occurred in only 62.4%

of the records. Further, there were 6,826 (14.5%) geographic headings among the 47,036 subject headings. Geographic headings occurred among 14.9% of the records.   **(766)**

Ibid. . . . *showed that* by inspection of the data there seemed to be a relationship between LC class and the decision whether or not to assign a subject heading. For example, of 6,649 records classified in the LC "P" class, 56.2% received no subject headings, while of 1,959 records classified in the LC "Q" class, 1.1% received no subject headings.   **(766)**

Ibid. . . . *showed that* by inspection of the data there seemed to be a relationship between LC class and type of subject heading assigned. For example:

> LC classes D, E, F, and J (history and political science) had higher than average percentages of records with geographic headings (66.2%, 43.2%, 77.7%, and 35.2%, respectively);

> LC classes C, E, and N (art, literature, music, philosophy, and religion) had higher than average percentages of records with personal name headings (39.9%, 23.4%, and 24.5%, respectively);

> LC classes Q, R, S, and T (science and technology) had higher than average percentages of records with topical headings (96.9%, 77.0%, 78.9%, and 93.8%, respectively).   **(766)**

Title Changes

Academic

■ A study reported in 1982 concerning the impact of AACR 2 on the card catalog in a medium-sized (740,000 volumes) academic library, based on a random sample of 909 catalog records (1,714 headings) taken from a year's pre-AACR 2 OCLC archival tapes and searched in the post-AACR 2 OCLC LC name authority file, *showed that* 217 (12.7%) different headings required changes under AACR 2 rules. 43% of these "unique" headings were verified in the online name authority file as of January 1981.   **(770)**

Ibid. . . . *showed that* the distribution of changes to be made by type of heading was as follows:

personal (1,246 headings)	98 (7.9%) changes
corporate (125 headings)	53 (42.4%) changes

continued

geographical (153 headings)   20 (13.1%) changes
uniform title (34 headings)   1 (2.9%) changes
series (156 headings)   45 (28.8%) changes

However, since not every heading that required a change under AACR 2 was already represented in the catalog, the number of conflicts was less than the number of changes. The number of conflicts by type of heading was as follows:

personal (1,246 headings)   85 (6.8%) conflicts
corporate (125 headings)   27 (21.6%) conflicts
geographical (153 headings)   15 (9.8%) conflicts
uniform title (34 headings)   1 (2.9%) conflicts
series (156 headings)   42 (26.9%) conflicts   **(770)**

Ibid. . . . *showed that* a summary review of the literature came up with the following rates of difference ("headings which would be constructed differently under AACR 2") and rates of conflict ("AACR 2 headings for names already entered in the catalog under a different form"):

of 295 records and 541 headings studied at Johns Hopkins University, the rate of difference was 17.3% and the rate of conflict was 11%;

of 484 records studied at Duke University the rate of conflict was 15.5%;

of 330 titles and 577 headings at Emory University the rate of difference was 15%;

of 300 titles and 447 headings at the University of Minnesota the rate of difference was 3%;

of 258 headings at the University of Washington the rate of difference was 30%;

of 325 titles and 644 entries at Southern Illinois University, Carbondale, the rate of difference was 20.3%.   **(770)**

2.

Catalogs

AACR 2

General

■ A 1978 study of OCLC's online union catalog preparatory to converting to AACR 2 form of name headings and uniform titles, involving a 1% test file (41,212 records) and a thorough review of AACR 2 rules, *showed that* AACR 2 contained 454 "significant" rule changes or new rules, of which 56% would benefit neither librarian nor patron, 23% of which would benefit librarians, and 21% of which would benefit patrons.   **(337)**

Ibid. . . . *showed that* 39% of the total records in the online union catalog were ultimately converted to AACR 2 form.   **(337)**

■ A survey reported in 1982 of Canadian libraries selected from the *CLA Directory* and its supplement (sample size: 203; responding: 85; usable: 69 or 34.0%) concerning implementation of AACR 2 *showed that*, of the 53 libraries who adopted AACR 2, 77% reported they would interfile the AACR 2 entries in their old catalogs, 7 [%] reported they would freeze their catalogs, and 9% reported they would close their catalogs.   **(299)**

Academic

■ A study reported in 1980 of 2 card catalogs (University of Wisconsin, Whitewater, 170,000 titles; University of Illinois, Urbana, 3,000,000 titles) investigating the number of personal authors for which there was only 1 title in the collection (sample size: Whitewater, 2,762 authors; Urbana, 2,345 authors) *showed that* a sample of 1,366 personal authors selected from 6 months of recent cataloging revealed that 52.12% had established headings. Based on Library of Congress estimates that 11% of the headings would have to be revised under AACR 2, 5.7% of all headings for new titles would have to be revised initially so that different works by the same author would file together.   **(758)**

■ A study reported in 1982 concerning the impact of AACR 2 on the card catalog in a medium-sized (740,000 volumes) academic library, based on a random sample of 909 catalog records (1,714 headings) taken from a year's pre-AACR 2 OCLC archival tapes and searched in the post-AACR 2 OCLC LC name authority file, *showed that* 217 (12.7%) different headings required changes under AACR 2 rules. 43% of these "unique" headings were verified in the online name authority file as of January 1981.   **(770)**

Ibid. . . . *showed that* the distribution of changes to be made by type of heading was as follows:

personal (1,246 headings)	98 (7.9%) changes
corporate (125 headings)	53 (42.4%) changes
geographical (153 headings)	20 (13.1%) changes
uniform title (34 headings)	1 (2.9%) changes
series (156 headings)	45 (28.8%) changes

However, since not every heading that required a change under AACR 2 was already represented in the catalog the number of conflicts was less than the number of changes. The number of conflicts by type of heading was as follows:

personal (1,246 headings)	85 (6.8%) conflicts	
corporate (125 headings)	27 (21.6%) conflicts	
geographical (153 headings)	15 (9.8%) conflicts	
uniform title (34 headings)	1 (2.9%) conflicts	
series (156 headings)	42 (26.9%) conflicts	**(770)**

Ibid. . . . *showed that* not all conflicts needed to be changed in order to be interfiled with pre-AACR 2 entries in the card catalog. Specifically, assuming that 5 kinds of differences could be ignored (punctuation, abbreviation, spelling, qualifier, and forname), 31.8% of the conflicts could be interfiled.   **(770)**

Ibid. . . . *showed that* a summary review of the literature came up with the following rates of difference ("headings which would be constructed differently under AACR 2") and rates of conflict ("AACR 2 headings for names already entered in the catalog under a different form"):

of 295 records and 541 headings studied at Johns Hopkins University, the rate of difference was 17.3% and the rate of conflict was 11%;

of 484 records studied at Duke University the rate of conflict was 15.5%;

of 330 titles and 577 headings at Emory University the rate of difference was 15%;

of 300 titles and 447 headings at the University of Minnesota the rate of difference was 3%;

of 258 headings at the University of Washington the rate of difference was 30%;

of 325 titles and 644 entries at Southern Illinois University, Carbondale, the rate of difference was 20.3%.   **(770)**

Book

Academic

■ A study reported in 1972 comparing the ability of 20 University of Chicago graduate students to search 10 entries in a large book catalog (*National Union Catalog, Pre-1956 Imprints*) vs. 10 entries in a large card catalog (UC main card catalog) *showed that* the average search time per item was less in the card catalog ("consistently less than 19 seconds") than in the book catalog ("consistently greater than 25 seconds"). However, the book catalog (3.1 million entries) was substantially larger than the card catalog (1.4 million entries). **(249)**

■ A study reported in 1972 comparing the ability of 20 University of Chicago graduate students to search 6 entries in each of an essentially identical book and card catalog (Center for Research Libraries catalogs) *showed that* for 16 students the total search time using the book catalog was longer than when using the card catalog, for 2 students the time was identical, and for 2 students searching the book catalog took less total time than when searching the card catalog. The differences in search time were statistically significant at the .05 level. **(249)**

Public

■ A 1981-82 study of media cataloging practices in 932 public libraries (responding: 466 or 50%; usable: 448 or 48%) across the U.S. serving communities of all sizes *showed that*, of the public catalogs, 85% were in card form, 9% in COM form, and 2% in book form. 38% of the libraries reported integrating all entries in the public catalog including media, while 62% reported using different catalogs for print and nonprint materials. **(161)**

Special

■ A 1977 survey of U.S. law libraries over 10,000 volumes taken from the 1976 *Directory of Law Libraries* (sample size: 1,080; responding: 373 or 35%) *showed that*, of 368 law libraries, 359 (98%) libraries reported having a card catalog, 5 libraries reported having book catalogs, 2 reported using both book and card catalogs, and 1 library reported using a computer-produced microfiche catalog. [The remaining library is not accounted for.] **(366)**

Card—General Issues

Academic

■ A study reported in 1972 of the author/title section of the card catalog in the Norlin Library of the University of Colorado (population: 1,000,000 cards; sample size: 2,500 cards) *showed that* there was a filing error in the sample of 1.1%. 52% of the errors were due to lack of knowledge of the filing rules, and 48% were mechanical or simple alphabetical mistakes.

(210)

Ibid. . . . *showed that* in the sample 10.14% of the cross-references were blind.

(210)

Ibid. . . . *showed that* in the sample 1.48% of the cards were judged to be mutilated, i.e., call numbers or other essential information was torn off or completely obscured by dirt and wear.

(210)

■ A study reported in 1980 of 2 card catalogs (University of Wisconsin, Whitewater, 170,000 titles; University of Illinois, Urbana, 3,000,000 titles) investigating the number of personal authors for which there was only 1 title in the collection (sample size: Whitewater, 2,762 authors; Urbana, 2,345 authors) *showed that* the incidence of single-work authors was 69.33% (67.60% to 71.05% confidence interval at .95 probability) at Whitewater and 63.5% (61.4% to 65.6% confidence interval at .95 probability) at Urbana.

(758)

Public

■ A 1981-82 study of media cataloging practices in 932 public libraries (responding: 466 or 50%; usable: 448 or 48%) across the U.S. serving communities of all sizes, *showed that*, of the public catalogs, 85% were in card form, 9% in COM form, and 2% in book form. 38% of the libraries reported integrating all entries in the public catalog including media, while 62% reported using different catalogs for print and nonprint materials.

(161)

Special

■ A 1977 survey of U.S. law libraries over 10,000 volumes taken from the 1976 *Directory of Law Libraries* (sample size: 1,080; responding: 373 or 35%) *showed that*, of 368 law libraries, 359 (98%) libraries reported having a card catalog, 5 libraries reported having book catalogs, 2 reported using both book and card catalogs, and 1 library reported using a computer-produced microfiche catalog. [The remaining library is not accounted for.] **(366)**

Card—Filing

General

■ A survey reported in 1982 of Canadian libraries selected from the *CLA Directory* and its supplement (sample size: 203; responding: 85; usable: 69 or 34.0%) concerning implementation of AACR 2 *showed that*, of the 53 libraries who adopted AACR 2, 77% reported they would interfile the AACR 2 entries in their old catalogs, 7 [%] reported they would freeze their catalogs, and 9% reported they would close their catalogs. **(299)**

Academic

■ A 1959 study at the Flint College of the University of Michigan Library and the Flint Community Junior College Library involving the costs of a divided catalog (university catalog held 25,000 volumes and 79,000 cards; community college catalog held 29,000 volumes and 76,000 cards) *showed that*, based on filing 2,580 cards in the university catalog and 7,740 cards in the community college catalog, it was considerably cheaper to alphabetize, file,and revise in the divided catalog than in the dictionary catalog. Specifically, the total savings in time ranged between 39% for the community college and 45% for the university library. **(581)**

■ A survey of 12 university libraries (11 responding) during a 3-month period in 1965 and a survey of 11 public libraries during a similar period in 1967 to determine the kinds of reference assistance needed at the card catalog (647 problems reported with 284 from university libraries and 363 from public libraries), reported together in 1968, *showed that* the 3 most frequent problems with the card catalog in university libraries were subject headings (18% of university total), filing arrangement (17% of university total), and "see" or "see also" references (15% of the university total). In public libraries the 3 most frequent problems were filing arrangement (23% of public total), call number (15% of public total), and subject headings (13% of public total). **(134)**

■ A study reported in 1970 at the University of Michigan, involving alphabetizing and filing National Union Catalog cards into the National Union Catalog (14 groups ranging from 600 cards per group to 2,275 cards

per group alphabetized forwards, i.e., alphabetized into 26 groups on the
basis of the first letter, then each of those groups alphabetized into 26
groups based on the second letter, etc., and 3 groups ranging from 601 to
1,274 cards per group alphabetized by a backwards sort, i.e., alphabetized
into 26 subgroups on the basis of a letter 3 or 4 letters to the right of the
first letter and then sorted into further subgroups by resorting on letters
increasingly close to the beginning of the word), *showed that* when
combined with filing, forwards sorting was more efficient than backwards
sorting. Specifically, based on optimal sorting and filing sized groups
(1,037 cards), the forward-sorted and filed cards took an average of .37
minutes to sort and file, while the backward-sorted groups took an average
in excess of .4 minutes per card to sort and file.   **(590)**

■ A study reported in 1972 of the author/title section of the card catalog
in the Norlin Library of the University of Colorado (population: 1,000,000
cards; sample size: 2,500 cards) *showed that* there was a filing error in the
sample of 1.1%. 52% of the errors were due to lack of knowledge of the
filing rules, and 48% were mechanical or simple alphabetical mistakes.
                                                                       (210)

■ In 1976 the UBC Library (British Columbia) reported that time studies
showed that it took an hour to file 100 author/title cards and half an hour to
file 100 classed or subject file cards.   **(056)**

■ A 1977 survey of U.S. law libraries over 10,000 volumes taken from the
1976 *Directory of Law Libraries* (sample size: 1,080; responding: 373 or
35%) *showed that*, of 123 academic law libraries and 250 remaining law
libraries, 98% of the academic law libraries and 66% of the remaining law
libraries reported using the Anglo-American Cataloging rules, while 78%
of the academic law libraries and 61% of the remaining law libraries
reported using the ALA filing rules.   **(366)**

Public

■ A survey of 12 university libraries (11 responding) during a 3-month
period in 1965 and a survey of 11 public libraries during a similar period in
1967 to determine the kinds of reference assistance needed at the card
catalog (647 problems reported with 284 from university libraries and 363
from public libraries), reported together in 1968, *showed that* the 3 most
frequent problems with the card catalog in university libraries were subject
headings (18% of university total), filing arrangement (17% of university
total), and "see" or "see also" references (15% of the university total). In
public libraries the 3 most frequent problems were filing arrangement

(23% of public total), call number (15% of public total), and subject headings (13% of public total). **(134)**

Special

■ A 1977 survey of U.S. law libraries over 10,000 volumes taken from the 1976 *Directory of Law Libraries* (sample size: 1,080; responding: 373 or 35%) *showed that*, of 123 academic law libraries and 250 remaining law libraries, 98% of the academic law libraries and 66% of the remaining law libraries reported using the Anglo-American Cataloging rules, while 78% of the academic law libraries and 61% of the remaining law libraries reported using the ALA filing rules. **(366)**

Card—Patron Use Patterns

Academic

■ A 1967-70 study in the Main Library at Yale University involving 2,100 interviews at the card catalog during a 1-year period *showed that* weekly charting of card catalog use and book circulation revealed by inspection that card catalog use and book borrowing always remained in the same proportion. **(248)**

Ibid. . . . *showed that* use of the card catalog during the academic year was as follows: Yale freshmen (8.3% of catalog use), other Yale undergraduates (27.7%), graduate/postgraduate students (35.6%), Yale faculty (7.3%), Yale staff (2.9%), and other (18.1%). **(248)**

Ibid. . . . *showed that* known-item searches to determine if the library held the item and, if so, where, accounted for 73% of the catalog use, subject searches accounted for 16%, author searches (to determine what works are available for a known author or publishing body) accounted for 6%, and bibliographic searches (to make use of data on the catalog card rather than locate a book) accounted for 5%. Follow-up questioning about known-item searches suggested that many of these were really subject searches using a known item to identify an appropriate call number or subject heading. The real or "underlying" percentage of known-item and subject searches in the card catalog may be more like 56 and 33, respectively. **(248)**

Ibid. . . . *showed that* 84% of the card catalog searches were successful, that 5% of the searches were unsuccessful for the patron even though library staff later located the document in the card catalog, that 10% of the searches were for documents that probably exist but that were not in the card catalog at the time, and that 1% of the searches were for documents too vaguely or inaccurately described to follow up on. **(248)**

Ibid. . . . *showed that* that the 4 most popular approaches to searching the card catalog were: author name (personal or corporate, 62.0%), title (28.5%), subject (4.5%), and editor (4.0%). **(248)**

■ A survey in 1976 of 999 library users at San Jose State University Library *showed that* of 288 card catalog users only 74 (26%) asked for help and of individuals who had only partial or no success in locating materials in the catalog only 34% had requested help. **(010)**

■ A 1979 study at Iowa State University concerning queueing at the public card catalog during a month and a half period and involving 2,327 sample counts of patrons at the catalog *showed that* the correlation between card catalog use and exit counts, books circulated, and number of individuals checking out books, while statistically significant at the .001 level or better in all 3 cases, was so low as to be negligible. The highest $R2$ (exit count with card catalog use), for example, was .075. With a 1-hour differential between card catalog use counts and number of books circulated, the correlation began to be substantial with an $R2$ of 22%. (No significance level given.) **(497)**

Ibid. . . . *showed that*, when the Friday and Sunday counts (there were no Saturday counts) of card catalog patrons were ignored, there was no statistically significant difference among the daily means during Monday through Thursday. For example, the average number of arrivals at the card catalog during a 10-minute period during any of these 4 days ranged from 11.9 patrons (Wednesday) to 12.9 patrons (Monday). **(497)**

Ibid. . . . *showed that* there were statistically significant differences between patron counts at the card catalog by hour of the day, especially when Friday and Sunday (there were no Saturday counts) were excluded. Arrivals at the card catalog during 10-minute periods averaged 9.7 patrons at 10:00 a.m. and rose regularly until a high of 18.0 patrons was reached at 2:00 p.m. and then fell to 8.8 patrons at 4:00 p.m. (No significance level was given.) **(497)**

■ A 1980 study of patron use of the serial card catalog at the University of Illinois, Urbana (sample size: 452 patrons; usable responses: 445 patrons) involving faculty, students, and staff *showed that* 94% of the materials

sought were English-language materials, with 27 (6%) in other languages.
(505)

Ibid. . . . *showed that* the top 2 sources of 192 serial citations that patrons obtained through use of an index, abstract, or bibliography were *Readers' Guide* (accounting for 54 or 28% of the citations) and *Business Periodicals Index* (accounting for 17 or 9% of the citations). **(505)**

Ibid. . . . *showed that* the sources of the 445 serial citations that patrons brought to the serial card catalog were as follows:

class reading list	42 (9%)	citations
index, abstract, or bibliography	192 (43%)	citations
bibliography or footnote in		
book or journal	127 (29%)	citations
online literature search	40 (9%)	citations
other/no answer	44 (10%)	citations **(505)**

Ibid. . . . *showed that* 366 (83%) of the searches undertaken by patrons in the serial card catalog were successful, i.e., a citation was matched to a catalog entry. Further, the success rate of the frequent catalog user (daily or once/twice per week) was not statistically significantly better than the success rate of the infrequent catalog user. Specifically, 167 (46%) of the frequent catalog users and 199 (54%) of the infrequent catalog users were successful in their searches. **(505)**

Ibid. . . . *showed that* of 427 searches there was no statistically significant difference in success rates between patrons who wrote their citations down (or Xeroxed them) and those who did not. For example, 246 (70%) of the patrons who found their citations in the card catalog had written them down compared to 52 (69%) of the patrons who did not find their citations in the card catalog but who had written them down. Conversely, 93 (26%) of the patrons found their citations in the card catalog without writing them down compared to 20 (27%) of the patrons who did not find their citations in the card catalog but also did not write the citation down. **(505)**

Ibid. . . . *showed that* of the 79 (18%) unsuccessful searches in the serial card catalog the reasons for failure were as follows:

not owned by the library	24 (5%)	citations
patron missed the entry	22 (5%)	citations

continued

        patron had incomplete entry   5 (1%) citations
        serial record failures   28 (6%) citations

Of those not owned by the library, 20 of the 24 titles were verified as correct in spelling and existing in print, i.e., not simply incorrect citations.

(505)

■ A 1981 survey of faculty, students, staff, and community users of the University of Cincinnati Libraries (sample size: 4,074; responding: 912 or 22.4%, including 436 or 39% faculty response and 218 or 11% student response) *showed that*, when asked their most frequent access point used in the public card catalog, faculty and library staff reported "author," while community users, university administrators, and students reported "subject." Further, subgroups among the faculty reported differently from the 57% overall report of author access. For example, 74% of the Arts and Sciences faculty reported "author" as the most frequent point of access, while 60% of the faculty in the College of Business Administration and College of Education reported "subject" as the most frequent point of access. **(522)**

Card—Rearrangement

Academic

■ A 1959 study at the Flint College of the University of Michigan Library and the Flint Community Junior College Library involving the costs of a divided catalog (university catalog held 25,000 volumes and 79,000 cards; community college catalog held 29,000 volumes and 76,000 cards) *showed that* 141 hours (49 hours to divide and 92 hours to revise) were required to rearrange the university dictionary catalog into author/title and subject sections, while 56 hours (32 hours to divide and 24 hours to revise) were required to rearrange the community college dictionary catalog into author/title and subject sections. **(581)**

Ibid. . . . *showed that*, based on filing 2,580 cards in the university catalog and 7,740 cards in the community college catalog, it was considerably cheaper to alphabetize, file, and revise in the divided catalog than in the dictionary catalog. Specifically, the total savings in time ranged between 39% for the community college and 45% for the university library.

(581)

■ A study reported in 1972 at Cornell University concerning a major expansion of the public card catalog (rearranging 4,979 drawers of cards into 6,084 drawers) *showed that* the project required 62 hours of professional time (10% of the total hours), 206 hours of clerical time (34% of the total hours), and 335 hours of student time (56% of the total hours). **(600)**

Card-Book Comparison

Academic

■ A study reported in 1972 comparing the ability of 20 University of Chicago graduate students to search 10 entries in a large book catalog (*National Union Catalog, Pre-1956 Imprints*) vs. 10 entries in a large card catalog (UC main card catalog) *showed that* the average search time per item was less in the card catalog ("consistently less than 19 seconds") than in the book catalog ("consistently greater than 25 seconds"). However, the book catalog (3.1 million entries) was substantially larger than the card catalog (1.4 million entries). **(249)**

■ A study reported in 1972 comparing the ability of 20 University of Chicago graduate students to search 6 entries in each of an essentially identical book and card catalog (Center for Research Libraries catalogs) *showed that* for 16 students the total search time using the book catalog was longer than when using the card catalog, for 2 students the time was identical, and for 2 students searching the book catalog took less total time than when searching the card catalog. (The differences in search time were statistically significant at the .05 level.) **(249)**

Card-Online Comparison

Academic

■ A comparison reported in 1982 of title searches on an online catalog vs. a card catalog at Ohio State University *showed that* patrons were more successful in using departmental card catalogs (1/4 to 1/2 million cards) than in using a central online catalog (3.5 million records). The same held true though to a lesser degree for a skilled librarian. Success rate in the card catalog ran 9-20% higher for patron groups and 4% higher for an experienced librarian. **(045)**

Ibid. . . . *showed that* considering only successful searches, patron groups as well as an experienced librarian generally took longer to find the same materials in the online catalog than in the card catalog. **(045)**

■ A 1982 online survey of MELVYL patrons from all 9 UC campuses conducted over a 2-month period for each 25th user of the system (1,259 questionnaires collected: 72.2 questionnaires complete and usable) *showed that* 68.3% of the respondents reported that the computer catalog was better than other library (i.e., card) catalogs, 17.3% reported that it was equal to other library catalogs, and 14.4% reported that it was worse than other library catalogs. **(349)**

Public

■ A 1980 survey of card catalog and information desk patrons in the Pikes Peak Library District Library over a 2-week period (sample size: 97; responding: 91) *showed that* 85.4% reported a preference for online catalog searching over the traditional manual approach to the card catalog. The main reason given for preferring the online catalog was its ease of use and the speed with which searches could be conducted. **(345)**

COM

Academic

■ A comparison reported in 1975 of circulation statistics at the Georgia Tech library for Spring quarter 1971 and Spring quarter 1972, before and after they had installed microfiche catalogs for the collection in 35 academic and research departments and an accompanying twice-daily book delivery service, *showed that* faculty book circulation as a percentage of total book circulation increased from 13% to 16%, a statistically significant change. [No significance level given.] **(106)**

Ibid. . . . *showed that* the new system changed the way faculty retrieved books from the library. Phone requests increased from 0 to 21.6% of total checkouts, books obtained by going to the library decreased from 88% to 71.6% of total checkouts, and books obtained by sending someone else to the library decreased from 10.5% to 2.7%. **(106)**

■ A survey of 50 faculty patrons who had not used a new system of departmental microfiche catalogs of the total collection and twice-daily book delivery system at Georgia Tech that was reported in 1975 *showed that* the following were the reasons for not using the new system:

	NUMBER
inertia	13
I like to go to the library.	14
I have not had occasion to use the new system.	9

continued

It is more convenient for me to go to the library.   15
I like to browse or look at the books I select.   8
I do not fully understand the (new system).   6
(Some faculty gave more than one response.)   **(106)**

■ A study at the University of Oregon during 1976-77 of 790 library patrons *showed that* acceptance of the new fiche catalog declined with use. Over the period of a year the percentage of respondents who gave the new fiche catalog an easier rating dropped from 29% to 21%, while those who rated the new fiche catalog harder to use increased from 42% to 53%.
(020)

Ibid. . . . *showed that* 37% reported the new fiche catalog was both harder and slower to use than the card catalog, whereas only 19% rated the new fiche catalog superior on both counts.   **(020)**

Ibid. . . . *showed that* more than 1/3 (36%) were unaware of or had not used the catalog fiche supplements updating the basic COM fiche catalog.
(020)

Ibid. . . . *showed that* acceptance of the new COM fiche catalog varied inversely with academic standing. Acceptance was highest among freshmen (35%) and dropped steadily by class through seniors (21%) to graduate students (16%), to faculty (14%). Staff acceptance was 9%.
(020)

Ibid. . . . *showed that* over the course of a year the percentage of patrons who felt the basic microfiche catalog highly legible dropped from 35% to 15%, while the percentage of those who felt the basic microfiche catalog unacceptable rose from 14% to 36%. Catalog film quality was unchanged.
(020)

Ibid. . . . *showed that* 20% of respondents reported physical difficulties using the new microfiche catalog (e.g., eyestrain, headaches, nausea, pains in neck, back, etc.).   **(020)**

■ A preliminary study in 1977 of the University of Toronto *showed that* no category of user (undergrad, grad, faculty, staff) reported much difficulty in using either mircofilm or microfiche catalogs, though microfilm was slightly preferred. Specifically, only 2.3% of the users of the microfilm catalog and 7.2% of the users of the microfiche catalog reported them "difficult to use." **(006)**

■ A 1979 survey of library automation in post-secondary educational institutions in Canada (survey size: 423 libraries; responding: 283 or 67%) *showed that*, of an average of 256 respondents for each of the following items, the distribution of automated activities was as follows (multiple responses allowed):

cataloging	47.2% respondents
online bibliographic searching	34.2% respondents
COM catalog	24.2% respondents
circulation	19.8% respondents
ordering	16.5% respondents
photo-sense ID	7.7% respondents
online catalog	3.2% respondents **(556)**

■ A 1980 survey of North American medical school libraries concerning automation of internal library operations (population: 139; responding: 93 or 69%) *showed that* 8 (8.6%) respondents reported online catalogs, 15 (16.1%) reported either batch or online automated circulation systems, and 20 (21.5%) reported using machine records to produce book or computer output microform (COM) catalogs. Further, 9 (9.7%) respondents reported plans to have online catalogs within a year or 2 of the survey, while 11 (11.8%) reported plans for automated circulation within a year or 2 of the survey. **(741)**

■ A study reported in 1981 at San Jose State University Library comparing graduate library school students' lookup speeds of 16 entries (3 author, 8 title/added entries, and 5 subject entries) in fiche vs. microfilm forms of a dictionary public library catalog with 436,791 entries (using a Micro-Desing 4020 fiche reader and an Information Design ROM 3 film reader) *showed that* the average speed of the film users was 16.7 minutes compared to 25.3 minutes for the fiche users. (This was a statistically significant difference at the .01 level.) **(340)**

Public

■ A 1981-82 study of media cataloging practices in 932 public libraries (responding: 466 or 50%; usable 448 or 48%) across the U.S. serving communities of all sizes *showed that*, of the public catalogs, 85% are in card form, 9% in COM form, and 2% in book form. 38% of the libraries

reported integrating all entries in the public catalog including media, while 62% reported using different catalogs for print and nonprint materials.
(161)

Special

■ A 1977 survey of U.S. law libraries over 10,000 volumes taken from the 1976 *Directory of Law Libraries* (sample size: 1,080; responding: 373 or 35%) *showed that*, of 368 law libraries, 359 (98%) libraries reported having a card catalog, 5 libraries reported having book catalogs, 2 reported using both book and card catalogs and 1 library reported using a computer-produced microfiche catalog. [The remaining library was not accounted for]
(366)

■ A 1980 survey of North American medical school libraries concerning automation of internal library operations (population: 139; responding: 93 or 69%), *showed that* 8 (8.6%) respondents reported online catalogs, 15 (16.1%) reported either batch or online automated circulation systems, and 20 (21.5%) reported using machine records to produce book or computer output microform (COM) catalogs. Further, 9 (9.7%) respondents reported plans to have online catalogs within a year or 2 of the survey, while 11 (11.8%) reported plans for automated circulation within a year or 2 of the survey.
(741)

COM—Microfilm-Microfiche Comparison

General

■ A 1979 study comparing lookup time of the same catalog (Anoka County Library, Minnesota, with a collection size of 110,000 titles with almost 500,000 entries) in fiche format (using a nmi-90 fiche reader) vs. microfilm format (ROM 3 mechanized reader) *showed that* an arbitrarily selected group of 36 UC Berkeley patrons (an additional 3 did not complete enough of the lookups to be included) carrying out 252 trials revealed that the fiche catalog required an average of 7.6% longer lookup time. A lookup task that would take 20 minutes using a ROM film reader would take 21 to 22 minutes in a fiche reader.
(267)

Ibid. . . . *showed that* 40 library staff at UC Berkeley carrying out 240 trials revealed that the fiche catalog required on average a 5.7% longer lookup time.
(267)

Ibid. . . . *showed that*, of 39 respondents in the patron group and 31 respondents in the library staff group, 10 (26%) of the patron group favored the fiche reader vs. 14 (45%) of the library staff group, 10 (26%) of the patron group had no preference vs. 1 (3%) of the library staff group, and 19 (49%) of the patron group favored the ROM vs. 16 (52%) of the library staff group.   **(267)**

■ A study reported in 1981 at San Jose State University Library comparing graduate library school students' lookup speeds of 16 entries (3 author, 8 title/added entries, and 5 subject entries) in fiche vs. microfilm forms of a dictionary public library catalog with 436,791 entries (using a Micro-Desing 4020 fiche reader and an Information Design ROM 3 film reader) *showed that* the average speed of the film users was 16.7 minutes compared to 25.3 minutes for the fiche users. (This was a statistically significant difference at the .01 level.)   **(340)**

Cross-References

General

■ A 1974 survey of libraries world-wide concerning scripts used and script conversion practices employed in their catalogs (sample size: 231; responding: 146 or 63%) *showed that* 5 (3%) libraries provided cross-references from non-Roman to romanized entries,while 5 (3%) libraries provided cross-references from romanized entries to non-Roman entries.   **(356)**

Academic

■ A study reported in 1972 of the author/title section of the card catalog in the Norlin Library of the University of Colorado (population: 1,000,000 cards; sample size: 2,500 cards) *showed that* in the sample 10.14% of the cross-references were blind.   **(210)**

Special

■ A survey reported in 1975 of subject heading use in a wide range of law libraries selected from the 1972 edition of the American Association of Law Libraries *Directory of Law Libraries* (sample size: 256; responding: 204; usable: 200 or 78.1%) *showed that* the following cross-reference structure was kept in the public card catalog:

full structure (see and see
  also references)   97 (48.5%) respondents
see references and selected
  see also references   71 (35.5%) respondents
see references only   20 (10.0%) respondents
none   12 (6.0%) respondents   **(393)**

Dictionary

Academic

■ A survey reported in 1969 of medical school and selected medical research libraries (survey size: 102 libraries; responding: 92 or 90%) *showed that* there was a strong trend toward divided catalogs. Specifically, 38 (41%) libraries reported dictionary card catalogs, while 54 (59%) libraries reported divided card catalogs. These figures included 12 new (established within 10 years of the study) libraries of which 1 (8%) reported a dictionary catalog and 11 (92%) reported a divided catalog. Further, of the 54 libraries reporting divided catalogs, 31 (57%) had changed to the divided catalog within the last 10 years.   **(679)**

Ibid. . . . *showed that* the 54 libraries that reported divided catalogs reported the following methods of division:

author-title/subject   42 (77.8%) libraries
name-title/subject   7 (13.0%) libraries
author/title/subject   3 (5.6%) libraries
other   1 (1.9%) libraries

(Name-title catalog was defined to include persons and places as subject headings as well as as authors.)   **(679)**

Ibid. . . . *showed that* the subject heading authority used by the 54 libraries with divided catalogs was as follows: MeSH, exclusively or in combination with LC subject headings (41 or 75.9% libraries); LC subject headings exclusively (9 or 16.7% libraries); and other (2 or 3.7% libraries).   **(679)**

■ A 1980 survey of law school libraries with collections in excess of 175,000 volumes (sample size: 50; responding: 37 or 70%) *showed that* 24 libraries reported a divided catalog with authors and titles together and all subjects together, 8 reported a dictionary catalog, and 5 reported a divided catalog in 3 divisions with authors, titles, and subjects organized separately. **(369)**

Special

■ A survey reported in 1969 of medical school and selected medical research libraries (survey size: 102 libraries; responding: 92 or 90%) *showed that* there was a strong trend toward divided catalogs. Specifically, 38 (41%) libraries reported dictionary card catalogs, while 54 (59%) libraries reported divided card catalogs. These figures included 12 new (established within 10 years of the study) libraries of which 1 (8%) reported a dictionary catalog and 11 (92%) reported a divided catalog. Further, of the 54 libraries reporting divided catalogs, 31 (57%) had changed to the divided catalog within the last 10 years. **(679)**

Ibid. . . . *showed that* the 54 libraries that reported divided catalogs reported the following methods of division:

author-title/subject	42 (77.8%)	libraries
name-title/subject	7 (13.0%)	libraries
author/title/subject	3 (5.6%)	libraries
other	1 (1.9%)	libraries

(Name-title catalog was defined to include persons and places as subject headings as well as as authors.) **(679)**

Ibid. . . . *showed that* the subject heading authority used by the 54 libraries with divided catalogs was as follows: MeSH, exclusively or in combination with LC subject headings (41 or 75.9% libraries); LC subject headings exclusively (9 or 16.7% libraries); and other (2 or 3.7% libraries). **(679)**

■ A survey reported in 1975 of subject heading use in a wide range of law libraries selected from the 1972 edition of the American Association of Law Libraries *Directory of Law Libraries* (sample size: 256; responding: 204; usable: 200 or 78.1%) *showed that* 101 (50.5%) respondents had a dictionary catalog, while 96 (48%) had a divided catalog. 3 (1.5%) respondents did not clearly state which kind of catalog they had. **(393)**

■ A 1977 survey of U.S. law libraries over 10,000 volumes taken from the 1976 *Directory of Law Libraries* (sample size: 1,080; responding: 373 or 35%) *showed that* 55% of the responding libraries reported owning a divided catalog, 43% reported owning a dictionary catalog, and 2% did not indicate either form. The "most common" divided catalog was a 2-way author/title and subject division, with only 6 respondents reporting a 3-way divided catalog. **(366)**

■ A 1980 survey of law school libraries with collections in excess of 175,000 volumes (sample size: 50; responding: 37 or 70%) *showed that* 24 libraries reported a divided catalog with authors and titles together and all subjects together, 8 reported a dictionary catalog, and 5 reported a divided catalog in 3 divisions with authors, titles, and subjects organized separately. **(369)**

Dictionary-Divided Catalog Comparison

Academic

■ A 1959 study at the Flint College of the University of Michigan Library and the Flint Community Junior College Library involving the costs of a divided catalog (university catalog held 25,000 volumes and 79,000 cards; community college catalog held 29,000 volumes and 76,000 cards) *showed that* 141 hours (49 hours to divide and 92 hours to revise) were required to rearrange the university dictionary catalog into author/title and subject sections, while 56 hours (32 hours to divide and 24 hours to revise) were required to rearrange the community college dictionary catalog into author/title and subject sections. **(581)**

Ibid. . . . *showed that*, based on filing 2,580 cards in the university catalog and 7,740 cards in the community college catalog, it was considerably cheaper to alphabetize, file, and revise in the divided catalog than in the dictionary catalog. Specifically, the total savings in time ranged between 39% for the community college and 45% for the university library. **(581)**

■ A 1967 study comparing a dictionary catalog at 1 university with a divided catalog (author/title and subject) at another university by using undergraduates to search entries *showed that* there was no statistically significant difference in average success rates between the 2 catalogs in subject searching or known-item searching. **(199)**

Divided

Academic

■ A survey reported in 1969 of medical school and selected medical research libraries (survey size: 102 libraries; responding: 92 or 90%) *showed that* there was a strong trend toward divided catalogs. Specifically, 38 (41%) libraries reported dictionary card catalogs, while 54 (59%) libraries reported divided card catalogs. These figures included 12 new (established within 10 years of the study) libraries of which 1 (8%) reported a dictionary catalog and 11 (92%) reported a divided catalog. Further, of the 54 libraries reporting divided catalogs, 31 (57%) had changed to the divided catalog within the last 10 years. **(679)**

Ibid. . . . *showed that* the 54 libraries that reported divided catalogs reported the following methods of division:

author-title/subject	42 (77.8%) libraries
name-title/subject	7 (13.0%) libraries
author/title/subject	3 (5.6%) libraries
other	1 (1.9%) libraries

(Name-title catalog was defined to include persons and places as subject headings as well as as authors.) **(679)**

Ibid. . . . *showed that* the subject heading authority used by the 54 libraries with divided catalogs was as follows: MeSH, exclusively or in combination with LC subject headings (41 or 75.9% libraries); LC subject headings exclusively (9 or 16.7% libraries); and other (2 or 3.7% libraries). **(679)**

■ A 1975 survey of North American medical school libraries concerning subject cataloging practices (survey size: 134 libraries; responding: 114 or 85%) *showed that*, of 78 respondents who used MeSH as the primary authority for subject headings and who also had divided catalogs, 54 (69%) reported they used a guidecard to distinguish subject headings filed in the subject section of the catalog, while 24 (31%) reported they did not. **(712)**

Ibid. . . . *showed that*, of 78 respondents who used MeSH as the primary authority for subject headings and who also had divided catalogs, 76 (97%) reported they did not file MeSH terms in the public catalog unless there were catalog cards for them, while 2 (3%) reported they filed all MeSH terms regardless of whether there were cards for that heading. **(712)**

Ibid. . . . *showed that*, of 78 respondents who used MeSH as the primary authority for subject headings and who also had divided catalogs, 14 (18%) reported that they distinguished between form and topical subheading guidecards in a physical way in the catalog, while 62 (79%) reported they did not, and 2 (3%) did not respond. Of those that did distinguish, the following methods were used: cut of tab on card (10 respondents), color of tab (8 respondents), and color of type (1 respondent). **(712)**

Ibid. . . . *showed that*, of 65 respondents who used MeSH as the primary authority for subject headings and who also had divided catalogs, 18 (27.7%) reported that if language and geographic subheadings were combined with form subheadings the first filing term would be the language/geographic term (e.g., French—Dictionaries), while 47 (72.3%) reported that the order would be reversed. **(712)**

Ibid. . . . *showed that*, of 62 respondents who used MeSH as the primary authority for subject headings and who also had divided catalogs, 56 (90.3%) reported that if language and geographic subheadings were combined with topical subheadings the first filing term would be the topical term followed by the language/geographic term (e.g., Manpower—France), while 6 (9.7%) reported that the order would be reversed.
(712)

Ibid. . . . *showed that*, of 78 respondents who used MeSH as the primary authority for subject headings and who also had divided catalogs, 56 (72%) respondents reported updating the subject catalog and authority file annually to correspond to the new MeSH, 20 (26%) reported "other," and 2 (2%) did not respond. **(712)**

Ibid. . . . *showed that*, of 78 respondents who used MeSH as the primary authority for subject headings and who also had divided catalogs, the following methods were used to update the catalog (multiple responses allowed):

56 (71.8%) reported "changing or shifting subject cards from the old headings to the new and pulling deleted MeSH terms";

8 (10.3%) reported "making no changes in the existing catalog but making cross references from old to new terms";

15 (19.2%) reported "other method";

2 (2.6%) gave no response. **(712)**

■ A 1980 survey of law school libraries with collections in excess of 175,000 volumes (sample size: 50; responding: 37 or 70%) *showed that* 24 libraries reported a divided catalog with authors and titles together and all subjects together, 8 reported a dictionary catalog, and 5 reported a divided catalog in 3 divisions with authors, titles, and subjects organized separately.   **(369)**

Special

■ A survey reported in 1969 of medical school and selected medical research libraries (survey size: 102 libraries; responding: 92 or 90%) *showed that* there was a strong trend toward divided catalogs. Specifically, 38 (41%) libraries reported dictionary card catalogs, while 54 (59%) libraries reported divided card catalogs. These figures included 12 new (established within 10 years of the study) libraries of which 1 (8%) reported a dictionary catalog and 11 (92%) reported a divided catalog. Further, of the 54 libraries reporting divided catalogs, 31 (57%) had changed to the divided catalog within the last 10 years.   **(679)**

Ibid. . . . *showed that* the 54 libraries that reported divided catalogs reported the following methods of division:

author-title/subject	42 (77.8%)	libraries
name-title/subject	7 (13.0%)	libraries
author/title/subject	3 (5.6%)	libraries
other	1 (1.9%)	libraries

(Name-title catalog was defined to include persons and places as subject headings as well as as authors.)   **(679)**

Ibid. . . . *showed that* the subject heading authority used by the 54 libraries with divided catalogs was as follows: MeSH, exclusively or in combination with LC subject headings (41 or 75.9% libraries); LC subject headings exclusively (9 or 16.7% libraries); and other (2 or 3.7% libraries).   **(679)**

■ A 1975 survey of North American medical school libraries concerning subject cataloging practices (survey size: 134 libraries; responding: 114 or 85%) *showed that*, of 78 respondents who used MeSH as the primary authority for subject headings and who also had divided catalogs, 54 (69%) reported they used a guidecard to distinguish subject headings filed in the subject section of the catalog, while 24 (31%) reported they did not.   **(712)**

Ibid. . . . *showed that*, of 78 respondents who used MeSH as the primary authority for subject headings and who also had divided catalogs, 76 (97%) reported they did not file MeSH terms in the public catalog unless there were catalog cards for them, while 2 (3%) reported they filed all MeSH terms regardless of whether there were cards for that heading. **(712)**

Ibid. . . . *showed that*, of 78 respondents who used MeSH as the primary authority for subject headings and who also had divided catalogs, 14 (18%) reported that they distinguished between form and topical subheading guidecards in a physical way in the catalog, while 62 (79%) reported they did not, and 2 (3%) did not respond. Of those that did distinguish, the following methods were used: cut of tab on card (10 respondents), color of tab (8 respondents), and color of type (1 respondent). **(712)**

Ibid. . . . *showed that*, of 65 respondents who used MeSH as the primary authority for subject headings and who also had divided catalogs, 18 (27.7%) reported that if language and geographic subheadings were combined with form subheadings the first filing term would be the language/geographic term (e.g., French—Dictionaries), while 47 (72.3%) reported that the order would be reversed. **(712)**

Ibid. . . . *showed that*, of 62 respondents who used MeSH as the primary authority for subject headings and who also had divided catalogs, 56 (90.3%) reported that if language and geographic subheadings were combined with topical subheadings the first filing term would be the topical term followed by the language/geographic term (e.g., Manpower—France), while 6 (9.7%) reported that the order would be reversed.
(712)

Ibid. . . . *showed that*, of 78 respondents who used MeSH as the primary authority for subject headings and who also had divided catalogs, 56 (72%) respondents reported updating the subject catalog and authority file annually to correspond to the new MeSH, 20 (26%) reported "other," and 2 (2%) did not respond. **(712)**

Ibid. . . . *showed that*, of 78 respondents who used MeSH as the primary authority for subject headings and who also had divided catalogs, the following methods were used to update the catalog (multiple responses allowed):

> 56 (71.8%) reported "changing or shifting subject cards from
> the old headings to the new and pulling deleted MeSH terms";

8 (10.3%) reported "making no changes in the existing catalog but making cross references from old to new terms";

15 (19.2%) reported "other method";

2 (2.6%) gave no response.　　　　　　　　　　　　　　**(712)**

■ A survey reported in 1975 of subject heading use in a wide range of law libraries selected from the 1972 edition of the American Association of Law Libraries *Directory of Law Libraries* (sample size: 256; responding: 204; usable: 200 or 78.1%) *showed that* 101 (50.5%) respondents had a dictionary catalog, while 96 (48%) had a divided catalog. 3 (1.5%) respondents did not clearly state which kind of catalog they had.　　**(393)**

■ A 1977 survey of U.S. law libraries over 10,000 volumes taken from the 1976 *Directory of Law Libraries* (sample size: 1,080; responding: 373 or 35%) *showed that* 55% of the responding libraries reported owning a divided catalog, 43% reported owning a dictionary catalog, and 2% did not indicate either form. The "most common" divided catalog was a 2-way author/title and subject division, with only 6 respondents reporting a 3-way divided catalog.　　　　　　　　　　　　　　　　　　**(366)**

■ A 1980 survey of law school libraries with collections in excess of 175,000 volumes (sample size: 50; responding: 37 or 70%) *showed that* 24 libraries reported a divided catalog with authors and titles together and all subjects together, 8 reported a dictionary catalog, and 5 reported a divided catalog in 3 divisions with authors, titles, and subjects organized separately.　　　　　　　　　　　　　　　　　　　　　　　　**(369)**

Entries

General

■ An analysis of the number of added entries assigned cataloged material listed in the *National Union Catalog* during the period 1950-73 *showed that* there was an increase in the average number of added entries per item, rising consistently from 1 added entry 1950 to 1.5 added entries in 1973. Over this period there was a drop in the number of titles receiving no added entries from 22.6% to 8.6%.　　　　　　　　　　　**(055)**

Ibid. . . . *showed that* the average number of added entries per main entry increased from 1 to 1.5, a statistically significant increase.　　**(055)**

■ A 1974 survey of libraries world-wide concerning scripts used and script conversion practices employed in their catalogs (sample size: 231; responding: 146 or 63%) *showed that*, of 134 respondents, 76 (56%) romanized the whole entry, 44 (32%) romanized both the author and the title, and 24 (18%) romanized either the author's name or the title.

(356)

Ibid. . . . *showed that* those parts of the entry that are translated by responding libraries were as follows: corporate author (11 or 8% respondents always translated, 26 or 18% sometimes translated), title (16 or 11% always translated, 15 or 10% sometimes translated), and whole entry (1 or less than 1% always translated, 6 or 4% sometimes translated).

(356)

Ibid. . . . *showed that* 5 (3%) libraries provided cross-references from non-Roman to romanized entries, while 5 (3%) libraries provided cross-references from romanized entries to non-Roman entries.

(356)

Ibid. . . . *showed that* 12 (8%) libraries used no kind of script conversion in their catalogs.

(356)

Academic

■ A survey of 12 university libraries (11 responding) during a 3-month period in 1965 and a survey of 11 public libraries during a similar period in 1967 to determine the kinds of reference assistance needed at the card catalog (647 problems reported with 284 from university libraries and 363 from public libraries), reported together in 1968, *showed that* the 3 most frequent problems with the card catalog in university libraries were subject headings (18% of university total), filing arrangement (17% of university total), and "see" or "see also" references (15% of the university total). In public libraries the 3 most frequent problems were filing arrangement (23% of public total), call number (15% of public total), and subject headings (13% of public total).

(134)

■ A preliminary study of catalog use at the University of Toronto in 1977 *showed that* brief bibliographic entries were suffficient for most users and that full bibliographic entries were more important to library staff. Specifically, estimated use of the full bibliographic record was as follows (the remaining percentage was use of the brief entry record):

Estimated Use:
undergraduate	0.9%
graduate/faculty	4.6%
ibrary staff	14.2%
overall average	6.6%

Actual Use:
overall average	7.7%	**(006)**

Ibid. . . . *showed that* users tend to overestimate their use of author and subject access points and underestimate their use of the title access point. (The remaining percentage was use of the full bibliographic record.)

	ESTIMATED USATE	ACTUAL USAGE	
author	43.2%	36.7%	
title	27.2%	32.4%	
subject	23.0%	21.3%	**(006)**

■ A study reported in 1980 of 2 card catalogs (University of Wisconsin, Whitewater, 170,000 titles; University of Illinois, Urbana, 3,000,000 titles) investigating the number of personal authors for which there was only 1 title in the collection (sample size: Whitewater, 2,762 authors; Urbana, 2,345 authors) *showed that* the incidence of single-work authors was 69.33% (67.60% to 71.05% confidence interval at .95 probability) at Whitewater and 63.5% (61.4% to 65.6% confidence interval at .95 probability) at Urbana.   **(758)**

ISBD

Academic

■ A study reported in 1979 at the Undergraduate Library of the University of Illinois, Urbana, comparing catalog cards formatted according to the unrevised 1967 AACR chapter 6 rules with cards formatted according to ISBD (International Standard Bibliographic Description) presented to 48 students, *showed that* students were able to find completely correct information on the ISBD formatted cards 68.5% of the time compared to 64.1% of the time for the chapter 6 rules formatted cards. Further, incorrect answers were provided 9.8% of the time for ISBD cards and 17.4% of the time for chapter 6 cards, while response time averaged 8 seconds for ISBD cards and 9 seconds for chapter 6 cards.   **(477)**

Maintenance

General

■ A survey reported in 1982 of Canadian libraries selected from the *CLA Directory* and its supplement (sample size: 203; responding: 85; usable: 69 or 34.0%) concerning implementation of AACR 2 *showed that*, of the 53 libraries who adopted AACR 2, 77% reported they would interfile the AACR 2 entries in their old catalogs, 7 [%] reported they would freeze their catalogs, and 9% reported they would close their catalogs. **(299)**

■ A survey reported in 1983 of operational online catalogs in the United States (survey size: 20 systems) *showed that* 16 (80.0%) systems created their data base by loading tapes, while 14 (70.0%) maintained their data base by loading tapes. 6 (30.0%) systems had an online interface to OCLC, while a total of 13 (65.0%) allowed records to be input and edited by direct keying. **(773)**

Academic

■ A 1959 study at the Flint College of the University of Michigan Library and the Flint Community Junior College Library involving the costs of a divided catalog (university catalog held 25,000 volumes and 79,000 cards; community college catalog held 29,000 volumes and 76,000 cards) *showed that* 141 hours (49 hours to divide and 92 hours to revise) were required to rearrange the university dictionary catalog into author/title and subject sections, while 56 hours (32 hours to divide and 24 hours to revise) were required to rearrange the community college dictionary catalog into author/title and subject sections. **(581)**

Ibid. . . . *showed that*, based on filing 2,580 cards in the university catalog and 7,740 cards in the community college catalog, it was considerably cheaper to alphabetize, file, and revise in the divided catalog than in the dictionary catalog. Specifically, the total savings in time ranged between 39% for the community college and 45% for the university library. **(581)**

■ A study reported in 1972 of the author/title section of the card catalog in the Norlin Library of the University of Colorado (population: 1,000,000 cards; sample size: 2,500 cards) *showed that* there was a filing error in the sample of 1.1%. 52% of the errors were due to lack of knowledge of the filing rules, and 48% were mechanical or simple alphabetical mistakes. **(210)**

Ibid. . . . *showed that* in the sample 10.14% of the cross-references were blind.   **(210)**

Ibid. . . . *showed that* in the sample 1.48% of the cards were judged to be mutilated, i.e., call numbers or other essential information was torn off or completely obscured by dirt and wear.   **(210)**

■ A 1975 survey of North American medical school libraries concerning subject cataloging practices (survey size: 134 libraries; responding: 114 or 85%) *showed that*, of 78 respondents who used MeSH as the primary authority for subject headings and who also had divided catalogs, 54 (69%) reported they used a guidecard to distinguish subject headings filed in the subject section of the catalog, while 24 (31%) reported they did not.
                                                                       (712)

Ibid. . . . *showed that*, of 78 respondents who used MeSH as the primary authority for subject headings and who also had divided catalogs, 76 (97%) reported they did not file MeSH terms in the public catalog unless there were catalog cards for them, while 2 (3%) reported they filed all MeSH terms regardless of whether there were cards for that heading.   **(712)**

Ibid. . . . *showed that*, of 78 respondents who used MeSH as the primary authority for subject headings and who also had divided catalogs, 14 (18%) reported that they distinguished between form and topical subheading guidecards in a physical way in the catalog, while 62 (79%) reported they did not, and 2 (3%) did not respond. Of those that did distinguish, the following methods were used: cut of tab on card (10 respondents), color of tab (8 respondents), and color of type (1 respondent).   **(712)**

Ibid. . . . *showed that*, of 65 respondents who used MeSH as the primary authority for subject headings and who also had divided catalogs, 18 (27.7%) reported that if language and geographic subheadings were combined with form subheadings the first filing term would be the language/geographic term (e.g., French—Dictionaries), while 47 (72.3%) reported that the order would be reversed.   **(712)**

Ibid. . . . *showed that*, of 62 respondents who used MeSH as the primary authority for subject headings and who also had divided catalogs, 56 (90.3%) reported that if language and geographic subheadings were combined with topical subheadings the first filing term would be the topical term followed by the language/geographic term (e.g., Manpower—

France), while 6 (9.7%) reported that the order would be reversed.
(712)

Ibid. . . . *showed that*, of 78 respondents who used MeSH as the primary authority for subject headings and who also had divided catalogs, 56 (72%) respondents reported updating the subject catalog and authority file annually to correspond to the new MeSH, 20 (26%) reported "other," and 2 (2%) did not respond.
(712)

Ibid. . . . *showed that*, of 78 respondents who used MeSH as the primary authority for subject headings and who also had divided catalogs, the following methods were used to update the catalog (multiple responses allowed):

56 (71.8%) reported "changing or shifting subject cards from the old headings to the new and pulling deleted MeSH terms";

8 (10.3%) reported "making no changes in the existing catalog but making cross references from old to new terms";

15 (19.2%) reported "other method";

2 (2.6%) gave no response.
(712)

■ A study reported in 1982 concerning the impact of AACR 2 on the card catalog in a medium-sized (740,000 volumes) academic library, based on a random sample of 909 catalog records (1,714 headings) taken from a year's pre-AACR 2 OCLC archival tapes and searched in the post-AACR 2 OCLC LC name authority file, *showed that* not all conflicts needed to be changed in order to interfile with pre-AACR 2 entries in the card catalog. Specifically, assuming that 5 kinds of differences could be ignored (punctuation, abbreviation, spelling, qualifier, and forname), 31.8% of the conflicts could be interfiled.
(770)

Public

■ A report issued in 1974 of the experience of the Houston Public Library in inventorying its collection (236,519 titles) *showed that* catalog cards could be pulled from the catalog at the rate of 40 cards per hour per person.
(097)

Special

■ A 1975 survey of North American medical school libraries concerning subject cataloging practices (survey size: 134 libraries; responding: 114 or 85%) *showed that*, of 78 respondents who used MeSH as the primary authority for subject headings and who also had divided catalogs, 54 (69%)

reported they used a guidecard to distinguish subject headings filed in the subject section of the catalog, while 24 (31%) reported they did not.
                                                                                       (712)

Ibid. . . . *showed that*, of 78 respondents who used MeSH as the primary authority for subject headings and who also had divided catalogs, 76 (97%) reported they did not file MeSH terms in the public catalog unless there were catalog cards for them, while 2 (3%) reported they filed all MeSH terms regardless of whether there were cards for that heading.   **(712)**

Ibid. . . . *showed that*, of 78 respondents who used MeSH as the primary authority for subject headings and who also had divided catalogs, 14 (18%) reported that they distinguished between form and topical subheading guidecards in a physical way in the catalog, while 62 (79%) reported they did not, and 2 (3%) did not respond. Of those that did distinguish, the following methods were used: cut of tab on card (10 respondents), color of tab (8 respondents), and color of type (1 respondent).   **(712)**

Ibid. . . . *showed that*, of 65 respondents who used MeSH as the primary authority for subject headings and who also had divided catalogs, 18 (27.7%) reported that if language and geographic subheadings were combined with form subheadings the first filing term would be the language/geographic term (e.g., French—Dictionaries), while 47 (72.3%) reported that the order would be reversed.   **(712)**

Ibid. . . . *showed that*, of 62 respondents who used MeSH as the primary authority for subject headings and who also had divided catalogs, 56 (90.3%) reported that if language and geographic subheadings were combined with topical subheadings the first filing term would be the topical term followed by the language/geographic term (e.g., Manpower—France), while 6 (9.7%) reported that the order would be reversed.
                                                                                       (712)

Ibid. . . . *showed that*, of 78 respondents who used MeSH as the primary authority for subject headings and who also had divided catalogs, 56 (72%) respondents reported updating the subject catalog and authority file annually to correspond to the new MeSH, 20 (26%) reported "other," and 2 (2%) did not respond.   **(712)**

Ibid. . . . *showed that*, of 78 respondents who used MeSH as the primary authority for subject headings and who also had divided catalogs, the following methods were used to update the catalog (multiple responses allowed):

56 (71.8%) reported "changing or shifting subject cards from the old headings to the new and pulling deleted MeSH terms";

8 (10.3%) reported "making no changes in the existing catalog but making cross references from old to new terms";

15 (19.2%) reported "other method";

2 (2.6%) gave no response. **(712)**

Media Materials

Academic

■ A 1979 survey of U.S. community college libraries selected from the 1978 *Community, Junior and Technical College Directory* (sample size: 98; responding: 52; usable: 48 or 48.98%) *showed that* for audiovisual materials:

24 (50.0%) libraries did full cataloging and interfiled entries in the central catalog;

8 (16.7%) libraries did full cataloging but filed audiovisual entries in a separate catalog;

1 (2.1%) library did full cataloging and filed audiovisual entries in separate drawers of the central catalog;

6 (12.5%) libraries did full cataloging but filed audiovisual entries in a separate catalog in the AV center;

9 (18.8%) libraries did full cataloging and filed audiovisual entries both in the central catalog and in a separate catalog in the AV center. **(498)**

Public

■ A 1972 survey of chief library administrators in public comprehensive community colleges (population: 586; usable responses: 75.9% [no raw number given]) *showed that* books and audiovisual materials were listed in a central coordinated or union catalog in 67.2% of the institutions. **(452)**

■ A 1981-82 study of media cataloging practices in 932 public libraries (responding: 466 or 50%; usable: 448 or 48%) across the U.S. serving communities of all sizes *showed that*, of the public catalogs, 85% were in card form, 9% in COM form, and 2% in book form. 38% of the libraries reported integrating all entries in the public catalog including media, while

62% reported using different catalogs for print and nonprint materials.
(161)

Online

General

■ A study reported in 1972 at Ohio State University involving biblio-graphic search keys for large collections, i.e., using a 4-5 search key (first 4 letters of the author's last name and the first 5 letters of the first significant word in the title) to search 1,000 actual requests in a collection of 857,725 titles representing 2.6 million volumes, *showed that* 35.9% of the time 1 or less items were matched, while 87.8% of the time 10 or less items were matched. With a 99% confidence interval the upper limit for the 4-5 search key retrieving 10 or less items was 90.2%.   **(323)**

■ A 1978 study of OCLC's online union catalog preparatory to convert-ing to AACR 2 form of name headings and uniform titles, involving a 1% test file (41,212 records) and a thorough review of AACR 2 rules, *showed that* AACR 2 contained 454 "significant" rule changes or new rules, of which 56% would benefit neither librarian nor patron, 23% of which would benefit librarians, and 21% of which would benefit patrons.   **(337)**

Ibid. . . . *showed that* 39% of the total records in the online union catalog were ultimately converted to AACR 2 form.   **(337)**

■ A study reported in 1981 of OCLC's online union catalog to investigate the scope of its music holdings by checking 4 major lists of materials ("Books Recently Published" column of *Notes*; "Music Received" column of *Notes*; "New Listings" column of the *Schwann-1 Record and Tape Guide*; and *A Basic Music Library: Essential Scores and Books*) in the catalog *showed that*, of the 317 books listed in the December 1979 "Books Recently Published" column and searched 1 year later, 312 (98.42%) were found in the OCLC union catalog, while of the 287 books listed in the September 1980 "Books Recently Published" column and searched 7 months later, 272 (94.78%) were found in the OCLC union catalog.
(757)

Ibid. . . . *showed that*, of the 420 items listed in the December 1979 "Music Received" column and searched 1 year later, 255 (60.71%) were found in the OCLC union catalog, while of the 351 items listed in the September 1980 "Music Received" column and searched 1-2 months later,

109 (31.05%) were found in the OCLC union catalog.   **(757)**

Ibid. . . . *showed that*, of the 276 items listed in the December 1979 "New Listings" column and searched 14 months later, 162 (58.7%) were found in the OCLC union catalog, while of the 282 items listed in the September 1980 "New Listings" column and searched 1-2 months later, 64 (22.7%) were found in the OCLC union catalog.   **(757)**

Ibid. . . . *showed that*, of the 941 items listed in *A Basis Music Library*, 861 (91.5%) were found, including 231 (94.29%) of the study scores, 195 (96.53%) of the performing editions, and 114 (82.01%) of the instrumental methods and studies. Further, "a large number of specific editions not found in the search" were represented in the OCLC union catalog by other editions.   **(757)**

■ A survey reported in 1983 of operational online catalogs in the United States (survey size: 20 systems) *showed that* all 20 systems included access by author, title, and subject. In addition the following access points were allowed:

call number access	15 (75.0%) systems
LC card number access	13 (65.0%) systems
ISBN/ISSN access	11 (55.0%) systems
OCLC number access	5 (25.0%) systems
document number access	3 (15.0%) systems
CODEN number	2 (10.0%) systems

Further, the number of access points per system ranged from 12 (Avatar Systems) to 4 (Northwestern University) with a median of 7 access points and an average of 7.9 access points.   **(773)**

Ibid. . . . *showed that* the number of display formats offered per system ranged from 1 to 5 (index, brief [2 kinds], full, and MARC) and were distributed as follows:

1 display format	2 (10.0%) systems
2 display formats	7 (35.0%) systems
3 display formats	8 (40.0%) systems
4 display formats	2 (10.0%) systems
5 display formats	1 (5.0%) systems

Further, 16 (80%) systems had a brief bibliographic display (generally including brief author, title, imprint, and call number), while 18 (90%) systems had a full bibliographic display (including all or most of the bibliographic information found on a catalog card). In "only 1 or 2 cases" was the full display arranged as on a catalog card; most systems used a tabular form with the information elements labeled.   **(773)**

Ibid. . . . *showed that* only 8 (40.0%) of the systems had "some form of authority control," and only 3 of the 8 "consolidated variant records for the same title and retained those variations in the master file."   **(773)**

Ibid. . . . *showed that* 16 (80.0%) systems created their data base by loading tapes, while 14 (70.0%) maintained their data base by loading tapes. 6 (30.0%) systems had an online interface to OCLC, while a total of 13 (65.0%) allowed records to be input and edited by direct keying.
                                                                              (773)

Ibid. . . . *showed that* the size of the online catalogs varied greatly although there was some clustering. 2 systems contained approximately 35,000 records, 7 contained 400,000-500,000 records and 3 contained 700,000-750,000 records. The remaining systems ranged in size from 69,000 records to 2,500,000 records.   **(773)**

Ibid. . . . *showed that* neither of the 2 basic approaches to searching online catalogs (menu and command) had become dominant [number of systems providing each or both not given].   **(773)**

Academic

■ A 1978 study at Ohio State University Library involving 2 full days' transactions in the OCLC data base for each of the OSU terminals (1,153 searches of the data base) *showed that* of 158 searches by the public the 2 most frequent types of searches were by name/title (77 or 48.7% of the searches by the public of which 22 or 28.6% were successful) and by title (44 or 27.8% of the searches by the public of which 20 or 45.4% were successful).   **(336)**

■ A 1979 survey of library automation in post-secondary educational institutions in Canada (survey size: 423 libraries; responding: 283 or 67%) *showed that*, of an average of 256 respondents for each of the following items, the distribution of automated activities was as follows (multiple responses allowed):

cataloging	47.2% respondents
online bibliographic searching	34.2% respondents
COM catalog	24.2% respondents

continued

circulation	19.8% respondents
ordering	16.5% respondents
photo-sense ID	7.7% respondents
online catalog	3.2% respondents

(556)

■ A 1980 survey of North American medical school libraries concerning automation of internal library operations (population: 139; responding: 93 or 69%) *showed that* 8 (8.6%) respondents reported online catalogs, 15 (16.1%) reported either batch or online automated circulation systems, and 20 (21.5%) reported using machine records to produce book or computer output microform (COM) catalogs. Further, 9 (9.7%) respondents reported plans to have online catalogs within a year or 2 of the survey, while 11 (11.8%) reported plans for automated circulation within a year or 2 of the survey. **(741)**

■ A 1981 survey of faculty, students, staff, and community users of the University of Cincinnati Libraries (sample size: 4,074; responding: 912 or 22.4%, including 436 or 39% faculty response and 218 or 11% student response) *showed that*, when asked which should be automated first of 3 possibilities, faculty, university administrators, and community users picked the public card catalog as first priority with circulation second and periodicals third, while students and library staff picked circulation as first priority with the public card catalog second and periodicals third. **(522)**

■ A comparison reported in 1982 of title searches on an online catalog vs. a card catalog at Ohio State University *showed that* patrons were more successful in using departmental card catalogs (1/4 to 1/2 million cards) than in using a central online catalog (3.5 million records). The same held true though to a lesser degree for a skilled librarian. Success rate in the card catalog ran 9-20% higher for patron groups and 4% higher for an experienced librarian. **(045)**

Ibid. . . . *showed that*, considering only successful searches, patron groups as well as an experienced librarian generally took longer to find the same materials in the online catalog than in the card catalog. **(045)**

Ibid. . . . *showed that* the percentage of patron failure in the following problem areas for the online catalog was:

| title appearing as subject | 75% |
| hyphenated words | 67% |

continued

words not on stoplist	50%
all words in title on stoplist	50%
too many matches	43%
words on stoplist	41%
person's name begins title	40%
abbreviations	40%
foreign titles	33%
1-word titles	25%

(045)

■ A 1982 online survey of MELVYL patrons from all 9 UC campuses, conducted over a 2-month period for each 25th user of the system (1,259 questionnaires collected; 72.2 questionnaires complete and usable), *showed that* in relation to what they were looking for during the search in which they were queried, 32.7% of the respondents judged MELVYL "very satisfactory," 33.5% judged it "somewhat satisfactory," 14.9% judged it "somewhat unsatisfactory," and 18.9% judged it " very unsatisfactory."   **(349)**

Ibid. . . . *showed that* respondents' university affiliations were:

freshman/sophmore	23.2% respondents
junior/senior	39.0% respondents
graduate—master's level	6.4% respondents
graduate—doctoral level	7.6% respondents
graduate—professional school	1.9% respondents
faculty	3.2% respondents
staff	2.6% respondents
other	16.1% respondents

(349)

Ibid. . . . *showed that* respondents' academic areas were:

art/humanities	24.2% respondents
physical/biological sciences	22.7% respondents
social sciences	19.3% respondents
engineering	14.1% respondents
medical and health sciences	5.8% respondents
business management	4.7% respondents
major undeclared	4.0% respondents
law	2.9% respondents
education	2.0% respondents
interdisciplinary	0.2% respondents

(349)

Ibid. . . . *showed that* the average length of time a patron spent at the terminal was 8 minutes 41 seconds, while the average number of commands issued during a session was 22.297. **(349)**

Ibid. . . . *showed that* the patrons conducted an average of 5.66 searches per session. **(349)**

Ibid. . . . *showed that* the help facilities were used in 14.28% of the sessions, with those patrons who did use the help facilities averaging 1.59 unqualified help requests and 2.63 help requests with a specific glossary term. Only 2.6% of the patrons made the same error 3 times in a row. **(349)**

Ibid. . . . *showed that* 75.22% of the patrons made no errors at all during their sessions (this includes command syntax errors, logical errors, and unrecognizable commands). The remaining 24.77% of the patrons made an average of 2.85 errors during their sessions. **(349)**

Ibid. . . . *showed that* the 3 most frequently used searches in the COMMAND mode were subject (51.6%), personal author (21.5%), and title (18.8%), while the 3 most frequently used searches in the LOOKUP mode were subject/title (63.4%), personal author/corporate author (15.4%), and title/personal author/corporate author (13.2%). **(349)**

Ibid. . . . *showed that* 70.8% of the respondents reported that their general attitude toward the computer catalog was "very favorable," 22.1% reported their attitude as "somewhat favorable," 3.2% reported "somewhat unfavorable," and 3.9% reported "very unfavorable." **(349)**

Ibid. . . . *showed that* 68.3% of the respondents reported that the computer catalog was better than other library (i.e., card) catalogs, 17.3% reported that it was equal to other library catalogs, and 14.4% reported that it was worse than other library catalogs. **(349)**

Public

■ A 1980 survey of card catalog and information desk patrons in the Pikes Peak Library District Library over a 2-week period (sample size: 97;

responding: 91) *showed that* 85.4% reported a preference for online catalog searching over the traditional manual approach to the card catalog. The main reason given for preferring the online catalog was its ease of use and the speed with which searches could be conducted. **(345)**

Special

■ A 1980 survey of North American medical school libraries concerning automation of internal library operations (population: 139; responding: 93 or 69%) *showed that* 8 (8.6%) respondents reported online catalogs, 15 (16.1%) reported either batch or online automated circulation systems, and 20 (21.5%) reported using machine records to produce book or computer output microform (COM) catalogs. Further, 9 (9.7%) respondents reported plans to have online catalogs within a year or 2 of the survey, while 11 (11.8%) reported plans for automated circulation within a year or 2 of the survey. **(741)**

Organization—General Issues

General

■ A survey reported in 1972 of 50 depository libraries selected at random from the 1970 issue of the *Monthly Catalog* (36 or 72% responding) concerning subject access to government documents *showed that* 19% of responding libraries compiled separate subject indexes or catalogs for their U.S. government documents. **(140)**

■ A survey reported in 1982 of Canadian libraries selected from the *CLA Directory* and its supplement (sample size: 203; responding: 85; usable: 69 or 34.0%) concerning implementation of AACR 2 *showed that*, of the 53 libraries who adopted AACR 2, 77% reported they would interfile the AACR 2 entries in their old catalogs, 7 [%] reported they would freeze their catalogs, and 9% reported they would close their catalogs. **(299)**

Academic

■ A 1959 study at the Flint College of the University of Michigan Library and the Flint Community Junior College Library involving the costs of a divided catalog (university catalog held 25,000 volumes and 79,000 cards; community college catalog held 29,000 volumes and 76,000 cards) *showed that* 141 hours (49 hours to divide and 92 hours to revise) were required to rearrange the university dictionary catalog into author/title and subject sections, while 56 hours (32 hours to divide and 24 hours to revise) were required to rearrange the community college dictionary catalog into author/title and subject sections. **(581)**

Ibid. . . . *showed that*, based on filing 2,580 cards in the university catalog and 7,740 cards in the community college catalog, it was considerably cheaper to alphabetize, file, and revise in the divided catalog than in the dictionary catalog. Specifically, the total savings in time ranged between 39% for the community college and 45% for the university library.

(581)

■ A 1967 survey by the Institute of Higher Education at Teachers College, Columbia University, of innovative programs in libraries in academic institutions with liberal arts programs (sample size: 1,193; responding 781 or 65%) *showed that* 308 (39%) of the libraries reported multimedia cards in their card catalogs, 193 (25%) have special catalogs for multimedia materials, and 170 (22%) reported using various media in programs of library instruction. **(190)**

■ A 1967 study comparing a dictionary catalog at 1 university with a divided catalog (author/title and subject) at another university by using undergraduates to search entries *showed that* there was no statistically significant difference in average success rates between the 2 catalogs in subject searching or known-item searching. **(199)**

■ A survey reported in 1969 of medical school and selected medical research libraries (survey size: 102 libraries; responding: 92 or 90%) *showed that* there was a strong trend toward divided catalogs. Specifically, 38 (41%) libraries reported dictionary card catalogs, while 54 (59%) libraries reported divided card catalogs. These figures included 12 new (established within 10 years of the study) libraries of which 1 (8%) reported a dictionary catalog and 11 (92%) reported a divided catalog. Further, of the 54 libraries reporting divided catalogs, 31 (57%) had changed to the divided catalog within the last 10 years. **(679)**

Ibid. . . . *showed that* the 54 libraries that reported divided catalogs reported the following methods of division:

author-title/subject	42 (77.8%)	libraries
name-title/subject	7 (13.0%)	libraries
author/title/subject	3 (5.6%)	libraries
other	1 (1.9%)	libraries

(Name-title catalog includes persons and places as headings as well as authors.) **(679)**

Ibid. . . . *showed that* the subject heading authority used by the 54 libraries with divided catalogs was as follows: MeSH, exclusively or in combination with LC subject headings (41 or 75.9% libraries); LC subject headings exclusively (9 or 16.7% libraries); and other (2 or 3.7% libraries). **(679)**

■ A 1972 survey of chief library administrators in public comprehensive community colleges (population: 586; usable responses: 75.9% [no raw number given]) *showed that* books and audiovisual materials were listed in a central coordinated or union catalog in 67.2% of the institutions. **(452)**

■ A 1975 survey of North American medical school libraries concerning subject cataloging practices (survey size: 134 libraries; responding: 114 or 85%) *showed that* 96 (84%) respondents reported a divided catalog, while 18 (16%) reported dictionary catalogs. **(712)**

■ A 1977 survey of U.S. law libraries over 10,000 volumes taken from the 1976 *Directory of Law Libraries* (sample size: 1,080; responding: 373 or 35%) *showed that*, of 123 academic law libraries and 250 remaining law libraries, 98% of the academic law libraries and 66% of the remaining law libraries reported using the Anglo-American Cataloging rules, while 78% of the academic law libraries and 61% of the remaining law libraries reported using the ALA filing rules. **(366)**

■ A 1979 survey of U.S. community college libraries selected from the 1978 *Community, Junior and Technical College Directory* (sample size: 98; responding: 52; usable: 48 or 48.98%) *showed that* for audiovisual materials:

24 (50.0%) libraries did full cataloging and interfiled entries in the central catalog;

8 (16.7%) libraries did full cataloging but filed audiovisual entries in a separate catalog;

1 (2.1%) library did full cataloging and filed audiovisual entries in separate drawers of the central catalog;

6 (12.5%) libraries did full cataloging but filed audiovisual entries in a separate catalog in the AV center;

9 (18.8%) libraries did full cataloging and filed audiovisual entries both in the central catalog and in a separate catalog in the AV center. **(498)**

■ A 1980 survey of law school libraries with collections in excess of 175,000 volumes (sample size: 50; responding: 37 or 70%) *showed that* 24 libraries reported a divided catalog with authors and titles together and all subjects together, 8 reported a dictionary catalog, and 5 reported a divided catalog in 3 divisions with authors, titles, and subjects organized separately. **(369)**

Special

■ A survey reported in 1969 of medical school and selected medical research libraries (survey size: 102 libraries; responding: 92 or 90%) *showed that* there was a strong trend toward divided catalogs. Specifically, 38 (41%) libraries reported dictionary card catalogs, while 54 (59%) libraries reported divided card catalogs. These figures included 12 new (established within 10 years of the study) libraries of which 1 (8%) reported a dictionary catalog and 11 (92%) reported a divided catalog. Further, of the 54 libraries reporting divided catalogs, 31 (57%) had changed to the divided catalog within the last 10 years. **(679)**

Ibid. . . . *showed that* the 54 libraries that reported divided catalogs reported the following methods of division:

author-title/subject	42 (77.8%) libraries
name-title/subject	7 (13.0%) libraries
author/title/subject	3 (5.6%) libraries
other	1 (1.9%) libraries

(Name-title catalog includes persons and places as headings as well as as authors.) **(679)**

Ibid. . . . *showed that* the subject heading authority used by the 54 libraries with divided catalogs was as follows: MeSH, exclusively or in combination with LC subject headings (41 or 75.9% libraries); LC subject headings exclusively (9 or 16.7% libraries); and other (2 or 3.7% libraries). **(679)**

■ A 1975 survey of North American medical school libraries concerning subject cataloging practices (survey size: 134 libraries; responding: 114 or

85%) *showed that* 96 (84%) respondents reported a divided catalog, while 18 (16%) reported dictionary catalogs.   **(712)**

■ A survey reported in 1975 of subject heading use in a wide range of law libraries selected from the 1972 edition of the American Association of Law Libraries *Directory of Law Libraries* (sample size: 256; responding: 204; usable: 200 or 78.1%) *showed that* 101 (50.5%) respondents had a dictionary catalog, while 96 (48%) had a divided catalog. 3 (1.5%) respondents did not clearly state which kind of catalog they had.   **(393)**

■ A 1977 survey of U.S. law libraries over 10,000 volumes taken from the 1976 *Directory of Law Libraries* (sample size: 1,080; responding: 373 or 35%) *showed that* 55% of the responding libraries reported owning a divided catalog, 43% reported owning a dictionary catalog, and 2% did not indicate either form. The "most common" divided catalog was a 2-way author/title and subject division, with only 6 respondents reporting a 3-way divided catalog.   **(366)**

Ibid. . . . *showed that*, of 123 academic law libraries and 250 remaining law libraries, 98% of the academic law libraries and 66% of the remaining law libraries reported using the Anglo-American Cataloging rules, while 78% of the academic law libraries and 61% of the remaining law libraries reported using the ALA filing rules.   **(366)**

■ A 1980 survey of law school libraries with collections in excess of 175,000 volumes (sample size: 50; responding: 37 or 70%) *showed that* 24 libraries reported a divided catalog with authors and titles together and all subjects together, 8 reported a dictionary catalog, and 5 reported a divided catalog in 3 divisions with authors, titles, and subjects organized separately.   **(369)**

Organization—MeSH

Academic

■ A 1975 survey of North American medical school libraries concerning subject cataloging practices (survey size: 134 libraries; responding: 114 or 85%) *showed that*, of 78 respondents who used MeSH as the primary authority for subject headings and who also had divided catalogs, 54 (69%) reported they used a guidecard to distinguish subject headings filed in the

subject section of the catalog, while 24 (31%) reported they did not.
(712)

Ibid. . . . *showed that*, of 78 respondents who used MeSH as the primary authority for subject headings and who also had divided catalogs, 76 (97%) reported they did not file MeSH terms in the public catalog unless there were catalog cards for them, while 2 (3%) reported they filed all MeSH terms regardless of whether there were cards for that heading. **(712)**

Ibid. . . . *showed that* the type of subject authority used was as follows:

MeSH exclusively	30 (26%)	libraries
MeSH supplemented by LC	57 (50%)	libraries
LC exclusively	23 (20%)	libraries
LC supplemented by MeSH	2 (2%)	libraries
no response	2 (2%)	libraries **(712)**

Ibid. . . . *showed that*, of 78 respondents who used MeSH as the primary authority for subject headings and who also had divided catalogs, 77 (99%) reported using MeSH subheadings in the catalog (1 or 1% reported they did not) and 76 (99% of the 77) reported using both form and topical subheadings, while 1 (1% of the 77) reported using topical subheadings only. **(712)**

Ibid. . . . *showed that*, of 78 respondents who used MeSH as the primary authority for subject headings and who also had divided catalogs, the following use of guidecards for subheadings was reported:

all subheadings	54 (69%)	libraries
topical subheadings	0	libraries
form subheadings	2 (3%)	libraries
no guidecards used for subheadings	17 (22%)	libraries
no response	5 (6%)	libraries **(712)**

Ibid. . . . *showed that*, of 78 respondents who used MeSH as the primary authority for subject headings and who also had divided catalogs, 14 (18%) reported that they distinguished between form and topical subheading guidecards in a physical way in the catalog, while 62 (79%) reported they did not, and 2 (3%) did not respond. Of those that did distinguish, the following methods were used: cut of tab on card (10 respondents), color of tab (8 respondents), and color of type (1 respondent).   **(712)**

Ibid. . . . *showed that*, of 78 respondents who used MeSH as the primary authority for subject headings and who also had divided catalogs, the following methods were used to subdivide main subject headings in the catalog into topical and form categories:

combined and interfiled alphabetically	70 (90%)	libraries
all form subheadings first, then topical subheadings	5 (6%)	libraries
all topical subheadings first, then form subheadings	1 (1%)	libraries
no response	2 (3%)	libraries **(712)**

Ibid. . . . *showed that*, of 78 respondents who used MeSH as the primary authority for subject headings and who also had divided catalogs, 63 (81%) respondents reported they modified subject headings by combining several subheadings, while 15 (19%) reported they did not. Of those that did combine subheadings, the maximum number combined was as follows:

2 subheadings	8 respondents
3 subheadings	33 respondents
4 subheadings	15 respondents
5 subheadings	2 respondents
no policy or no limit	5 respondents **(712)**

Ibid. . . . *showed that*, of 78 respondents who used MeSH as the primary authority for subject headings and who also had divided catalogs, language and geographic subheadings were considered by respondents to be the following:

form subheadings	11 (14%)	libraries
topical subheadings	4 (5%)	libraries
do not distinguish	60 (77%)	libraries
no response	3 (4%)	libraries **(712)**

Ibid. . . . *showed that*, of 65 respondents who used MeSH as the primary authority for subject headings and who also had divided catalogs, 18 (27.7%) reported that if language and geographic subheadings were combined with form subheadings the first filing term would be the language/geographic term (e.g., French—Dictionaries), while 47 (72.3%) reported that the order would be reversed. **(712)**

Ibid. . . . *showed that*, of 62 respondents who used MeSH as the primary authority for subject headings and who also had divided catalogs, 56 (90.3%) reported that if language and geographic subheadings were combined with topical subheadings the first filing term would be the topical term followed by the language/geographic term (e.g., Manpower—France), while 6 (9.7%) reported that the order would be reversed.
(712)

Ibid. . . . *showed that*, of 78 respondents who used MeSH as the primary authority for subject headings and who also had divided catalogs, 56 (72%) respondents reported updating the subject catalog and authority file annually to correspond to the new MeSH, 20 (26%) reported "other," and 2 (2%) did not respond. **(712)**

Ibid. . . . *showed that*, of 78 respondents who used MeSH as the primary authority for subject headings and who also had divided catalogs, the following methods were used to update the catalog (multiple responses allowed):

56 (71.8%) reported "changing or shifting subject cards from the old headings to the new and pulling deleted MeSH terms";

8 (10.3%) reported "making no changes in the existing catalog but making cross references from old to new terms";

15 (19.2%) reported "other method";

2 (2.6%) gave no response. **(712)**

Special

■ A 1975 survey of North American medical school libraries concerning subject cataloging practices (survey size: 134 libraries; responding: 114 or 85%) *showed that*, of 78 respondents who used MeSH as the primary authority for subject headings and who also had divided catalogs, 54 (69%) reported they used a guidecard to distinguish subject headings filed in the subject section of the catalog, while 24 (31%) reported they did not.
(712)

Ibid. . . . *showed that*, of 78 respondents who used MeSH as the primary authority for subject headings and who also had divided catalogs, 76 (97%) reported they did not file MeSH terms in the public catalog unless there

were catalog cards for them, while 2 (3%) reported they filed all MeSH
terms regardless of whether there were cards for that heading.   **(712)**

Ibid. . . . *showed that* the type of subject authority used was as follows:

MeSH exclusively	30 (26%) libraries
MeSH supplemented by LC	57 (50%) libraries
LC exclusively	23 (20%) libraries
LC supplemented by MeSH	2 (2%) libraries
no response	2 (2%) libraries **(712)**

Ibid. . . . *showed that*, of 78 respondents who used MeSH as the primary
authority for subject headings and who also had divided catalogs, 77 (99%)
reported using MeSH subheadings in the catalog (1 or 1% reported they
did not) and 76 (99% of the 77) reported using both form and topical
subheadings, while 1 (1% of the 77) reported using topical subheadings
only.   **(712)**

Ibid. . . . *showed that*, of 78 respondents who used MeSH as the primary
authority for subject headings and who also had divided catalogs, the
following use of guidecards for subheadings was reported:

all subheadings	54 (69%) libraries
topical subheadings	0 libraries
form subheadings	2 (3%) libraries
no guidecards used for	
subheadings	17 (22%) libraries
no response	5 (6%) libraries **(712)**

Ibid. . . . *showed that*, of 78 respondents who used MeSH as the primary
authority for subject headings and who also had divided catalogs, 14 (18%)
reported that they distinguished between form and topical subheading
guidecards in a physical way in the catalog, while 62 (79%) reported they
did not, and 2 (3%) did not respond. Of those that did distinguish, the
following methods were used: cut of tab on card (10 respondents), color of
tab (8 respondents), and color of type (1 respondent).   **(712)**

Ibid. . . . *showed that*, of 78 respondents who used MeSH as the primary
authority for subject headings and who also had divided catalogs, the
following methods were used to subdivide main subject headings in the
catalog into topical and form categories:

combined and interfiled
 alphabetically   70 (90%) libraries
all form subheadings first,
 then topical subheadings 5 (6%) libraries
all topical subheadings first,
 then form subheadings   1 (1%) libraries
no response   2 (3%) libraries **(712)**

Ibid. . . . *showed that*, of 78 respondents who used MeSH as the primary authority for subject headings and who also had divided catalogs, 63 (81%) respondents reported they modified subject headings by combining several subheadings, while 15 (19%) reported they did not. Of those that did combine subheadings, the maximum number combined was as follows:

2 subheadings	8 respondents
3 subheadings	33 respondents
4 subheadings	15 respondents
5 subheadings	2 respondents
no policy or no limit	5 respondents **(712)**

Ibid. . . . *showed that*, of 78 respondents who used MeSH as the primary authority for subject headings and who also had divided catalogs, language and geographic subheadings were considered by respondents to be the following:

form subheadings	11 (14%) libraries
topical subheadings	4 (5%) libraries
do not distinguish	60 (77%) libraries
no response	3 (4%) libraries **(712)**

Ibid. . . . *showed that*, of 65 respondents who used MeSH as the primary authority for subject headings and who also had divided catalogs, 18 (27.7%) reported that if language and geographic subheadings were combined with form subheadings the first filing term would be the language/geographic term (e.g., French—Dictionaries), while 47 (72.3%) reported that the order would be reversed. **(712)**

Ibid. . . . *showed that*, of 62 respondents who used MeSH as the primary authority for subject headings and who also had divided catalogs, 56 (90.3%) reported that if language and geographic subheadings were combined with topical subheadings the first filing term would be the topical

term followed by the language/geographic term (e.g., Manpower—France), while 6 (9.7%) reported that the order would be reversed.
(712)

Ibid. . . . *showed that*, of 78 respondents who used MeSH as the primary authority for subject headings and who also had divided catalogs, 56 (72%) respondents reported updating the subject catalog and authority file annually to correspond to the new MeSH, 20 (26%) reported "other," and 2 (2%) did not respond.   **(712)**

Ibid. . . . *showed that*, of 78 respondents who used MeSH as the primary authority for subject headings and who also had divided catalogs, the following methods were used to update the catalog (multiple responses allowed):

56 (71.8%) reported "changing or shifting subject cards from the old headings to the new and pulling deleted MeSH terms";

8 (10.3%) reported "making no changes in the existing catalog but making cross references from old to new terms";

15 (19.2%) reported "other method";

2 (2.6%) gave no response.   **(712)**

Scripts

General

■ A 1974 survey of libraries world-wide concerning scripts used and script conversion practices employed in their catalogs (sample size: 231; responding: 146 or 63%) *showed that* the Cyrillic romanization schemes used by 90 respondents were as follows:

Library of Congress or adaptions thereof	33 (36.7%)
International Organization for Standardization or adaptions thereof	28 (31.1%)
Preussische Instruktionen	13 (14.4%)
own	7 (7.8%)
British Standards Institution	5 (5.6%)
British Museum	2 (2.2%)
other published schemes	2 (2.2%)**(356)**

Ibid. . . . *showed that* the romanization schemes used for Japanese by 56 respondents were as follows: Hepburn (51 or 91.1%), own (4 or [7.1%]), and Kunrei-shiki (1 or [1.8%]).   **(356)**

Ibid. . . . *showed that* the romanization schemes used for Devanagari (India) by 44 respondents were as follows:

Library of Congress or adaptions thereof	19 (43.2%)
own	10 (22.7%)
other published schemes	7 (16.0%)
Preussische Instruktionen	6 (13.6%)
British Museum	2 (4.5%) **(356)**

Ibid. . . . *showed that* the romanization schemes used for Arabic by 76 respondents were as follows:

Library of Congress or adaptions thereof	29 (37.7%)
own	13 (16.9%)
International Organization for Standardization	12 (15.6%)
Preussische Instruktionen	11 (14.2%)
other published	7 (9.1%)
British Museum	4 (5.2%)
British Standards Institution	1 (1.3%) **(356)**

Ibid. . . . *showed that* the romanization schemes used for Chinese by 69 respondents were:

Wade-Giles	57 (82.6%)
own	7 (10.1%)
Pin-Yin	2 (2.9%)
Kunrei-shiki	2 (2.9%)
other published	1 (1.5%) **(356)**

Ibid. . . . *showed that* the romanization schemes used for Korean by 45 respondents were:

McCune-Reischauer	37 (82.3%)
own	4 (8.9%)
Kunrei-shiki	2 (4.4%)
other published	2 (4.4%) **(356)**

Ibid. . . . *showed that* the romanization schemes used for Greek by 67 respondents were:

Library of Congress or adaptions thereof	30 (44.8%)
own	13 (19.4%)
International Organization for Standardization or adaptions thereof	12 (17.9%)

continued

Preussische Instruktionen	9 (13.4%)
British Museum	1 (1.5%)
British Standards Institution	1 (1.5%)
other published	1 (1.5%) **(356)**

Ibid. . . . *showed that* the romanization schemes used for Hebrew by 67 respondents were:

Library of Congress or adaptions thereof	27 (40.3%)
Preussische Instruktionen	13 (19.4%)
own	12 (17.9%)
International Organization for Standardization	9 (13.4%)
other published	4 (6.0%)
British Museum	1 (1.5%) **(356)**

Ibid. . . . *showed that* 98 (67.1%) libraries reported romanizing all their scripts, 20 (13.7%) libraries reported that Cyrillic and/or Greek were romanized but that separate catalogs were used for other scripts, and 28 (19.2%) libraries reported that separate catalogs were used for each script. **(356)**

Ibid. . . . *showed that* of 134 respondents, 76 (56%) romanized the whole entry, 44 (32%) romanized both the author and the title, and 24 (18%) romanized either the author's name or the title. **(356)**

Ibid. . . . *showed that* those parts of the entry that are translated by responding libraries were as follows: corporate author (11 or 8% respondents always translated, 26 or 18% sometimes translated), title (16 or 11% always translated, 15 or 10% sometimes translated), and whole entry (1 or less than 1% always translated, 6 or 4% sometimes translated). **(356)**

Ibid. . . . *showed that* 5 (3%) libraries provided cross-references from non-Roman to romanized entries, while 5 (3%) libraries provided cross-references from romanized entries to non-Roman entries. **(356)**

Ibid. . . . *showed that* 12 (8%) libraries used no kind of script conversion in their catalogs. **(356)**

■ A study reported in 1978 concerning book publishing in non-Roman scripts based on book production figures reported in the *UNESCO*

Statistical Yearbook (1974) *showed that* of 566,000 titles reported published in 1973 the 10 most frequently used scripts (accounting for 99.2% of the reported publishing) were:

Roman	404,000	(71.3%)	titles
Cyrillic	81,000	(14.3%)	titles
Japanese	35,500	(6.3%)	titles
Chinese	11,200	(1.9%)	titles
Devanagari	8,800	(1.6%)	titles
Arabic	7,500	(1.3%)	titles
Korean	7,400	(1.3%)	titles
Greek	2,300	(0.4%)	titles
Thai	2,200	(0.4%)	titles
Hebrew	2,000	(0.4%)	titles

(641)

Search Keys

General

■ A study reported in 1972 at Ohio State University involving bibliographic search keys for large collections, i.e., using a 4-5 search key (first 4 letters of the author's last name and the first 5 letters of the first significant word in the title) to search 1,000 actual requests in a collection of 857,725 titles representing 2.6 million volumes, *showed that* 35.9% of the time 1 or less items were matched, while 87.8% of the time 10 or less items were matched. With a 99% confidence interval the upper limit for the 4-5 search key retrieving 10 or less items was 90.2%. **(323)**

■ A study reported in 1973 at the Ohio College Library Center of 167,745 MARC II personal author entries *showed that* adding a search key element for the author's middle initial was more efficient in reducing the number of inappropriate matches in a file than increasing the size of the search key strings for the first and last name. For example, 90% of the time a 3-2 search key (the 3 first letters from the author's surname and the first 2 letters of the author's forename) would retrieve 26 or fewer different names, a 4-1 search key would retrieve 25 or fewer different names and a 3-1-1 search key would retrieve 16 or fewer different names. Likewise a 5-1 search key would retrieve 18 or fewer different names, and 4-2 search key would retrieve 12 or fewer different names and a 3-2-1 search key would retrieve 8 or fewer different names. **(324)**

Ibid. . . . *showed that* a second example illustrating the above statement is the number of times a single name would be retrieved by a search key. A

3-2 or 4-1 search key would retrieve a single name 34.8% and 35.7% of the time, respectively, while a 3-1-1 search key would retrieve a single name 44.5% of the time. Likewise, a 5-1 or 4-2 search key would retrieve a single name 44.9% and 49.9% of the time, respectively, while a 3-2-1 search key would retrieve a single name 57.1% of the time.   **(324)**

■ A study reported in 1976 comparing use of 2 title search keys in the MARC monographic data base (500,000+ records) at the University of California, Berkeley, *showed that* use of a 3-1-1-1 search key (the 3 first letters from the title's first significant word and the first letter from the next 3 significant words) identified "approximately 46%" of the titles uniquely, i.e., only 1 title was selected. However, such a key grouped 11.2% of the titles in groups of 10 or greater. The use of a 4-2-2-2 search key identified "approximately 75%" of the titles uniquely with only 2.1% of the titles being grouped in clusters of 10 or more.   **(328)**

■ A study reported in 1977 concerning the effectiveness of truncated search keys in retrieving records by author, using a data base of 200,000 personal author records and another data base of 200,000 corporate author records both taken from the OCLC online union catalog, *showed that*, of 10 different search keys, the most discriminating was a 4-3-1 combination (i.e., personal author: first 4 characters of the author's last name, first 3 characters of the author's first name, and the first character of the author's middle name; corporate author: first 4 characters of the first word, first 3 characters of the second word, and first character of the third word), which retrieved a single personal author name 98.2% of the time and a single corporate author name 81.7% of the time. This compared to the 4-3-0 combination, which retrieved a single author name 92.9% of the time and a single corporate author name 75.6% of the time.   **(614)**

■ A study reported in 1978 of 2,451 corporate author entry MARC II format records taken from the OCLC data base *showed that* a search key using a 2-2-2-2-2 configuration (2 first letters of first significant word, 2 first letters of next significant word, etc.) identified 1,746 records uniquely, 244 records with 2 to 7 matches, and 5 records with 10 to 21 matches.   **(333)**

■ A 1978 study at Ohio State University Library involving 2 full days' transactions in the OCLC data base for each of the OSU terminals (1,153 searches of the data base) *showed that* the use of the personal author (by itself), ISBN, ISSN, and CODEN search keys "was very limited for all library functions. Corporate-author search keys were not used at all. "   **(336)**

■ A 1980 study comparing the Library Computer System (University of Illinois) and the Washington Library Network by searching 152 periodical titles in both systems *showed that* the number of keywords used in the search had little effect in determining the likelihood of success of finding the item on the first search. The correlation for WLN searches was −.3717 (significance level .001),while the correlation for LCS was −.1555 (significance level .03). This explained 18% of the variance for WLN searches and 2% of the variance for LCS searches. **(348)**

■ A 1982 study of the OCLC union catalog to investigate the extent of record duplication, based on 100 records randomly selected from the OCLC data base and subsequently searched in the OCLC data base for duplicates by using the alphabetic and numeric search keys generated from the selected record, *showed that*, based on an average of 3.6 alphabetic searches per record, 23% of the search keys evoked the response "[search key] produces more than 50 entries." **(772)**

Subject Access—General Issues

General

■ A survey reported in 1972 of 50 depository libraries selected at random from the 1970 issue of the *Monthly Catalog* (36 or 72% responding) concerning subject access to government documents *showed that* 19% of responding libraries compiled separate subject indexes or catalogs for their U.S. government documents. **(140)**

■ A comparison of the average number of subject headings assigned 500 items each in 1973 in *Research in Education, Current Index To Journals in Education*, and the *National Union Catalog: Authors showed that* there was greater subject access via the indexes with an average of 4.9, 4.5, and 1.3 subject headings per item, respectively. **(055)**

■ A 1976-77 study over a 31-week period comparing subject retrieval in terms of both recall (probability that a relevant item will be retrieved) and precision (probability that a retrieved item will be relevant), using Library of Congress subject headings and the British Library's PRECIS terms (both found in UK MARC tapes for this period) and involving 42 users and 61 search profiles resulting in 5,326 usable citations, *showed that* use of PRECIS terms resulted in a statistically significant higher recall rate (81.9% citations) than use of LCSH terms (76.2% citations). However, use of LCSH terms resulted in a statistically significant higher precision rate

(29.6% citations) than use of PRECIS terms (27.9% citations). (Both findings significant at the .05 level.) **(654)**

Ibid. . . . *showed that* searching on article titles as well as on subject terms improved the recall rate for both LCSH (from 76.2% to 90.0% citations) and PRECIS (from 81.9% to 93.0% citations). In both cases this was a statistically significant increase in percentage of citations retrieved (significant at the .05 level). However, the increase eliminated any statistically significant difference between LCSH and PRECIS recall rates. Further, the use of title searching lowered the precision rate slightly, from 19.6% citations to 26.7% citations for LCSH and from 27.9% to 25.7% citations for PRECIS. In both cases this was a statistically significant decrease in percentage of citations (significant at the .05 level). However, here too the change eliminated any statistically significant difference between LCSH and PRECIS precision rates. **(654)**

Ibid. . . . *showed that*, while LCSH and PRECIS appear to work equally well in the pure/applied sciences, PRECIS had a "clear recall advantage" over LCSH for social science books. For example, recall rates in the social sciences for LCSH was 75.8% citations compared to 84.2% citations for PRECIS—a statistically significant difference (significant at the .05 level). However, recall rates in the pure/applied sciences were 75.5% citations for LCSH and 78.1% citations for PRECIS—not a statistically significant difference. **(654)**

■ A survey reported in 1983 of operational online catalogs in the United States (survey size: 20 systems) *showed that* all 20 systems include access by author, title, and subject. In addition the following access points were allowed:

call number access	15 (75.0%) systems
LC card number access	13 (65.0%) systems
ISBN/ISSN access	11 (55.0%) systems
OCLC number access	5 (25.0%) systems
document number access	3 (15.0%) systems
CODEN number	2 (10.0%) systems

Further, the number of access points per system ranged from 12 (Avatar Systems) to 4 (Northwestern University) with a median of 7 access points and an average of 7.9 access points. **(773)**

Academic

■ A 1963 study of 501 searches in the card catalog of the Yale Medical library during 1 working week in Fall 1963 (a historically busy period) *showed that*, of 501 searches, 64 or 12.8% were subject searches. **(171)**

■ A 1967 study comparing a dictionary catalog at 1 university with a divided catalog (author/title and subject) at another university by using undergraduates to search entries *showed that* there was no statistically significant difference in average success rates between the 2 catalogs in subject searching or known-item searching.   **(199)**

■ A survey of 12 university libraries (11 responding) during a 3-month period in 1965 and a survey of 11 public libraries during a similar period in 1967 to determine the kinds of reference assistance needed at the card catalog (647 problems reported with 284 from university libraries and 363 from public libraries), reported together in 1968, *showed that* the 3 most frequent problems with the card catalog in university libraries were subject headings (18% of university total), filing arrangement (17% of university total), and "see" or "see also" references (15% of the university total). In public libraries the 3 most frequent problems were filing arrangement (23% of public total), call number (15% of public total), and subject headings (13% of public total).   **(134)**

■ A survey reported in 1969 of medical school and selected medical research libraries (survey size: 102 libraries; responding: 92 or 90%) *showed that* the subject heading authority used by the 54 libraries with divided catalogs was as follows:

MeSH, exclusively or in combination with LC subject headings (41 or 75.9% libraries);

LC subject headings exclusively (9 or 16.7% libraries);

and other (2 or 3.7% libraries).   **(679)**

■ A comparison of the average number of subject headings assigned 500 items each in 1973 in *Research in Education, Current Index To Journals in Education*, and the *National Union Catalog: Authors showed that* there was greater subject access via the indexes with an average of 4.9, 4.5, and 1.3 subject headings per item, respectively.   **(055)**

■ A 1975 survey of North American medical school libraries concerning subject cataloging practices (survey size: 134 libraries; responding: 114 or 85%) *showed that* the type of subject authority used was as follows:

MeSH exclusively	30 (26%)	libraries
MeSH supplemented by LC	57 (50%)	libraries
LC exclusively	23 (20%)	libraries
LC supplemented by MeSH	2 (2%)	libraries
no response	2 (2%)	libraries **(712)**

■ A study reported in 1977 at the University of California, Berkeley, comparing the importance of subject familiarity (knowledge of a specified academic field) versus catalog familiarity (knowledge of the structure of the Library of Congress subject headings) in thinking of an appropriate term for subject searching in the library catalog when presented an abstract and book title and involving 22 psychology students (subject familiarity), 22 economics students (subject familiarity), and 17 library students (catalog familiarity), *showed that* catalog familiarity was more important than subject familiarity to a statistically significant degreee in selecting an appropriate subject term [significance level not given]. Specifically, scores for library students in determining subject terms for psychology and economics materials were higher than scores for students in those disciplines determining subject terms in their own discipline.   **(615)**

Ibid. . . . *showed that*, although the difference was not statistically significant, psychology and economics students scored higher in selecting appropriate subject terms for the opposite discipline than they did in their own discipline.   **(615)**

Ibid. . . . *showed that* students were more likely to achieve the illusion of success in using the library catalog than real success. This was demonstrated by the discrepancy between basic matching (exact matches between subject heading assigned by the library to a particular item and the subject heading chosen by the student) and "existence matching" (a marginal match in which the subject heading chosen by the student existed in the catalog but was not the subject heading assigned by the library). Specifically, the number of terms that constituted basic matches versus existence matches for the 3 groups were as follows:

    economics students   21% basic; 62% existence matches
    psychology students   22% basic; 60% existence matches
    library students   35% basic; 64% existence matches   **(615)**

Public

■ A survey of 12 university libraries (11 responding) during a 3-month period in 1965 and a survey of 11 public libraries during a similar period in 1967 to determine the kinds of reference assistance needed at the card catalog (647 problems reported with 284 from university libraries and 363 from public libraries), reported together in 1968, *showed that* the 3 most frequent problems with the card catalog in university libraries were subject headings (18% of university total), filing arrangement (17% of university total), and "see" or "see also" references (15% of the university total). In public libraries the 3 most frequent problems were filing arrangement

(23% of public total), call number (15% of public total), and subject headings (13% of public total). **(134)**

Special

■ A 1963 study of 501 searches in the card catalog of the Yale Medical library during 1 working week in Fall 1963 (a historically busy period) *showed that*, of 501 searches, 64 or 12.8% were subject searches. **(171)**

■ A survey reported in 1969 of medical school and selected medical research libraries (survey size: 102 libraries; responding: 92 or 90%) *showed that* the subject heading authority used by the 54 libraries with divided catalogs was as follows:

MeSH, exclusively or in combination with LC subject headings (41 or 75.9% libraries);

LC subject headings exclusively (9 or 16.7% libraries);

and other (2 or 3.7% libraries). **(679)**

■ A 1975 survey of North American medical school libraries concerning subject cataloging practices (survey size: 134 libraries; responding: 114 or 85%) *showed that* the type of subject authority used was as follows:

MeSH exclusively	30 (26%)	libraries
MeSH supplemented by LC	57 (50%)	libraries
LC exclusively	23 (20%)	libraries
LC supplemented by MeSH	2 (2%)	libraries
no response	2 (2%)	libraries **(712)**

Subject Access—MeSH

General

■ A 1963 study of 501 searches in the card catalog of the Yale Medical library during 1 working week in Fall 1963 (a historically busy period) *showed that*, of 501 searches, 64 or 12.8% were subject searches. **(171)**

■ A 1967 study comparing a dictionary catalog at 1 university with a divided catalog (author/title and subject) at another university by using undergraduates to search entries *showed that* there was no statistically significant difference in average success rates between the 2 catalogs in subject searching or known-item searching. **(199)**

■ A survey of 12 university libraries (11 responding) during a 3-month period in 1965 and a survey of 11 public libraries during a similar period in 1967 to determine the kinds of reference assistance needed at the card catalog (647 problems reported with 284 from university libraries and 363 from public libraries), reported together in 1968, *showed that* the 3 most frequent problems with the card catalog in university libraries were subject headings (18% of university total), filing arrangement (17% of university total), and "see" or "see also" references (15% of the university total). In public libraries the 3 most frequent problems were filing arrangement (23% of public total), call number (15% of public total), and subject headings (13% of public total).   **(134)**

■ A comparison of the average number of subject headings assigned 500 items each in 1973 in *Research in Education, Current Index To Journals in Education*, and the *National Union Catalog: Authors showed that* there was greater subject access via the indexes with an average of 4.9, 4.5, and 1.3 subject headings per item, respectively.   **(055)**

Academic

■ A survey reported in 1969 of medical school and selected medical research libraries (survey size: 102 libraries; responding: 92 or 90%) *showed that* the subject heading authority used by the 54 libraries with divided catalogs was as follows: MeSH, exclusively or in combination with LC subject headings (41 or 75.9% libraries); LC subject headings exclusively (9 or 16.7% libraries); and other (2 or 3.7% libraries).   **(679)**

■ A 1975 survey of North American medical school libraries concerning subject cataloging practices (survey size: 134 libraries; responding: 114 or 85%) *showed that* the type of subject authority used was as follows:

MeSH exclusively	30 (26%) libraries
MeSH supplemented by LC	57 (50%) libraries
LC exclusively	23 (20%) libraries
LC supplemented by MeSH	2 (2%) libraries
no response	2 (2%) libraries **(712)**

Ibid. . . . *showed that*, of 78 respondents who used MeSH as the primary authority for subject headings and who also had divided catalogs, 77 (99%) reported using MeSH subheadings in the catalog (1 or 1% reported they did not) and 76 (99% of the 77) reported using both form and topical subheadings, while 1 (1% of the 77) reported using topical subheadings only.   **(712)**

Ibid. . . . *showed that*, of 78 respondents who used MeSH as the primary authority for subject headings and who also had divided catalogs, the following use of guidecards for subheadings was reported:

all subheadings	54 (69%)	libraries
topical subheadings	0	libraries
form subheadings	2 (3%)	libraries
no guidecards used for subheadings	17 (22%)	libraries
no response	5 (6%)	libraries **(712)**

Ibid. . . . *showed that*, of 78 respondents who used MeSH as the primary authority for subject headings and who also had divided catalogs, 14 (18%) reported that they distinguished between form and topical subheading guidecards in a physical way in the catalog, while 62 (79%) reported they did not, and 2 (3%) did not respond. Of those that did distinguish, the following methods were used: cut of tab on card (10 respondents), color of tab (8 respondents), and color of type (1 respondent). **(712)**

Ibid. . . . *showed that*, of 78 respondents who used MeSH as the primary authority for subject headings and who also had divided catalogs, the following methods were used to subdivide main subject headings in the catalog into topical and form categories:

combined and interfiled alphabetically	70 (90%)	libraries
all form subheadings first, then topical subheadings	5 (6%)	libraries
all topical subheadings first, then form subheadings	1 (1%)	libraries
no response	2 (3%)	libraries **(712)**

Ibid. . . . *showed that*, of 78 respondents who used MeSH as the primary authority for subject headings and who also had divided catalogs, 63 (81%) respondents reported they modified subject headings by combining several subheadings, while 15 (19%) reported they did not. Of those that did combine subheadings, the maximum number combined was as follows:

2 subheadings	8 respondents
3 subheadings	33 respondents
4 subheadings	15 respondents
5 subheadings	2 respondents
no policy or no limit	5 respondents **(712)**

Ibid. . . . *showed that*, of 78 respondents who used MeSH as the primary authority for subject headings and who also had divided catalogs, language and geographic subheadings were considered by respondents to be the following:

form subheadings	11 (14%)	libraries
topical subheadings	4 (5%)	libraries
do not distinguish	60 (77%)	libraries
no response	3 (4%)	libraries **(712)**

Ibid. . . . *showed that*, of 65 respondents who used MeSH as the primary authority for subject headings and who also had divided catalogs, 18 (27.7%) reported that if language and geographic subheadings were combined with form subheadings the first filing term would be the language/geographic term (e.g., French—Dictionaries), while 47 (72.3%) reported that the order would be reversed. **(712)**

Ibid. . . . *showed that*, of 62 respondents who used MeSH as the primary authority for subject headings and who also had divided catalogs, 56 (90.3%) reported that if language and geographic subheadings were combined with topical subheadings the first filing term would be the topical term followed by the language/geographic term (e.g., Manpower—France), while 6 (9.7%) reported that the order would be reversed. **(712)**

Ibid. . . . *showed that*, of 78 respondents who used MeSH as the primary authority for subject headings and who also had divided catalogs, 56 (72%) respondents reported updating the subject catalog and authority file annually to correspond to the new MeSH, 20 (26%) reported "other," and 2 (2%) did not respond. **(712)**

Ibid. . . . *showed that*, of 78 respondents who used MeSH as the primary authority for subject headings and who also had divided catalogs, the following methods were used to update the catalog (multiple responses allowed):

56 (71.8%) reported "changing or shifting subject cards from the old headings to the new and pulling deleted MeSH terms";

8 (10.3%) reported "making no changes in the existing catalog but making cross references from old to new terms";

15 (19.2%) reported "other method";

2 (2.6%) gave no response. **(712)**

Ibid. . . . *showed that*, of 78 respondents who used MeSH as the primary authority for subject headings and who also had divided catalogs, 54 (69%) reported they used a guidecard to distinguish subject headings filed in the subject section of the catalog, while 24 (31%) reported they did not.

(712)

Ibid. . . . *showed that*, of 78 respondents who used MeSH as the primary authority for subject headings and who also had divided catalogs, 76 (97%) reported they did not file MeSH terms in the public catalog unless there were catalog cards for them, while 2 (3%) reported they filed all MeSH terms regardless of whether there were cards for that heading. **(712)**

Special

■ A survey reported in 1969 of medical school and selected medical research libraries (survey size: 102 libraries; responding: 92 or 90%) *showed that* the subject heading authority used by the 54 libraries with divided catalogs was as follows: MeSH, exclusively or in combination with LC subject headings (41 or 75.9% libraries); LC subject headings exclusively (9 or 16.7% libraries); and other (2 or 3.7% libraries). **(679)**

■ A 1975 survey of North American medical school libraries concerning subject cataloging practices (survey size: 134 libraries; responding: 114 or 85%) *showed that* the type of subject authority used was as follows:

MeSH exclusively	30 (26%) libraries	
MeSH supplemented by LC	57 (50%) libraries	
LC exclusively	23 (20%) libraries	
LC supplemented by MeSH	2 (2%) libraries	
no response	2 (2%) libraries	**(712)**

Ibid. . . . *showed that*, of 78 respondents who used MeSH as the primary authority for subject headings and who also had divided catalogs, 77 (99%) reported using MeSH subheadings in the catalog (1 or 1% reported they did not) and 76 (99% of the 77) reported using both form and topical subheadings, while 1 (1% of the 77) reported using topical subheadings only.   **(712)**

Ibid. . . . *showed that*, of 78 respondents who used MeSH as the primary authority for subject headings and who also had divided catalogs, the following use of guidecards for subheadings was reported:

all subheadings	54 (69%)	libraries
topical subheadings	0	libraries
form subheadings	2 (3%)	libraries
no guidecards used for subheadings	17 (22%)	libraries
no response	5 (6%)	libraries	**(712)**

Ibid. . . . *showed that*, of 78 respondents who used MeSH as the primary authority for subject headings and who also had divided catalogs, 14 (18%) reported that they distinguished between form and topical subheading guidecards in a physical way in the catalog, while 62 (79%) reported they did not, and 2 (3%) did not respond. Of those that did distinguish, the following methods were used: cut of tab on card (10 respondents), color of tab (8 respondents), and color of type (1 respondent).   **(712)**

Ibid. . . . *showed that*, of 78 respondents who used MeSH as the primary authority for subject headings and who also had divided catalogs, the following methods were used to subdivide main subject headings in the catalog into topical and form categories:

combined and interfiled alphabetically	70 (90%)	libraries
all form subheadings first, then topical subheadings	5 (6%)	libraries
all topical subheadings first, then form subheadings	1 (1%)	libraries
no response	2 (3%)	libraries	**(712)**

Ibid. . . . *showed that*, of 78 respondents who used MeSH as the primary authority for subject headings and who also had divided catalogs, 63 (81%) respondents reported they modified subject headings by combining several subheadings, while 15 (19%) reported they did not. Of those that did combine subheadings, the maximum number combined was as follows:

2 subheadings	8 respondents
3 subheadings	33 respondents

continued

4 subheadings	15 respondents
5 subheadings	2 respondents
no policy or no limit	5 respondents **(712)**

Ibid. . . . *showed that*, of 78 respondents who used MeSH as the primary authority for subject headings and who also had divided catalogs, language and geographic subheadings were considered by respondents to be the following:

form subheadings	11 (14%)	libraries
topical subheadings	4 (5%)	libraries
do not distinguish	60 (77%)	libraries
no response	3 (4%)	libraries **(712)**

Ibid. . . . *showed that*, of 65 respondents who used MeSH as the primary authority for subject headings and who also had divided catalogs, 18 (27.7%) reported that if language and geographic subheadings were combined with form subheadings the first filing term would be the language/geographic term (e.g., French—Dictionaries), while 47 (72.3%) reported that the order would be reversed. **(712)**

Ibid. . . . *showed that*, of 62 respondents who used MeSH as the primary authority for subject headings and who also had divided catalogs, 56 (90.3%) reported that if language and geographic subheadings were combined with topical subheadings the first filing term would be the topical term followed by the language/geographic term (e.g., Manpower—France), while 6 (9.7%) reported that the order would be reversed.

(712)

Ibid. . . . *showed that*, of 78 respondents who used MeSH as the primary authority for subject headings and who also had divided catalogs, 56 (72%) respondents reported updating the subject catalog and authority file annually to correspond to the new MeSH, 20 (26%) reported "other," and 2 (2%) did not respond. **(712)**

Ibid. . . . *showed that* of 78 respondents who used MeSH as the primary authority for subject headings and who also had divided catalogs, the following methods were used to update the catalog (multiple responses allowed):

56 (71.8%) reported "changing or shifting subject cards from the old headings to the new and pulling deleted MeSH terms";

8 (10.3%) reported "making no changes in the existing catalog but making cross references from old to new terms";

15 (19.2%) reported "other method";

2 (2.6%) gave no response.   (712)

Ibid. . . . *showed that*, of 78 respondents who used MeSH as the primary authority for subject headings and who also had divided catalogs, 54 (69%) reported they used a guidecard to distinguish subject headings filed in the subject section of the catalog, while 24 (31%) reported they did not.
                                                                                              (712)

Ibid. . . . *showed that*, of 78 respondents who used MeSH as the primary authority for subject headings and who also had divided catalogs, 76 (97%) reported they did not file MeSH terms in the public catalog unless there were catalog cards for them, while 2 (3%) reported they filed all MeSH terms regardless of whether there were cards for that heading.   (712)

Use Patterns—General Issues

Academic

■   A 1967-70 study in the Main Library at Yale University, involving 2,100 interviews at the card catalog during a 1-year period, *showed that* weekly charting of card catalog use and book circulation revealed by inspection that card catalog use and book borrowing always remained in the same proportion.   (248)

Ibid. . . . *showed that* use of the card catalog during the academic year was as follows: Yale freshmen (8.3% of catalog use), other Yale undergraduates (27.7%), graduate/postgraduate students (35.6%), Yale faculty (7.3%), Yale staff (2.9%), and other (18.1%).   (248)

■   A survey reported in 1970 at the University of Michigan based on random interviews of catalog users in the General Library, Undergraduate Library, and Medical Library (2,167 users interviewed; 1,489 usable interviews, i.e, users searching for a particular item) *showed that*, of the known-item searches, 67.9% of the respondents entered the catalog with an author's or editor's name, 26.2% entered with a title, and 5.9% with a subject heading. **(321)**

■ A 1979 study at the University of Illinois, Urbana, involving patron use of an online circulation system for known-item searching (interviews with 240 faculty, staff, student, and visiting patrons conducting 310 searches), *showed that* the length of 156 successful known-item searches was as follows:

0.2 minutes or less	16 (10%)	searches
1.0 minutes or less	82 (53%)	searches
2.0 minutes or less	117 (75%)	searches
3.7 minutes or less	139 (89%)	searches
7.5 minutes or less	156 (100%)	searches **(626)**

■ A 1980 study of patron use of the serial card catalog at the University of Illinois, Urbana (sample size: 452 patrons; usable responses: 445 patrons), involving faculty, students, and staff, *showed that* 94% of the materials sought were English-language materials, with 27 (6%) in other languages. **(505)**

Ibid. . . . *showed that* the top 2 sources of 192 serial citations which patrons obtained through use of an index, abstract, or bibliography were *Readers' Guide* (accounting for 54 or 28% of the citations) and *Business Periodicals Index* (accounting for 17 or 9% of the citations). **(505)**

Ibid. . . . *showed that* 366 (83%) of the searches undertaken by patrons in the serial card catalog were successful, i.e., a citation was matched to a catalog entry. Further, the success rate of the frequent catalog user (daily or once/twice per week) was not statistically significantly better than the success rate of the infrequent catalog user. Specifically, 167 (46%) of the frequent catalog users and 199 (54%) of the infrequent catalog users were successful in their searches. **(505)**

Ibid. . . . *showed that* of 427 searches there was no statistically significant difference in success rates between patrons who wrote their citations down (or Xeroxed them) and those who did not. For example, 246 (70%) of the patrons who found their citations in the card catalog had written them down compared to 52 (69%) of the patrons who did not find their citations in the card catalog but who had written them down. Conversely, 93 (26%) of the patrons found their citations in the card catalog without writing them down compared to 20 (27%) of the patrons who did not find their citations in the card catalog but also did not write the citation down. **(505)**

■ A 1982 online survey of MELVYL patrons from all 9 UC campuses conducted over a 2-month period for each 25th user of the system (1,259 questionnaires collected; 72.2 questionnaires complete and usable) *showed that* the average length of time a patron spent at the terminal was 8 minutes 41 seconds, while the average number of commands issued during a session was 22.297.   **(349)**

Ibid. . . . *showed that* the patrons conducted an average of 5.66 searches per session.   **(349)**

Ibid. . . . *showed that* the help facilities were used in 14.28% of the sessions, with those patrons who did use the help facilities averaging 1.59 unqualified help requests and 2.63 help requests with a specific glossary term. Only 2.6% of the patrons made the same error 3 times in a row.
                                                              (349)

Ibid. . . . *showed that* 75.22% of the patrons made no errors at all during their sessions (this included command syntax errors, logical errors, and unrecognizable commands). The remaining 24.77% of the patrons made an average of 2.85 errors during their sessions.   **(349)**

Ibid. . . . *showed that* respondents' university affiliations were:

freshman/sophmore	23.2%	respondents
junior/senior	39.0%	respondents
graduate—master's level	6.4%	respondents
graduate—doctoral level	7.6%	respondents
graduate—professional school	1.9%	respondents
faculty	3.2%	respondents
staff	2.6%	respondents
other	16.1%	respondents **(349)**

Ibid. . . . *showed that* respondents' academic areas were:

art/humanities	24.2%	respondents
physical/biological sciences	22.7%	respondents
social sciences	19.3%	respondents
engineering	14.1%	respondents
medical and health sciences	5.8%	respondents
business management	4.7%	respondents
major undeclared	4.0%	respondents

continued

law	2.9% respondents	
education	2.0% respondents	
interdisciplinary	0.2% respondents	**(349)**

Public

■ A 1980 survey of card catalog and information desk patrons in the Pikes Peak Library District Library over a 2-week period (sample size: 97; responding: 91) *showed that* 85.4% reported a preference for online catalog searching over the traditional manual approach to the card catalog. The main reason given for preferring the online catalog was its ease of use and the speed with which searches could be conducted.   **(345)**

Use Patterns—Problems

Academic

■ A survey reported in 1970 at the University of Michigan based on random interviews of catalog users in the General Library, Undergraduate Library, and Medical Library (2,167 users interviewed; 1,489 usable interviews, i.e, users searching for a particular item) *showed that*, of the 925 searches involving single, personal authorship or editorship that could be verified, 470 (50.8%) had complete and correct author/editor entries, while 455 did not. Of the incomplete/incorrect entries, 348 (76.5%) had mistakes and/or omissions in the first or middle name or in the initials (although the last name was accurate), 87 (19.1%) had mistakes and/or omissions in the last name, and 20 (4.4%) had the identity of the author/editor wrong (i.e., the error was not in incompleteness or misspelling).   **(321)**

Ibid. . . . *showed that*, of 87 errors in the last name, 49.4% involved errors in one of the first 4 letters of the name.   **(321)**

Ibid. . . . *showed that*, of the 925 searches involving single, personal authorship or editorship that could be verified, more errors were made with longer names than with shorter names. For example, 4.9% of the short names (names 5 or less letters long) had errors, 10.5% of the medium names (names 6 to 8 letters long) had errors, and 14.3% of the long names (9 to 12 letters long) had errors.   **(321)**

Ibid. . . . *showed that*, of the 104 errors contained in the 87 searches that had errors in the last name, 50 (48.1%) of the errors were replacement errors (i.e., where 1 letter or string of letters were replaced by an incorrect letter or string of letters), 34 (32.7%) of the errors were omission errors (i.e., a letter or string of letters was omitted), 18 (17.3%) of the errors were addition errors (i.e., where a letter or string of letters was added) and 2 (1.9%) of the errors were transposition errors.   **(321)**

■ A 1979 study at the University of Illinois, Urbana, involving patron use of an online circulation system for known-item searching (interviews with 240 faculty, staff, student, and visiting patrons conducting 310 searches), *showed that* of 222 searches there was no statistically significant difference in success rate between more experienced users (5 or more previous uses) of the online system and less experienced users (less than 5 previous uses) of the system. Specifically, both groups had the same number of unsuccessful searches (33), while the more experienced patrons had 83 successful searches compared to 73 for the less experienced patrons. However, experienced patrons did complete their successful searches more quickly than inexperienced patrons to a statistically significant degree with a correlation of r = .24 (significant at the .01 level).   **(626)**

■ A 1980 study of patron use of the serial card catalog at the University of Illinois, Urbana (sample size: 452 patrons; usable responses: 445 patrons) involving faculty, students, and staff *showed that* of the 79 (18%) unsuccessful searches in the serial card catalog the reasons for failure were as follows:

not owned by the library	24 (5%) citations
patron missed the entry	22 (5%) citations
patron had incomplete entry	5 (1%) citations
serial record failures	28 (6%) citations

Of those not owned by the library, 20 of the 24 titles were verified as correct in spelling and existing in print, i.e., not simply incorrect citations.
                                                                          (505)

■ A 1982 online survey of MELVYL patrons from all 9 UC campuses conducted over a 2-month period for each 25th user of the system (1,259 questionnaires collected; 72.2 questionnaires complete and usable) *showed that* the help facilities were used in 14.28% of the sessions, with those patrons who did use the help facilities averaging 1.59 unqualified help requests and 2.63 help requests with a specific glossary term. Only 2.6% of the patrons made the same error 3 times in a row.   **(349)**

Ibid. . . . *showed that* 75.22% of the patrons made no errors at all during their sessions (this included command syntax errors, logical errors, and unrecognizable commands). The remaining 24.77% of the patrons made an average of 2.85 errors during their sessions.   **(349)**

Use Patterns—Traffic

Academic

■ A 1979 study at Iowa State University, concerning queuing at the public card catalog during a month and a half period and involving 2,327 sample counts of patrons at the catalog, *showed that* the correlation between card catalog use and exit counts, books circulated, and number of individuals checking out books, while statistically significant at the .001 level or better in all 3 cases, was so low as to be negligible. The highest $R2$ (exit count with card catalog use), for example, was .075. With a 1-hour differential between card catalog use counts and number of books circulated the correlation began to be substantial, with an $R2$ of 22% (no significance level given).   **(497)**

Ibid. . . . *showed that*, when the Friday and Sunday counts (there were no Saturday counts) of card catalog patrons were ignored, there was no statistically significant difference among the daily means during Monday through Thursday. For example, the average number of arrivals at the card catalog during a 10-minute period during any of these 4 days ranged from 11.9 patrons (Wednesday) to 12.9 patrons (Monday).   **(497)**

Ibid. . . . *showed that* there were statistically significant differences between patron counts at the card catalog by hour of the day, especially when Friday and Sunday (there were no Saturday counts) were excluded. Arrivals at the card catalog during 10-minute periods each hour between 10 a.m. and 8 p.m. averaged 9.7 patrons at 10:00 a.m. and rose regularly until a high of 18.0 patrons was reached at 2:00 p.m. and then fell to 8.8 patrons at 4:00 p.m. with a rebound to 11.3 patrons at 8:00 p.m. (No significance level was given.)   **(497)**

Use Patterns—Type of Searches

Academic

■ A 1967-70 study in the Main Library at Yale University involving 2,100 interviews at the card catalog during a 1-year period *showed that* known-item searches to determine if the library held the item and, if so, where, accounted for 73% of the catalog use, subject searches accounted for 16%, author searches (to determine what works were available for a known author or publishing body) accounted for 6%, and bibliographic searches (to make use of data on the catalog card rather than locate a book) accounted for 5%. Follow-up questioning about known-item searches suggested that many of these are really subject searches using a known item to identify an appropriate call number or subject heading. The real or "underlying" percentage of known-item and subject searches in the card catalog may be more like 56 and 33, respectively.   **(248)**

Ibid. . . . *showed that* the 4 most popular approaches to searching the card catalog were: author name (personal or corporate, 62.0%), title (28.5%), subject (4.5%), and editor (4.0%).   **(248)**

■ A survey reported in 1970 at the University of Michigan based on random interviews of catalog users in the General Library, Undergraduate Library, and Medical Library (2,167 users interviewed; 1,489 usable interviews, i.e, users searching for a particular item) *showed that*, of the known-item searches, 67.9% of the respondents entered the catalog with an author's or editor's name, 26.2% entered with a title, and 5.9% with a subject heading.   **(321)**

■ A 1982 online survey of MELVYL patrons from all 9 UC campuses conducted over a 2-month period for each 25th user of the system (1,259 questionnaires collected; 72.2 questionnaires complete and usable) *showed that* the 3 most frequently used searches in the COMMAND mode were subject (51.6%), personal author (21.5%), and title (18.8%), while the 3 most frequently used searches in the LOOKUP mode were subject/title (63.4%), personal author/corporate author (15.4%), and title/personal author/corporate author (13.2%).   **(349)**

Public

■ A 1973 study in the Burnaby Public Library (British Columbia) involving patron use of the card catalog (survey size: 367 patrons) *showed that* 152 (42%) were looking for a specific publication (about which they knew something), 208 (57%) were looking for information on a topic or something to read but without a specific item in mind, 6 (1%) were using the catalog to find something out about a book rather than looking for a book, and none were using the catalog to find out something about an author.   **(542)**

Ibid. . . . *showed that*, of the 152 patrons who were looking for a specific publication about which they knew something, the information brought to the card catalog was as follows:

subject only	197 (54%) patrons
title only	59 (16%) patrons

continued

author only	55 (15%) patrons
author and title	34 (9%) patrons
title and subject	11 (3%) patrons
author and subject	8 (2%) patrons
author, title, and subject	3 (1%) patrons	**(542)**

Ibid. . . . *showed that*, for those patrons who had completed successful searches (282 patrons), the information they reported looking at on the catalog card was as follows:

call number only	180 (64%) patrons
call number, author, and title	20 (7%) patrons
author only	19 (7%) patrons
call number and title	17 (6%) patrons
call number and author	16 (6%) patrons
author and title	15 (5%) patrons
title only	10 (3%) patrons

Further, no patron reported looking for "subtitle, edition statement, publisher, place or date of publication, number of pages, or other information on the catalog card." **(542)**

User Access—Theoretical

Academic

■ A study reported in 1970 at the University of Chicago concerning the use of nonstandard catalog access points (104 individuals selected and read 440 books in the general area of psychology that they had not previously read and then were tested on what they remembered about the book 2 weeks later) *showed that* standard author/title/subject information sufficient to look the book up in a conventional card catalog was recalled in only 18% of the cases. **(606)**

Ibid. . . . *showed that*, when asked to recall 24 nonstandard features (e.g., color, type of binding, presence of charts, approximate number of pages, etc.) about each book read, the response rate for each feature ranged from 29% (whether the book contained a dedication) to 99% (level of readership for which the book was intended) with an overall median of 74%. Further, the accuracy for these responses, that is, the correct number of responses ranged from 24% (the number of pages in the book ±100 pages) to 97% (whether the book was a single-volume work) with an overall median of 72%. **(606)**

Ibid. . . . *showed that* the 4 most memorable nonstandard features (of 24) in descending order of importance were:

number of pages
whether the book included case studies
level of work
whether the book included figures

However, none of the nonstandard features was very memorable in that the average nonstandard feature was only recalled correctly 9% more often than would be expected by sheer guesswork, while the most memorable nonstandard feature was recalled correctly only 19% more often than would be expected by sheer guesswork.   **(606)**

Ibid. . . . *showed that* use of any 1 nonstandard feature would reduce the number of books that would need to be searched in a collection on the average by 21.4% with a range of reduction from 57% of the collection (date of the book) to a reduction of 3% (whether the book contained problems for the student to work on). The 5 nonstandard features that reduced the number of books that would need to be searched the most were:

date	57% of collection eliminated
type of work	49% of collection eliminated
number of pages (± 100)	43% of collection eliminated
type of binding	32% of collection eliminated
color	29% of collection eliminated **(606)**

■ A study reported in 1977 at the University of California, Berkeley, comparing the importance of subject familiarity (knowledge of a specified academic field) versus catalog familiarity (knowledge of the structure of the Library of Congress subject headings) in thinking of an appropriate term for subject searching in the library catalog when presented an abstract and book title and involving 22 psychology students (subject familiarity), 22 economics students (subject familiarity), and 17 library students (catalog familiarity), *showed that* catalog familiarity was more important than subject familiarity to a statistically significant degreee in selecting an appropriate subject term [significance level not given]. Specifically, scores for library students in determining subject terms for psychology and economics materials were higher than scores for students in those disciplines determining subject terms in their own discipline.   **(615)**

Ibid. . . . *showed that* although the difference was not statistically significant, psychology and economics students scored higher in selecting appropriate subject terms for the opposite discipline than they did in their own discipline. **(615)**

Ibid. . . . *showed that* students were more likely to achieve the illusion of success in using the library catalog than real success. This was demonstrated by the discrepancy between basic matching (exact matches between subject heading assigned by the library to a particular item and the subject heading chosen by the student) and "existence matching" (a marginal match in which the subject heading chosen by the student existed in the catalog but was not the subject heading assigned by the library). Specifically, the number of terms that constituted basic matches versus existence matches for the 3 groups were as follows:

economics students   21% basic; 62% existence matches
psychology students   22% basic; 60% existence matches
library students   35% basic; 64% existence matches **(615)**

User Success Rate

General

■ A study reported in 1981 of OCLC's online union catalog to investigate the scope of its music holdings by checking 4 major lists of materials ("Books Recently Published" column of *Notes*; "Music Received" column of *Notes*; "New Listings" column of the *Schwann-1 Record and Tape Guide*; and *A Basic Music Library: Essential Scores and Books*) in the catalog *showed that*, of the 317 books listed in the December 1979 "Books Recently Published" column and searched 1 year later, 312 (98.42%) were found in the OCLC union catalog, while of the 287 books listed in the September 1980 "Books Recently Published" column and searched 7 months later, 272 (94.78%) were found in the OCLC union catalog.
(757)

Ibid. . . . *showed that*, of the 420 items listed in the December 1979 "Music Received" column and searched 1 year later, 255 (60.71%) were found in the OCLC union catalog, while of the 351 items listed in the September 1980 "Music Received" column and searched 1-2 months later, 109 (31.05%) were found in the OCLC union catalog.   **(757)**

Ibid. . . . *showed that*, of the 276 items listed in the December 1979 "New Listings" column and searched 14 months later, 162 (58.7%) were found in the OCLC union catalog, while of the 282 items listed in the September

1980 "New Listings" column and searched 1-2 months later, 64 (22.7%) were found in the OCLC union catalog.   **(757)**

Ibid. . . . *showed that*, of the 941 items listed in *A Basic Music Library*, 861 (91.5%) were found, including 231 (94.29%) of the study scores, 195 (96.53%) of the performing editions, and 114 (82.01%) of the instrumental methods and studies. Further, "a large number of specific editions not found in the search" were represented in the OCLC union catalog by other editions.   **(757)**

Academic

■ A 1967 study comparing a dictionary catalog at 1 university with a divided catalog (author/title and subject) at another university by using undergraduates to search entries *showed that* there was no statistically significant difference in average success rates between the 2 catalogs in subject searching or known-item searching.   **(199)**

■ A survey of 12 university libraries (11 responding) during a 3-month period in 1965 and a survey of 11 public libraries during a similar period in 1967 to determine the kinds of reference assistance needed at the card catalog (647 problems reported with 284 from university libraries and 363 from public libraries), reported together in 1968, *showed that* the 3 most frequent problems with the card catalog in university libraries were subject headings (18% of university total), filing arrangement (17% of university total), and "see" or "see also" references (15% of the university total). In public libraries the 3 most frequent problems were filing arrangement (23% of public total), call number (15% of public total), and subject headings (13% of public total).   **(134)**

■ A 1967-70 study in the Main Library at Yale University involving 2,100 interviews at the card catalog during a 1-year period *showed that* 84% of the card catalog searches were successful, that 5% of the searches were unsuccessful for the patron even though library staff later located the document in the card catalog, that 10% of the searches were for documents that probably exist but that were not in the card catalog at the time, and that 1% of the searches were for documents too vaguely or inaccurately described to follow up on.   **(248)**

Ibid. . . . *showed that* the 4 most popular approaches to searching the card catalog were: author name (personal or corporate, 62.0%), title (28.5%), subject (4.5%), and editor (4.0%).   **(248)**

■ A study reported in 1970 at the University of Chicago concerning the use of nonstandard catalog access points (104 individuals selected and read 440 books in the general area of psychology that they had not previously read and then were tested on what they remembered about the book 2 weeks later) *showed that* standard author/title/subject information sufficient to look the book up in a conventional card catalog was recalled in only 18% of the cases. **(606)**

■ A survey in 1976 of 999 library users at San Jose State University Library *showed that* the biggest barrier to locating library materials was difficulties in using the card catalog and finding desired items already in circulation. 42% of the items not found by patrons in the card catalog were in the card catalog, and 42% of the books not located on the shelves were in circulation or in the Reserve Book Room. **(010)**

Ibid. . . . *showed that* there was a 77.52% success rate in locating desired items in the card catalog and a 76% success rate in locating the book in the bookstacks, for an overall success rate of 58.9%. **(010)**

■ A study reported in 1977 at the University of California, Berkeley, comparing the importance of subject familiarity (knowledge of a specified academic field) versus catalog familiarity (knowledge of the structure of the Library of Congress subject headings) in thinking of an appropriate term for subject searching in the library catalog when presented an abstract and book title and involving 22 psychology students (subject familiarity), 22 economics students (subject familiarity), and 17 library students (catalog familiarity), *showed that* catalog familiarity was more important than subject familiarity to a statistically significant degreee in selecting an appropriate subject term [significance level not given]. Specifically, scores for library students in determining subject terms for psychology and economics materials were higher than scores for students in those disciplines determining subject terms in their own discipline. **(615)**

Ibid. . . . *showed that*, although the difference was not statistically significant, psychology and economics students scored higher in selecting appropriate subject terms for the opposite discipline than they did in their own discipline. **(615)**

Ibid. . . . *showed that* students were more likely to achieve the illusion of success in using the library catalog than real success. This was demonstrated by the discrepancy between basic matching (exact matches between subject heading assigned by the library to a particular item and the subject heading chosen by the student) and "existence matching" (a marginal match in which the subject heading chosen by the student existed in the catalog but was not the subject heading assigned by the library). Specifically, the number of terms that constituted basic matches versus existence matches for the 3 groups were as follows:

economics students	21% basic; 62% existence matches
psychology students	22% basic; 60% existence matches
library students	35% basic; 64% existence matches **(615)**

■ A 1978 study at Ohio State University Library involving 2 full days' transactions in the OCLC data base for each of the OSU terminals (1,153 searches of the data base) *showed that* of 158 searches by the public the 2 most frequent types of searches were by name/title (77 or 48.7% of the searches by the public of which 22 or 28.6% were successful) and by title (44 or 27.8% of the searches by the public of which 20 or 45.4% were successful). **(336)**

■ A 1979 study at the University of Illinois, Urbana, involving patron use of an online circulation system for known-item searching (interviews with 240 faculty, staff, student, and visiting patrons conducting 310 searches), *showed that*, of 235 known-item searches, 8% of the location searches (call number previously looked up in card catalog and departmental library location sought only) and 16% of the original searches (online search was first attempt to find out if the library had an item) failed because of an error in using LCS. **(626)**

Ibid. . . . *showed that* the length of 156 successful known-item searches was as follows:

0.2 minutes or less	16 (10%)	searches
1.0 minutes or less	82 (53%)	searches
2.0 minutes or less	117 (75%)	searches
3.7 minutes or less	139 (89%)	searches
7.5 minutes or less	156 (100%)	searches **(626)**

Ibid. . . . *showed that* of 222 searches there was no statistically significant difference in success rate between more experienced users (5 or more previous uses) of the online system and less experienced users (less than 5 previous uses) of the system. Specifically, both groups had the same number of unsuccessful searches (33), while the more experienced patrons had 83 successful searches compared to 73 for the less experienced patrons. However, experienced patrons did complete their successful searches more quickly than inexperienced patrons to a statistically significant degree with a correlation of r = .24 (significant at the .01 level). **(626)**

Ibid. . . . *showed that*, of 120 original known-item searches (original search was the first attempt to find out whether the library had the item desired), the library owned the item in 91% of the cases, the patron could find the item on LCS (Library Circulation System, an online system) in 66% of the cases, and the copy was uncharged in 90% of the cases.
(626)

■ A 1980 study of patron use of the serial card catalog at the University of Illinois, Urbana (sample size: 452 patrons; usable responses: 445 patrons) involving faculty, students, and staff *showed that* 366 (83%) of the searches undertaken by patrons in the serial card catalog were successful, i.e., a citation was matched to a catalog entry. Further, the success rate of the frequent catalog user (daily or once/twice per week) was not statistically significantly better than the success rate of the infrequent catalog user. Specifically, 167 (46%) of the frequent catalog users and 199 (54%) of the infrequent catalog users were successful in their searches. **(505)**

Ibid. . . . *showed that* of 427 searches there was no statistically significant difference in success rates between patrons who wrote their citations down (or Xeroxed them) and those who did not. For example, 246 (70%) of the patrons who found their citations in the card catalog had written them down compared to 52 (69%) of the patrons who did not find their citations in the card catalog but who had written them down. Conversely, 93 (26%) of the patrons found their citations in the card catalog without writing them down compared to 20 (27%) of the patrons who did not find their citations in the card catalog but also did not write the citation down. **(505)**

■ A comparison reported in 1982 of title search capability on an online catalog vs. card catalog at Ohio State University *showed that* patrons were more successful in using departmental card catalogs (1/4 to 1/2 million cards) than in using a central online catalog (3.5 million records). The same held true though to a lesser degree for a skilled librarian. Success rate in the card catalog ran 9-20% higher for patron groups and 4% higher for an experienced librarian. **(045)**

Ibid. . . . *showed that* the percentage of patron failure in the following problem areas for the online catalog was:

title appearing as subject	75%
hyphenated words	67%

continued

words not on stoplist	50%
all words in title on stoplist	50%
too many matches	43%
words on stoplist	41%
person's name begins title	40%
abbreviations	40%
foreign titles	33%
1-word titles	25%

(045)

Public

■ A survey of 12 university libraries (11 responding) during a 3-month period in 1965 and a survey of 11 public libraries during a similar period in 1967 to determine the kinds of reference assistance needed at the card catalog (647 problems reported with 284 from university libraries and 363 from public libraries), reported together in 1968, *showed that* the 3 most frequent problems with the card catalog in university libraries were subject headings (18% of university total), filing arrangement (17% of university total), and "see" or "see also" references (15% of the university total). In public libraries the 3 most frequent problems were filing arrangement (23% of public total), call number (15% of public total), and subject headings (13% of public total).   **(134)**

■ A 1973 study in the Burnaby Public Library (British Columbia) involving patron use of the card catalog (survey size: 367 patrons) *showed that* 63% of the respondents were successful in finding the book for which they were looking after 1 search, while 289 (78%) patrons ultimately had "some measure of success" in using the catalog.   **(542)**

BIBLIOGRAPHY OF ARTICLES

Note: This Bibliography cites all articles summarized in the six-volume set of *Handbooks*. Entries in the Bibliography are sequentially arranged by the citation reference numbers that correspond to the numbers appearing at the end of each research summary throughout the six volumes. The numbers in boldface located at the end of some citations refer only to those research summaries contained in this volume. Alphabetic access to the Bibliography is provided through the Author Index.

1   Pamela Kobelski and Jean Trumbore. "Student Use of On-line Bibliographic Services," *Journal of Academic Librarianship* 4:1 (March 1978), 14-18.

2   John V. Richardson, Jr. "Readability and Readership of Journals in Library Science," *Journal of Academic Librarianship* 3:1 (March 1977), 20-22.

3   Elizabeth Gates Kesler. "A Campaign against Mutilation," *Journal of Academic Librarianship* 3:1 (March 1977), 29-30.

4   Bruce Miller and Marilyn Sorum. "A Two Stage Sampling Procedure for Estimating the Proportion of Lost Books in a Library," *Journal of Academic Librarianship* 3:2 (May 1977), 74-80.

5   Jeffrey St. Clair and Rao Aluri. "Staffing the Reference Desk: Professionals or Nonprofessionals," *Journal of Academic Librarianship* 3:3 (July 1977), 149-153.

6   Valentine DeBruin. "Sometimes Dirty Things Are Seen on the Screen," *Journal of Academic Librarianship* 3:5 (November 1977), 256-266.(**139, 140, 151, 152**)

7   Herbert S. White. "The View from the Library School," *Journal of Academic Librarianship* 3:6 (January 1970), 321.

8   Stella Bentley. "Collective Bargaining and Faculty Status," *Journal of Academic Librarianship* 4:2 (May 1978), 75-81.

9   Steven Seokho Chwe. "A Comparative Study of Job Satisfaction: Catalogers and Reference Librarians in University Libraries," *Journal of Academic Librarianship* 4:3 (July 1978), 139-143. (**48**)

10   Jo Bell Whitlatch and Karen Kieffer. "Service at San Jose State University: Survey of Document Availability," *Journal of Academic Librarianship* 4:4 (September 1978), 196-199. (**134, 201**)

11   Joan Grant and Susan Perelmuter. "Vendor Performance Evaluation," *Journal of Academic Librarianship* 4:5 (November 1978), 366-367.

12 Robert Goehlert. "Book Availability and Delivery Service," *Journal of Academic Librarianship* 4:5 (November 1978), 368-371.

13 Linda L. Phillips and Ann E. Raup. "Comparing Methods for Teaching Use of Periodical Indexes," *Journal of Academic Librarianship* 4:6 (January 1979), 420-423.

14 Margaret Johnson Bennett, David T. Buxton and Ella Capriotti. "Shelf Reading in a Large, Open Stack Library," *Journal of Academic Librarianship* 5:1 (March 1979), 4-8.

15 Sarah D. Knapp and C. James Schmidt. "Budgeting To Provide Computer-Based Reference Services: A Case Study," *Journal of Academic Librarianship* 5:1 (March 1979), 9-13.

16 Herbert S. White. "Library Materials Prices and Academic Library Practices: Between Scylla and Charybdis," *Journal of Academic Librarianship* 5:1 (March 1979), 20-23.

17 Dorothy P. Wells. "Coping with Schedules for Extended Hours: A Survey of Attitudes and Practices," *Journal of Academic Librarianship* 5:1 (March 1979), 24-27.

18 Johanna E. Tallman. "One Year's Experience with CONTU Guidelines for Interlibrary Loan Photocopies," *Journal of Academic Librarianship* 5:2 (May 1979), 71-74.

19 Robert Goehlert. "The Effect of Loan Policies on Circulation Recalls," *Journal of Academic Librarianship* 5:2 (May 1979), 79-82.

20 James R. Dwyer. "Public Response to an Academic Library Microcatalog," *Journal of Academic Librarianship* 5:3 (July 1979), 132-141. **(139)**

21 Paul Metz. "The Role of the Academic Library Director," *Journal of Academic Librarianship* 5:3 (July 1979), 148-152.

22 Anne B. Piternick. "Problems of Resource Sharing with the Community: A Case Study," *Journal of Academic Librarianship* 5:3 (July 1979), 153-158.

23 Shelley Phipps and Ruth Dickstein. "The Library Skills Program at the University of Arizona: Testing, Evaluation and Critique," *Journal of Academic Librarianship* 5:4 (September 1979), 205-214.

24 Michael Stuart Freeman. "Published Study Guides: What They Say about Libraries," *Journal of Academic Librarianship* 5:5 (November 1979), 252-255.

25 James H. Richards, Jr. "Missing Inaction," *Journal of Academic Librarianship* 5:5 (November 1979), 266-269.

26 Philip H. Kitchens. "Engineers Meet the Library," *Journal of Academic Librarianship* 5:5 (November 1979), 277-282.

27 Michael Rouchton. "OCLC Serials Records: Errors, Omissions, and Dependability," *Journal of Academic Librarianship* 5:6 (January 1980), 316-321. **(64, 65, 66, 67, 68, 104, 105, 106)**

28 Charles R. McClure. "Academic Librarians, Information Sources, and Shared Decision Making," *Journal of Academic Librarianship* 6:1 (March 1980), 9-15.

29 Marjorie E. Murfin. "The Myth of Accessibility: Frustration and Failure in Retrieving Periodicals," *Journal of Academic Librarianship* 6:1 (March 1980), 16-19.

30 Anthony W. Ferguson and John R. Taylor. "What Are You Doing? An Analysis of Activities of Public Service Librarians at a Medium-sized Research Library," *Journal of Academic Librarianship* 6:1 (March 1980), 24-29.

31 Regina Shelton. "Adaption: A One-Year Survey of Reserve Photocopying," *Journal of Academic Librarianship* 6:2 (May 1980), 74-76.

32 Dorothea M. Thompson. "The Correct Uses of Library Data Bases Can Improve Interlibrary Loan Efficiency," *Journal of Academic Librarianship* 6:2 (May 1980), 83-86.

33 Joan Repp and Julia A. Woods. "Student Appraisal Study and Allocation Formula: Priorities and Equitable Funding in a University Setting," *Journal of Academic Librarianship* 6:2 (May 1980), 87-90.

34 Elaine S. Friedman. "Patron Access to Online Cataloging Systems: OCLC in the Public Service Environment," *Journal of Academic Librarianship* 6:3 (July 1980), 132-139.

35 Edward C. Jestes. "Manual vs. Automated Circulation: A Comparison of Operating Costs in a University Library," *Journal of Academic Librarianship* 6:3 (July 1980), 144-150.

36 Kathleen A. Johnson and Barbara S. Plake. "Evaluation of PLATO Library Instructional Lessons: Another View," *Journal of Academic Librarianship* 6:3 (July 1980), 154-158.

37 Priscilla C. Yu. "International Gift and Exchange: The Asian Experience," *Journal of Academic Librarianship* 6:6 (January 1981), 333-338.

38 George W. Black, Jr. "Estimating Collection Size Using the Shelf List in a Science Library," *Journal of Academic Librarianship* (January 1981), 339-341.

39 Beth Macleod. "*Library Journal* and *Choice*: A Review of Reviews," *Journal of Academic Librarianship* 7:1 (March 1981), 23-28.

40 Frank Wm. Goudy. "HEA, Title II-C Grant Awards: A Financial Overview from FY 1978-79 through FY 1981-82," *Journal of Academic Librarianship* 8:5 (November 1982), 264-269.

41 Larry Hardesty and John Wright. "Student Library Skills and Attitudes and Their Change: Relationships to Other Selected Variables," *Journal of Academic Librarianship* 8:4 (September 1982), 216-220.

42 Penelope Pearson and Virginia Teufel. "Evaluating Undergraduate Library Instruction at the Ohio State University," *Journal of Academic Librarianship* 7:6 (January 1982), 351-357.

43 David S. Ferrioro. "ARL Directors as Proteges and Mentors," *Journal of Academic Librarianship* 7:6 (January 1982), 358-365.

44 Albert F. Maag. "So You Want to be a Director...," *Journal of Academic Librarianship* 7:4 (September 1981), 213-217.

45 Mary Noel Gouke and Sue Pease. "Title Searches in an Online Catalog and a Card Catalog: A Comparative Study of Patron Success in Two Libraries," *Journal of Academic Librarianship* 8:3 (July 1982), 137-143. **(137, 161, 162, 203, 204)**

46 John K. Mayeski and Marilyn T. Sharrow. "Recruitment of Academic Library Managers: A Survey," *Journal of Academic Librarianship* 8:3 (July 1982), 151-154.

47 Linda K. Rambler. "Syllabus Study: Key to a Responsive Academic Library," *Journal of Academic Librarianship* 8:3 (July 1982), 155-159.

48 Marion T. Reid. "Effectiveness of the OCLC Data Base for Acquisitions Verification," *Journal of Academic Librarianship* 2:6 (January 1977), 303-326.

49 James D. Culley, Denis F. Healy and Kermit G. Cudd. "Business Students and the University Library: An Overlooked Element in the Business Curriculum," *Journal of Academic Librarianship* 2:6 (January 1977), 293-296.

50 Edward Kazlauskas. "An Exploratory Study: A Kenesic Analysis of Academic Library Service Points," *Journal of Academic Librarianship* 2:3 (July 1976), 130-134.

51 Helen Gothberg. "Immediacy: A Study of Communication Effect on the Reference Process," *Journal of Academic Librarianship* 2:3 (July 1976), 126-129.

52 John Vasi. "Building Libraries for the Handicapped: A Second Look," *Journal of Academic Librarianship* 2:2 (May 1976), 82-83.

53 Elliot S. Palais. "The Significance of Subject Dispersion for the Indexing of Political Science Journals," *Journal of Academic Librarianship* 2:2 (May 1976), 72-76.

54 Ruth Carol Cushman. "Lease Plans—A New Lease on Life for Libraries," *Journal of Academic Librarianship* 2:1 (March 1976), 15-19.

55 Charles R. McClure. "Subject and Added Entries as Access to Information," *Journal of Academic Librarianship* 2:1 (March 1976), 9-14. **(45, 113, 150, 179, 181, 184)**

56 Marilyn L. Miller and Barbara B. Moran. "Expenditures for Resources in School Library Media Centers FY '82-'83," *School Library Journal* 30:2 (October 1983), 105-114. **(132)**

57 Karen Lee Shelley. "The Future of Conservation in Research Libraries," *Journal of Academic Librarianship* 1:6 (January 1976), 15-18.

58 Maryan E. Reynolds. "Challenges of Modern Network Development," *Journal of Academic Librarianship* 1:2 (May 1975), 19-22. **(44)**

59 Marjorie E. Martin and Clyde Hendrick. "Ripoffs Tell Their Story: Interviews with Mutilators in a University Library," *Journal of Academic Librarianship* 1:2 (May 1975), 8-12.

60 Audrey Tobias. "The Yule Curve Describing Periodical Citations by Freshmen: Essential Tool or Abstract Frill?" *Journal of Academic Librarianship* 1:1 (March 1975), 14-16.

61 Allan J. Dyson. "Organizing Undergraduate Library Instruction," *Journal of Academic Librarianship* 1:1 (March 1975), 9-13.

62 David F. Kohl. "High Efficiency Inventorying through Predictive Data," *Journal of Academic Librarianship* 8:2 (May 1982), 82-84.

63 Eleanor Phinney. "Trends in Public Library Adult Services," *ALA Bulletin* 57:3 (March 1963), 262-266.

64 Zelia J. French. "Library-Community Self-studies in Kansas," *ALA Bulletin* 56:1 (January 1962), 37-41.

65 Guy Garrison. "Nonresident Library Fees in Suburban Chicago," *ALA Bulletin* 55:6 (June 1961), 1013-1017.

66 James E. Bryan. "The Christmas Holiday Jam," *ALA Bulletin* 55:6 (June 1961), 526-530.

67 Joint Libraries Committee on Fair Use in Photocopying, American Library Association. "Fair Use in Photocopying: Report on Single Copies," *ALA Bulletin* 55:6 (June 1961), 571-573.

68 Henry J. Dubester. "Stack Use of a Research Library," *ALA Bulletin* 55:10 (November 1961), 891-893.

69 Mary Virginia Gaver. "Teacher Education and School Libraries," *ALA Bulletin* 60:1 (January 1966), 63-72.

70 Richard Waters. "Free Space: Can Public Libraries Receive It?" *ALA Bulletin* 58:3 (March 1964), 232-234.

71 Frank L. Schick. "Professional Library Manpower," *ALA Bulletin* 58:4 (April 1964), 315-317.

72 Milbrey Jones. "Socio-Economic Factors in Library Service to Students," *ALA Bulletin* 58:11 (December 1964), 1003-1006.

73 Elizabeth W. Stone. "Administrators Fiddle while Employees Burn or Flee," *ALA Bulletin* 63:2 (February 1969), 181-187.

74 Staff Organizations Round Table, American Library Association. "Opinions on Collective Bargaining," *ALA Bulletin* 63:6 (June 1969), 803-808.

75 Library Administration Division, American Library Association. "Library Employment of Minority Group Personnel," *ALA Bulletin* 63:7 (July-August 1969), 985-987.

76 Eli M. Oboler. "The Case for ALA Regional Annual Conferences," *ALA Bulletin* 63:8 (September 1969), 1099-1101.

77 Edward N. Howard. "Breaking the Fine Barrier," *ALA Bulletin* 63:11 (December 1969), 1541-1545.

78 Elin B. Christianson. "Variation of Editorial Material in Periodicals Indexed in *Reader's Guide*," *ALA Bulletin* 62:2 (February 1968), 173-182. **(104)**

79 Insurance for Libraries Committee, American Library Association. "The Makings of a Nationwide Scandal," *ALA Bulletin* 62:4 (April 1968), 384-386.

80 George L. Gardiner. "Collective Bargaining: Some Questions Asked," *ALA Bulletin* 62:8 (September 1968), 973-976.

81 Barbara M. Conant. "Trials and Tribulations of Textbook Price Indexing," *ALA Bulletin* 61:2 (February 1967), 197-199.

82 Henry T. Drennan and Sarah R. Reed. "Library Manpower," *ALA Bulletin* 61:8 (September 1967), 957-965.

83 Jerry L. Walker. "Changing Attitudes toward the Library and the Librarian," *ALA Bulletin* 61:8 (September 1967), 977-981.

84 William R. Monat. "The Community Library: Its Search for a Vital Purpose," *ALA Bulletin* 61:11 (December 1967), 1301-1310.

85 Irene A. Braden. "Pilot Inventory of Library Holdings," *ALA Bulletin* 62:9 (October 1968), 1129-1131.

86 Genevieve Casey. "Library Manpower in the Detroit Metropolitan Region," *American Libraries* 1:8 (September 1970), 787-789.

87 Nora Cambier, Barton Clark, Robert Daugherty and Mike Gabriel. "Books in Print 1969: An Analysis of Errors," *American Libraries* 1:9 (October 1970), 901-902.

88 Tom Childers and Beth Krevitt. "Municipal Funding of Library Services," *American Libraries* 3:1 (January 1972), 53-57.

89 Albert H. Rubenstein, David J. Werner, Gustave Rath, John A. Kernaghan, and Robert D. O'Keefe. "Search versus Experiment—the Role of the Research Librarian," *College and Research Libraries* 34:4 (July 1973), 280-286.

90 Frank F. Kuo. "A Comparison of Six Versions of Science Library Instruction," *College and Research Libraries* 34:4 (July 1973), 287-290.

91 Laurence Miller. "The role of Circulation Services in the Major University Library," *College and Research Libraries* 34:6 (November 1973), 463-471.

92 Ruth Hyman and Gail Schlachter. "Academic Status: Who Wants It?" *College and Research Libraries* 34:6 (November 1973), 472-478.

93 Larry E. Harrelson. "Large Libraries and Information Desks," *College and Research Libraries* 35:1 (January 1974), 21-27.

94 Robert B. Downs. "Library Resources in the United States," *College and Research Libraries* 35:2 (March 1974), 97-108.

95 Richard J. Beeler. "Late-Study Areas: A Means of Extending Library Hours," *College and Research Libraries* 35:3 (May 1974), 200-203.

96 Rolland E. Stevens. "A Study of Interlibrary Loan," *College and Research Libraries* 35:5 (September 1974), 336-343.

97 Jay B. Clark. "An Approach to Collection Inventory," *College and Research Libraries* 35:5 (September 1974), 354-359. **(155)**

98 Jan Baaske, Don Tolliver and Judy Westerberg. "Overdue Policies: A Comparison of Alternatives," *College and Research Libraries* 35:5 (September 1974), 354-359.

99 Clyde Hendrick and Marjorie E. Murfin. "Project Library Ripoff: A Study of Periodical Mutilation in a University Library," *College and Research Libraries* 35:6 (November 1974), 402-411.

100 Peter Marshall. "How Much, How Often?" *College and Research Libraries* 35:6 (November 1974), 453-456.

101 Robert Balay and Christine Andres. "Use of the Reference Service in a Large Academic Library," *College and Research Libraries* 36:1 (January 1975), 9-26.

102 Guy Walker. "Preservation Efforts in Larger U.S. Academic Libraries," *College and Research Libraries* 36:1 (January 1975), 39-44.

103 Susanne Patterson Wahba. "Job Satisfaction of Librarians: A Comparison between Men and Women," *College and Research Libraries* 36:1 (January 1975), 45-51.

104 Grant T. Skelley. "Characteristics of Collections Added to American Research Libraries 1940-1970: A Preliminary Investigation," *College and Reseach Libraries* 36:1 (January 1975), 52-60.

105 Laura M. Boyer and William C. Theimer, Jr. "The Use and Training of Nonprofessional Personnel at Reference Desks in Selected College and University Libraries," *College and Research Libraries* 36:3 (May 1975), 193-200.

106 Robert J. Greene. "LENDS: An Approach to the Centralization/ Decentralization Dilemma," *College and Research Libraries* 36:3 (May 1975), 201-207. **(138, 139)**

107 Frances L. Meals and Walter T. Johnson. "We Chose Microfilm," *College and Research Libraries* 21:3 (May 1960), 223-228.

108 George Caldwell. "University Libraries and Government Publications: A Survey," *College and Research Libraries* 22:1 (January 1961), 30-34. **(45)**

109 Allen Story. "Leo in Libraryland," *American Libraries* 7:9 (October 1976), 569-571.

110 Leslie R. Morris. "The Rise and Fall of the Library Job Market," *American Libraries* 12:9 (October 1981), 557-558.

111 Richard De Gennaro. "Escalating Journal Prices: Time To Fight Back," *American Libraries* 8:1 (January 1977), 69-74.

112 Joe A. Hewitt. "The Impact of OCLC," *American Libaries* 7:5 (May 1976), 268-275. **(42, 43, 47, 48, 57, 70, 74, 77, 78, 79, 97, 98, 106, 107, 108, 110, 112)**

113 Fritz Veit. "Book Order Procedures in the Publicly Controlled Colleges and Universities of the Midwest," *College and Research Libraries* 23:1 (January 1962), 33-40.

114 Keyes D. Metcalf. "Compact Shelving," *College and Research Libraries* 23:2 (March 1962), 103-111.

115 Natalie N. Nicholson and Eleanor Bartlett. "Who Uses University Libraries," *College and Research Libraries* 23:3 (May 1962), 217-259.

116 H. William Axford. "Rider Revisited," *College and Research Libraries* 23:4 (July 1962), 345-347.

117 E.J. Josey. "The Role of the College Library Staff in Instruction in the Use of the Library," *College and Research Libraries* 23:6 (November 1962), 492-498.

118 Edwin E. Williams. "Magnitude of the Paper-Deterioration Problems as Measured by a National Union Catalog Sample," *College and Research Libraries* 23:6 (November 1962), 499.

119 Stella Frank Mosborg. "Measuring Circulation Desk Activities Using a Random Alarm Mechanism," *College and Research Libraries* 41:5 (September 1980), 437-444.

120 Jean E. Koch and Judith M. Pask. "Working Papers in Academic Business Libraries," *College and Research Libraries* 41:6 (November 1980), 517-523. (82)

121 Paul Metz. "Administrative Succession in the Academic Library," *College and Research Libraries* 39:5 (September 1978), 358-364.

122 Libby Trudell and James Wolper. "Interlibrary Loan in New England," *College and Research Libraries* 39:5 (September 1978), 365-371.

123 Richard M. Dougherty. "The Evaluation of Campus Library Document Delivery Service," *College and Research Libraries* 34:1 (January 1973), 29-39.

124 Ung Chon Kim. "A Comparison of Two Out-of-Print Book Buying Methods," *College and Research Libraries* 34:5 (September 1973), 258-264.

125 Ann Gwyn, Anne McArthur and Karen Furlow. "Friends of the Library," *College and Research Libraries* 36:4 (July 1975), 272-282.

126 John J. Knightly. "Library Collections and Academic Curricula: Quantitative Relationships," *College and Research Libraries* 36:4 (July 1975), 295-301.

127 Alice S. Clark and Rita Hirschman. "Using the 'Guidelines': A Study of the State-Supported Two-Year College Libraries in Ohio," *College and Research Libraries* 36:5 (September 1975), 364-370.

128 Virginia E. Yagello and Gerry Gutherie. "The Effect of Reduced Loan Periods on High Use Items," *College and Research Libraries* 36:5 (September 1975), 411-414.

129 George Piternick. "Library Growth and Academic Quality," *College and Research Libraries* 24:3 (May 1963), 223-229.

130 Robert N. Broadus. "An Analysis of Faculty Circulation in a University Library," *College and Research Libraries* 24:4 (July 1963), 323-325.

131 Perry D. Morrison. "The Personality of the Academic Librarian," *College and Research Libraries* 24:5 (September 1963), 365-368.

132 W.J. Bonk. "What is Basic Reference?" *College and Research Libraries* 25:3 (May 1964), 5-8.

133 Jean Legg "The Periodical Scene," *RQ* 7:3 (Spring 1968), 129-132.

134 Richard H. Perrine. "Catalog Use Difficulties," *RQ* 7:4 (Summer 1968), 169-174. **(131, 132, 133, 151, 181, 182, 183, 184, 200, 204)**

135 Thelma E. Larson. "A Survey of User Orientation Methods," *RQ* 8:3 (Spring 1969), 182-187.

136 Phil Hoehn and Jean Hudson. "Academic Library Staffing Patterns," *RQ* 8:4 (Summer 1969), 242-244.

137 T.H. Milby. "Two Approaches to Biology," *RQ* 11:3 (Spring 1972), 231-235.

138 James B. Way. "Loose Leaf Business Services," *RQ* 9:2 (Winter 1969), 128-133.

139 Mary Jane Swope and Jeffrey Katzer. "Why Don't They Ask Questions?" *RQ* 12:2 (Winter 1972), 161-165.

140 Robert M. Simmons. "Finding That Government Document," *RQ* 12:2 (Winter 1972), 167-171. **(164, 179)**

141 Lee Regan. "Status of Reader's Advisory Service," *RQ* 12:3 (Spring 1973), 227-233.

142 Bruce Cossar. "Interlibrary Loan Costs," *RQ* 12:3 (Spring 1973), 243-246.

143 Mary R. Turtle and William C. Robinson. "The Relationship between Time Lag and Place of Publication in *Library and Information Science Abstracts* and *Library Literature*," *RQ* 14:1 (Fall 1974), 28-31.

144 Rosemary Magrill and Charles H. Davis. "Public Library SDI; A Pilot Study," *RQ* 14:2 (Winter 1974), 131-137.

145 Steve Parker and Kathy Essary. "A Manual SDI System for Academic Libraries," *RQ* 15:1 (Fall 1975), 47-54.

146 Carl F. Orgren and Barbara J. Olson. "Statewide Teletype Reference Service," *RQ* 15:3 (Spring 1976), 203-209.

147 Anne S. Mavor, Jose Orlando Toro and Ernest R. Deprospo. "An Overview of the National Adult Independent Learning Project," *RQ* 15:4 (Summer 1976), 293-308.

148 Danuta A. Nitecki. "Attitudes toward Automated Information Retrieval Services among RASD Members," *RQ* 16:2 (Winter 1976), 133-141.

149 Rhoda Garoogian. "Library Use of the New York Times Information Bank: A Preliminary Survey," *RQ* 16:1 (Fall 1976), 59-64.

150 Marcella Ciucki. "Recording of Reference/Information Service Activities: A Study of Forms Currently Used," *RQ* 16:4 (Summer 1977), 273-283.

151 Mollie Sandock. "A Study of University Students' Awareness of Reference Services," *RQ* 16:4 (Summer 1977), 284-296.

152 Kathleen Imhoff and Larry Brandwein. "Labor Collections and Services in Public Libraries throughout the United States, 1976," *RQ* 17:2 (Winter 1977), 149-158.

153 Cynthia Swenk and Wendy Robinson. "A Comparison of the Guides to Abstracting and Indexing Services Provided by Katz, Chicorel and Ulrich," *RQ* (Summer 1978), 317-319.

154 John P. Wilkinson and William Miller. "The Step Approach to Reference Service," *RQ* (Summer 1978), 293-299.

155 Gerald Johoda, Alan Bayer and William L. Needham. "A Comparison of On-Line Bibliographic Searches in One Academic and One Industrial Organization," *RQ* 18:1 (Fall 1978), 42-49.

156 Stephen P. Harter and Mary Alice S. Fields. "Circulation, Reference and the Evaluation of Public Library Service," *RQ* 18:2 (Winter 1978), 147-152.

157 Daniel Ream. "An Evaluation of Four Book Review Journals," *RQ* 19:2 (Winter 1979), 149-153.

158 Joseph W. Palmer. "Review Citations for Best-Selling Books," *RQ* 19:2 (Winter 1979), 154-158.

159 "An Evaluation of References to Indexes and Abstracts in Ulrich's 17th Edition," *RQ* 20:2 (Winter 1980), 155-159.

160 Victoria T. Kok and Anton R. Pierce. "The Reference Desk Survey: A Management Tool in an Academic Research Library," *RQ* 22:2 (Winter 1982), 181-187.

161 Sheila S. Intner. "Equality of Cataloging in the Age of AACR2," *American Libraries* 14:2 (February 1983), 102-103. (**5, 56, 83, 129, 130, 141, 157, 158**)

162 Joseph W. Palmer. "The Future of Public Library Film Service," *American Libraries* 13:2 (February 1982), 140-142.

163 Robert Grover and Mary Kevin Moore. "Print Dominates Library Service to Children," *American Libraries* 13:4 (April 1982), 268-269.

164 Richard H. Evensen and Mary Berghaus Levering. "Services Are 500% Better," *American Libraries* 10:6 (June 1979), 373.

165 Judith Schick. "Job Mobility of Men and Women Librarians and How It Affects Career Advancement," *American Libraries* 10:11 (December 1979), 643-647.

166 Elizabeth Rountree. "Users and Nonusers Disclose Their Needs," *American Libraries* 10:8 (September 1979), 486-487.

167 George Bobinski. "A Survey of Faculty Loan Policies," *College and Research Libraries* 24:6 (November 1963), 483-486. add

168 L. Miles Raisig and Frederick G. Kilgour. "The Use of Medical Theses as Demonstrated by Journal Citations, 1850-1960," *College and Research Libraries* 25:2 (March 1964), 93-102.

169 George H. Fadenrecht. "Library Facilities and Practices in Colleges of Veterinary Medicine," *College and Research Libraries* 25:4 (July 1964), 308-335.

170 Donald Thompson. "Working Conditions in Selected Private College Libraries," *College and Research Libraries* 25:4 (July 1964), 261-294.

171 Benedict Brooks and Frederick G. Kilgour. "Catalog Subject Searches in the Yale Medical Library," *College and Research Libraries* 25:6 (November 1964), 483-487. **(180, 183)**

172 Patrick Barkey. "Patterns of Student Use of a College Library," *College and Research Libraries* 26:2 (March 1965), 115-118.

173 Genevieve Porterfield. "Staffing of Interlibrary Loan Service," *College and Research Libraries* 26:4 (July 1965), 318-320.

174 Harold Mathis. "Professional or Clerical: A Cross-Validation Study," *College and Research Libraries* 26:6 (November 1965), 525-531.

175 David H. Doerrer. 'Overtime' and the Academic Librarian," *College and Research Libraries* 27:3 (May 1966), 194-239.

176 Lois L. Luesing. "Church Historical Collections in Liberal Arts Colleges," *College and Research Libraries* 27:5 (July 1966), 291-317. **(80)**

177 W.C. Blankenship. "Head Librarians: How Many Men? How Many Women?" *College and Research Libraries* 28:1 (January 1967), 41-48.

178 Morrison C. Haviland. "Loans to Faculty Members in University Libraries," *College and Research Libraries* 28:3 (May 1967), 171-174.

179 R. Vernon Ritter. "An Investigation of Classroom-Library Relationships on a College Campus as Seen in Recorded Circulation and GPA's," *College and Research Libraries* 29:1 (January 1968), 3-4.

180 Peter Spyers-Duran. "Faculty Studies: A Survey of Their Use in Selected Libraries," *College and Research Libraries* 29:1 (January 1968), 55-61.

181 Raymond Kilpela. "The University Library Committee," *College and Research Libraries* 29:2 (March 1968), 141-143.

182 W. Porter Kellam and Dale L. Barker. "Activities and Opportunities of University Librarians for Full Participation in the Educational Enterprise," *College and Research Libraries* 29:5 (May 1968), 195-199.

183 Lloyd A. Kramer and Martha B. Kramer. "The College Library and the Drop-Out," *College and Research Libraries* 29:4 (July 1968), 310-312.

184 Carl Hintz. "Criteria for Appointment to and Promotion in Academic Rank," *College and Research Libraries* 29:5 (September 1968), 341-346.

185 Desmond Taylor. "Classification Trends in Junior College Libraries," *College and Research Libraries* 29:6 (September 1968), 351-356. **(29, 33, 37, 103)**

186 Raj Madan, Eliese Hetler and Marilyn Strong. "The Status of Librarians in Four-Year State Colleges and Universities," *College and Research Libraries* 29:5 (September 1968), 381-386.

187 Victor Novak. "The Librarian in Catholic Institutions," *College and Research Libraries* 29:5 (September 1968), 403-410.

188 Barbara H. Phipps. "Library Instruction for the Undergraduate," *College and Research Libraries* 29:5 (September 1968), 411-423.

189 Ashby J. Fristoe. "Paperbound Books: Many Problems, No Solutions," *College and Research Libraries* 29:5 (September 1968), 437-442.

190 Sidney Forman. "Innovative Practices in College Libraries," *College and Research Libraries* 29:6 (November 1968), 486-492. **(33, 103, 165)**

191 Richard W. Trueswell. "Some Circulation Data from a Research Library," *College and Research Libraries* 29:6 (November 1968), 493-495.

192 Jane P. Kleiner. "The Information Desk: The Library's Gateway to Service," *College and Research Libraries* 29:6 (November 1968), 496-501.

193 J.E.G. Craig, Jr. "Characteristics of Use of Geology Literature," *College and Research Libraries* 3:3 (May 1969), 230-236.

194 Ronald A. Hoppe and Edward C. Simmel. "Book Tearing: The Bystander in the University Library," *College and Research Libraries* 3:3 (May 1969), 247-251.

195 Stephen L. Peterson. "Patterns of Use of Periodical Literature," *College and Research Libraries* 30:5 (September 1969), 422-430.

196 Mary B. Cassata. "Teach-in: The Academic Librarian's Key to Status," *College and Research Libraries* 31:1 (January 1970), 22-27.

197 E.J. Josey. "Community Use of Junior College Libraries—A Symposium," *College and Research Libraries* 31:3 (May 1970), 185-198.

198 Virgil F. Massman. "Academic Library Salaries in a Seven-State Area," *College and Research Libraries* 3:6 (November 1969), 477-482.

199 James Krikelas. "Subject Searches Using Two Catalogs: A Comparative Evaluation," *College and Research Libraries* 30:6 (November 1969), 506-517. **(145, 165, 181, 183, 200)**

200 James Wright. "Fringe Benefits for Academic Library Personnel," *College and Research Libraries* 31:1 (January 1970), 18-21.

201 Howard Clayton. "Femininity and Job Satisfaction among Male Library Students at One Midwestern University," *College and Research Libraries* 31:6 (November 1970), 388-398.

202 Philip V. Rzasa and John H. Moriarty. "The Types and Needs of Academic Library Users: A Case Study of 6,568 Responses," *College and Research Libraries* 31:6 (November 1970),403-409.

203 Bob Carmack and Trudi Loeber. "The Library Reserve System—Another Look," *College and Research Libraries* 32:2 (March 1971), 105-109.

204 C. James Schmidt and Kay Shaffer. "A Cooperative Interlibrary Loan Service for the State-Assisted University Libraries in Ohio," *College and Research Libraries* 32:3 (May 1971), 197-204.

205 Edward S. Warner. "A Tentative Analytical Approach to the Determination of Interlibrary Loan Network Effectiveness," *College and Research Libraries* 32:3 (May 1971), 217-221.

206 Irving Zelkind and Joseph Sprug. "Increased Control through Decreased Controls: A Motivational Approach to a Library Circulation Problem," *College and Research Libraries* 32:3 (May 1971), 222-226.

207 William E. McGrath. "Correlating the Subjects of Books Taken Out Of and Books Used Within an Open-Stack Library," *College and Research Libraries* 32:4 (July 1971), 280-285.

208 Thomas Kirk. "A Comparison of Two Methods of Library Instruction for Students in Introductory Biology," *College and Research Libraries* 32:6 (November 1971), 465-474.

209 Dawn McCaghy and Gary Purcell. "Faculty Use of Government Publications," *College and Research Libraries* 33:1 (January 1972), 7-12.

210 Joe A. Hewitt. "Sample Audit of Cards from a University Library Catalog," *College and Research Libraries* 33:1 (January 1972), 24-27. **(130, 132, 142, 153, 154)**

211 William E. McGrath. "The Significance of Books Used According to a Classified Profile of Academic Departments," *College and Research Libraries* 33:3 (May 1972), 212-219.

212 Carlos A. Cuadra and Ruth J. Patrick. "Survey of Academic Library Consortia in the U.S.," *College and Research Libraries* 33:4 (July 1972), 271-283.

213 Marjorie Johnson. "Performance Appraisal of Librarians—A Survey," *College and Research Libraries* 33:5 (September 1972), 359-367.

214 Marvin E. Wiggins. "The Development of Library Use Instruction Programs," *College and Research Libraries* 33:6 (November 1972), 473-479. **(44, 45)**

215 Margaret E. Monroe. "Community Development as a Mode of Community Analysis," *Library Trends* 24:3 (January 1976), 497-514.

216 Janet K. Rudd and Larry G. Carver. "Topographic Map Acquisition in U.S. Academic Libraries," *Library Trends* 29:3 Winter 1981), 375-390.

217 John Belland. "Factors Influencing Selection of Materials," *School Media Quarterly* 6:2 (Winter 1978), 112-119.

218 Virginia Witucke. "A Comparative Analysis of Juvenile Book Review Media," *School Media Quarterly* 8:3 (Spring 1980), 153-160.

219 M. Carl Drott and Jacqueline C. Mancall. "Magazines as Information Sources: Patterns of Student Use," *School Media Quarterly* 8:4 (Summer 1980), 240-250.

220 Jerry J. Watson and Bill C. Snider. "Book Selection Pressure on School Library Media Specialists and Teachers," *School Media Quarterly* 9:2 (Winter 1981), 95-101.

221 Jerry J. Watson and Bill C. Snider. "Educating the Potential Self-Censor," *School Media Quarterly* 9:4 (Summer 1981), 272-276.

222 Lucy Anne Wozny. "Online Bibliographic Searching and Student Use of Information: An Innovative Teaching Approach," *School Library Media Quarterly* 11:1 (Fall 1982), 35-42.

223 Carol A. Doll. "School and Public Library Collection Overlap and the Implications for Networking," *School Library Media Quarterly* 11:3 (Spring 1983), 193-199.

224 Arthur Tannenbaum and Eva Sidhom. "User Environment and Attitudes in an Academic Microform Center," *Library Journal* 101:18 (October 15, 1976), 2139-2143.

225 Timothy Hays, Kenneth D. Shearer and Concepcion Wilson. "The Patron Is Not the Public," *Library Journal* 102:16 (September 15, 1977), 1813-1818.

226 Wilma Lee Woolard. "The Combined School and Public Library: Can It Work?" *Library Journal* 103:4 (February 15, 1978), 435-438.

227 David C. Genaway. "Bar Coding and the Librarian Supermarket: An Analysis of Advertised Library Vacancies," *Library Journal* 103:3 (February 1, 1978), 322-325.

228 Hoyt Galvin. "Public Library Parking Needs," *Library Journal* 103:2 (November 15, 1978), 2310-2313.

229   Harold J. Ettelt. "Book Use at a Small (Very) Community College Library,"
          Library Journal 103:2 (November 15, 1978), 2314-2315.

230   Frederick G. Kilgour. "Interlibrary Loans On-Line," *Library Journal* 104:4
          (February 15, 1979), 460-463.

231   Paul Little. "The Effectiveness of Paperbacks," *Library Journal* 104:2
          (November 15, 1979), 2411-2416.

232   Ken Kister. "Encyclopedias and the Public Library: A National Survey,"
          Library Journal 104:8 (April 15, 1979), 890-893.

233   Arlene T. Dowell. "Discrepancies in CIP: How Serious Is the Problem,"
          Library Journal 104:19 (November 1, 1979), 2281-2287. **(25)**

234   Gary D. Byrd, Mary Kay Smith and Norene McDonald. "MINET in K.C.,"
          Library Journal 104:17 (October 1, 1979), 2044-2047.

235   Ray L. Carpenter. "The Public Library Patron," *Library Journal* 104:3
          (February 1, 1979), 347-351.

236   Cathy Schell. "Preventive Medicine: The Library Prescription," *Library
          Journal* 105:8 (April 15, 1980), 929-931.

237   Michael Gonzalez, Bill Greeley and Stephen Whitney. "Assessing the
          Library Needs of the Spanish-speaking," *Library Journal* 105:7 (April 1,
          1980), 786-789.

238   Thomas Childers. "The Test of Reference," *Library Journal* 105:8 (April 15,
          1980), 924-928.

239   Mary Noel Gouke and Marjorie Murfin. "Periodical Mutilization: The
          Insidious Disease," *Library Journal* 105:16 (September 15, 1980), 1795-1797.

240   Sheila Creth and Faith Harders. "Requirements for the Entry Level Librari-
          an," *Library Journal* 105:18 (October 15, 1980), 2168-2169.

241   Kathleen M. Heim and Leigh S. Estabrook. "Career Patterns of Librarians,"
          Drexel Library Quarterly 17:3 (Summer 1981), 35-51.

242   Margaret Peil. "Library Use by Low-Income Chicago Families," *Library
          Quarterly* 33:4 (October 1963), 329-333.

243   Herbert Goldhor and John McCrossan. "An Exploratory Study of the Effect
          of a Public Library Summer Reading Club on Reading Skills," *Library
          Quarterly* 36:1 (June 1966), 14-24.

244   Robert Sommer. "Reading Areas in College Libraries," *Library Quarterly*
          38:3 (July 1968), 249-260.

245   Isaac T. Littleton. "The Literature of Agricultural Economics: Its Biblio-
          graphic Organization and Use," *Library Quarterly* 39:2 (April 1969),
          140-152.

246 G. Edward Evans. "Book Selection and Book Collection Usage in Academic Libraries," *Library Quarterly* 40:3 (July 1970), 297-308.

247 Marilyn Werstein Greenberg. "A Study of Reading Motivation of Twenty-Three Seventh-Grade Students," *Library Quarterly* 40:3 (July 1970), 309-317.

248 Ben-Ami Lipetz. "Catalog Use in a Large Research Library," *Library Quarterly* 42:1 (January 1972), 129-130. (**133, 134, 190, 195, 196, 200**)

249 John Aubry. "A Timing Study of the Manual Searching of Catalogs," *Library Quarterly* 42:4 (October 1972), 399-415. (**129, 137**)

250 Kenneth H. Plate and Elizabeth W. Stone. "Factors Affecting Librarians' Job Satisfaction: A Report of Two Studies," *Library Quarterly* 44:2 (April 1974), 97-109.

251 Elizabeth Warner McElroy. "Subject Variety in Adult Reading: I. Factors Related to Variety in Reading," *Library Quarterly* 38:1 (April 1968), 154-167.

252 James C. Baughman. "A Structural Analysis of the Literature of Sociology," *Library Quarterly* 44:4 (October 1974), 293-308.

253 Edd E. Wheeler. "The Bottom Lines: Fifty Years of Legal Footnoting in Review," *Law Library Journal* 72:2 (Spring 1979), 245-259.

254 Daniel O'Connor and Phyllis Van Orden. "Getting into Print," *College and Research Libraries* 39:5 (September 1978), 389-396.

255 Howard Fosdick. "Library Education in Information Science: Present Trends," *Special Libraries* 69:3 (March 1978), 100-108.

256 Paula de Simone Watson. "Publication Activity among Academic Librarians," *College and Research Libraries* 38:5 (September 1977), 375-384.

257 Susan Andriette Ariew. "The Failure of the Open Access Residence Hall Library," *College and Research Libraries* 39:5 (September 1978), 372-380.

258 Mary Ellen Soper. "Characteristics and Use of Personal Collections," *Library Quarterly* (October 1976), 397-415.

259 Ronald R. Powell. "An Investigation of the Relationships Between Quantifiable Reference Service Variables and Reference Performance in Public Libraries," *Library Quarterly* 48:1 (January 1978), 1-19.

260 Mary Jo Lynch. "Reference Interviews in Public Libraries," *Library Quarterly* 48:2 (April 1978), 119-142.

261 William A. Satariano. "Journal Use in Sociology: Citation Analysis versus Readership Patterns," *Library Quarterly* 48:3 (July 1978), 293-300.

262   Paul Metz. "The Use of the General Collection in the Library of Congress," *Library Quarterly* 49:4 (October 1979), 415-434.

263   Michael Halperin and Maureen Strazdon. "Measuring Students' Preferences for Reference Service: A Conjoint Analysis," *Library Quarterly* 50:2 (April 1980), 208-224.

264   Herbert S. White. "Factors in the Decisions by Individuals and Libraries To Place or Cancel Subscriptions to Scholarly and Research Journals," *Library Quarterly* 50:3 (July 1980), 287-309.

265   George D'Elia. "The Development and Testing of a Conceptual Model of Public Library User Behavior," *Library Quarterly* 50:4 (October 1980), 410-430.

266   Donald A. Hicks. "Diversifying Fiscal Support by Pricing Public Library Services: A Policy Impact Analysis," *Library Quarterly* 50:4 (October 1980), 453-474.

267   Theodora Hodges and Uri Block. "Fiche or Film for COM Catalogs: Two Use Tests," *Library Quarterly* 52:2 (April 1982), 131-144. **(141, 142)**

268   Terry L. Weech and Herbert Goldhor. "Obtrusive versus Unobtrusive Evaluation of Reference Service in Five Illinois Public Libraries: A Pilot Study," *Library Quarterly* 52:4 (October 1982), 305-324.

269   Stephen E. Wiberley, Jr. "Journal Rankings From Citation Studies: A Comparison of National and Local Data From Social Work," *Library Quarterly* 52:4 (October 1982), 348-359.

270   George D'Elia and Sandra Walsh. "User Satisfaction with Library Service— A Measure of Public Library Performance?" *Library Quarterly* 53:2 (April 1983), 109-133.

271   Edward A. Dyl. "A Note on Price Discrimination by Academic Journals," *Library Quarterly* 53:2 (April 1983), 161-168.

272   Michael R. Kronenfeld and James A. Thompson. "The Impact of Inflation on Journal Costs," *Library Journal* 106:7 (April 1,1981), 714-717.

273   George D'Elia and Mary K. Chelton. "Paperback Books," *Library Journal* 107:16 (September 15, 1982), 1718-1721.

274   Patsy Hansel and Robert Burgin. "Hard Facts about Overdues," *Library Journal* 108:4 (February 15, 1983), 349-352.

275   Robert Dale Karr. "Becoming a Library Director," *Library Journal* 108:4 (February 15, 1983), 343-346.

276   Mary V. Gaver. "The Science Collection—New Evidence To Consider," *Junior Libraries* (later *School Library Journal*) 7:6 (February 1961), 4-7.

277   Dorothy G. Petersen. "Teachers' Professional Reading," *School Library Journal* 9:8 (April 1963), 24-27.

278 Linda Kraft. "Lost Herstory: The Treatment of Women in Children's Encyclopedias," *School Library Journal* 19:5 (January 1973), 26-35.

279 John Stewig and Margaret Higgs. "Girls Grow Up: A Study of Sexism in Children's Literature," *School Library Journal* 19:5 (January 1973), 44-49.

280 W. Bernard Lukenbill. "Fathers in Adolescent Novels," *School Library Journal* 20:6 (February 1974), 26-30.

281 Jacqueline C. Mancall and M. Carl Drott. "Tomorrow's Scholars: Patterns of Facilities Use," *School Library Journal* 20:7 (March 1980), 99-103.

282 John McCrossan. "Education of Librarians Employed in Small Public Libraries," *Journal of Education for Librarianship* 7:4 (Spring 1967), 237-245.

283 Gail Schlachter and Dennis Thomison. "The Library Science Doctorate: A Quantitative Analysis of Dissertations and Recipients," *Journal of Education for Librarianship* 15:2 (Fall 1974), 95-111.

284 Constance Rinehart and Rose Mary Magrill. "Characteristics of Applicants for Library Science Teaching Positions," *Journal of Education for Librarianship* 16:3 (Winter 1976), 173-182.

285 George W. Whitbeck. "Grade Inflation in the Library School—Myth or Reality," *Journal of Education for Librarianship* 17:4 (Spring 1977), 214-237.

286 Charles H. Davis. "Computer Programming for Librarians," *Journal of Education for Librarianship* 18:1 (Summer 1977), 41-52.

287 Helen M. Gothberg. "A Study of the Audio-Tutorial Approach to Teaching Basic Reference," *Journal of Education for Librarianship* 18:3 (Winter 1978), 193-202.

288 J. Periam Danton. "British and American Library School Teaching Staffs: A Comparative Inquiry," *Journal of Education for Librarianship* 19:2 (Fall 1978), 97-129.

289 Lucille Whalen. "The Role of the Assistant Dean in Library Schools," *Journal of Education for Librarianship* 20:1 (Summer 1979), 44-54.

290 A. Neil Yerkey. "Values of Library School Students, Faculty and Librarians: Premises for Understanding," *Journal of Education for Librarianship* 21:2 (Fall 1980), 122-134.

291 Judith B. Katz. "Indicators of Success: Queens College Department of Library Science," *Journal of Education for Librarianship* 19:2 (Fall 1978), 130-139.

292 Lawrence Auld, Kathleen H. Heim and Jerome Miller. "Market Receptivity for an Extended M.L.S.," *Journal of Education for Librarianship* 21:3 (Winter 1981), 235-245.

293 John Richardson, Jr. and Peter Hernon. "Theory vs. Practice: Student Preferences," *Journal of Education for Librarianship* 21:4 (Spring 1981), 287-300,

294 Richard I. Blue and James L. Divilbiss. "Optimizing Selection of Library School Students," *Journal of Education for Librarianship* 21:4 (Spring 1981), 301-312.

295 David H. Jonassen and Gerald G. Hodges. "Student Cognitive Styles: Implications for Library Educators," *Journal of Education for Librarianship* 22:3 (Winter 1982), 143-153.

296 Mary Kingsbury. "How Library Schools Evaluate Faculty Performance," *Journal of Education for Librarianship* 22:4 (Spring 1982), 219-238.

297 John W. Lee and Raymond L. Read. "The Graduate Business Student and the Library," *College and Research Libraries* 33:5 (September 1972), 403-407.

298 Carol Steer. "Authors Are Studied," *Canadian Library Journal* 39:3 (June 1982), 151-155.

299 Rashid Tayyeb. "Implementing AACR 2—A National Survey," *Canadian Library Journal* 39:6 (December 1982), 373-376. **(3, 127, 131, 153, 164)**

300 Dick Matzek and Scott Smith. "Online Searching in the Small College Library—The Economics and the Results," *Online* (March 1982), 21-29.

301 Mary Lee Bundy. "Metropolitan Public Library Use," *Wilson Library Bulletin* 41:9 (May 1967), 950-961.

302 John Shipman. "Signifying Renewal as Well as Change: One Library's Experience with the Center for Research Libraries," *Library Acquisitions: Practice and Theory* 2:5 (1978), 243-248.

303 Nathan R. Einhorn. "The Inclusion of the Products of Reprography in the International Exchange of Publications," *Library Acquisitions: Practice and Theory* 2:5 (1978), 227-236

304 Nancy J. Williamson. "Education for Acquisitions Librarians: A State of the Art Review," *Library Acquisitions: Practice and Theory* 2:3-4 (1978), 199-208.

305 Janet L. Flowers. "Time Logs for Searchers: How Useful?" *Library Acquisitions: Practice and Theory* 2:2 (1978), 77-83.

306 D.N. Wood. "Current Exchange of Serials at the British Library Lending Division," *Library Acquisitions: Practice and Theory* 3:2 (1979), 107-113.

307 Robert Goehlert. "Journal Use Per Monetary Unit: A Reanalysis of Use Data," *Library Acquisitions: Practice and Theory* 3:2 (1979), 91-98.

308 Margaret Landesman and Christopher Gates. "Performance of American Inprint Vendors: A Comparison at the University of Utah," *Library Acquisitions: Practice and Theory* 4:3-4 (1980), 187-192.

309 Kenton Pattie and Mary Ernst. "Chapter II Grants: Libraries Gain," *School Library Journal* 29:5 (January 1983), 17-19.

310 John Erlandson and Yvonne Boyer. "Acquistions of State Documents," *Library Acquisitions: Practice and Theory* 4:2 (1980), 117-127.

311 George V. Hodowanec. "Analysis of Variables Which Help To Predict Book and Periodical Use," *Library Acquisitions: Practice and Theory* 4:1 (1980), 75-85.

312 Darrell L. Jenkins. "Acquiring Acquisitions Librarians," *Library Acquisitions: Practice and Theory* 5:2 (1981), 81-87.

313 Steven E. Maffeo. "Invoice Payment by Library Acquisitions: A Controlled Time Study," *Library Acquisitions: Practice and Theory* 5:2 (1981), 67-71.

314 Joyce G. McDonough, Carol Alf O'Connor and Thomas A. O'Connor. "Moving the Backlog: An Optimum Cycle for Searching OCLC," *Library Acquisitions: Practice and Theory* 6:3 (1982), 265-270. (**16, 17, 60, 61**)

315 Paul B. Wiener. "Recreational Reading Services in Academic Libraries: An Overview," *Library Acquisitions: Practice and Theory* 6:1 (1982), 59-70.

316 Peter Hernon. "Use of Microformatted Government Publications," *Microform Review* 11:4 (Fall 1982), 237-252.

317 Charles R. McClure. "Online Government Documents Data Base Searching and the Use of Microfiche Documents Online by Academic and Public Depository Librarians," *Microfilm Review* 10:4 (Fall 1981), 245-259.

318 Peter Hernon and George W. Whitbeck. "Government Publications and Commercial Microform Publishers: A Survey of Federal Depository Libraries," *Microform Review* 6:5 (September 1977), 272-284.

319 Robert F. Jennings and Hathia Hayes. "The Use of Microfiche Copies of Children's Trade Books in Selected Fourth-Grade Classrooms," *Microform Review* 3:3 (July 1974), 189-193.

320 E.R. Norten. "New Books in Microform: A Survey," *Microform Review* 1:4 (October 1972), 284-288.

321 Renata Tagliacozzo, Manfred Kochen and Lawrence Rosenberg. "Orthographic Error Patterns of Author Names in Catalog Searches," *Journal of Library Automation* 3:2 (June 1970), 93-101. (**191, 193, 194, 196**)

322 Lorne R. Buhr. "Selective Dissemination of MARC: A User Evaluation," *Journal of Library Automation* 5:1 (March 1972), 39-50.

323 Gerry D. Guthrie and Steven D. Slifko. "Analysis of Search Key Retrieval on a Large Bibliographic File," *Journal of Library Automation* 6:2 (June 1972), 96-100. **(158, 177, 178)**

324 Alan L. Landgraf and Frederick G. Kilgour. "Catalog Records Retrieved by Personal Author Using Derived Search Keys," *Journal of Library Automation* 6:2 (June 1973), 103-108. **(177)**

325 Martha E. Williams. "Data Element Statistics for the MARC II Data Base," *Journal of Library Automation* 6:2 (June 1976), 89-100. **(48)**

326 Michael D. Cooper and Nancy A. DeWath. "The Cost of On-Line Bibliographic Searching," *Journal of Library Automation* 9:3 (September 1976), 195-209.

327 Edward John Kazlauskas. "The Application of the Instrumental Development Process to a Module on Flowcharting," *Journal of Library Automation* 9:3 (September 1976), 234-244.

328 Lawrence K. Legard and Charles P. Bourne. "An Improved Title Word Search Key for Large Catalog Files," *Journal of Library Automation* 9:4 (December 1976), 318-327. **(178)**

329 Ryan E. Hoover. "Patron Appraisal of Computer-Aided On-Line Bibliographic Retrieval Services," *Journal of Library Automation* 9:4 (December 1976), 335-350.

330 T.D.C. Kuch. "Analysis of the Literature of Library Automation through Citations in the *Annual Review of Information Science and Technology*," *Journal of Library Automation* 10:1 (March 1977), 82-84.

331 Isobel Jean Mosley. "Cost-Effectiveness Analysis of the Automation of a Circulation System," *Journal of Library Automation* 10:3 (September 1977), 240-254.

332 Michael D. Cooper and Nancy A. DeWath. "The Effect of User Fees on the Cost of On-Line Searching in Libraries," *Journal of Library Automation* 10:4 (December 1977), 304-319.

333 James W. Bourg, Douglas Lacy, James Llinas and Edward T. O'Neill. "Developing Corporate Author Search Keys," *Journal of Library Automation* 11:2 (June 1978), 106-125. **(178)**

334 Cynthia C. Ryans. "A Study of Errors Found in Non-MARC Cataloging in a Machine-Assisted System," *Journal of Library Automation* 11:2 (June 1978), 125-132. **(65)**

335 Joselyn Druschel. "Cost Analysis of an Automated and Manual Cataloging and Book Processing System," *Journal of Library Automation* 14:1 (March 1981), 24-49. **(44, 83)**

336 Kunj B. Bastogi and Ichiko T. Morita. "OCLC Search Key Usage Patterns in a Large Research Library," *Journal of Library Automation* 14:2 (June 1981), 90-99. (**76, 92, 106, 160, 178, 202**)

337 Georgia L. Brown. "AACR 2: OCLC's Implementation and Database Conversion," *Journal of Library Automation* 14:3 (September 1981), 161-173. (**3, 57, 127, 158**)

338 James R. Martin. "Automation and the Service Attitudes of ARL Circulation Managers," *Journal of Library Automation* 14:3 (September 1981), 190-194.

339 University of Oregon Library. "A Comparison of OCLC, RLG/RLIN and WLN," *Journal of Library Automation* 14:3 (September 1981), 215-217.

340 Terence Crowley. "Comparing Fiche and Film: A Test of Speed," *Journal of Library Automation* 14:4 (December 1981), 292-294. (**140, 142**)

341 Public Service Satellite Consortium. "Cable Library Survey Results," *Journal of Library Automation* 14:4 (December 1981), 304-313.

342 Dennis Reynolds. "Entry of Local Data on OCLC: The Options and Their Impact on the Processing of Archival Tapes," *Information Technology and Libraries* 1:1 (March 1982), 5-14. (**66, 70, 71, 90, 91, 93, 94**)

343 Joseph Ford. "Network Service Centers and Their Expanding Role," *Information Technology and Libraries* 1:1 (March 1982), 28-35.

344 Carolyn A. Johnson. "Retrospective Conversion of Three Library Collections," *Information Technology and Libraries* 1:2 (June 1982), 133-139. (**76**)

345 Lynn L. Magrath. "Computers in the Library: The Human Element," *Information Technology and Libraries* 1:3 (September 1982), 266-270. (**138, 163, 164**)

346 Izabella Taler. "Automated and Manual ILL: Time Effectiveness and Success Rate," *Information Technology and Libraries* 1:3 (September 1982), 277-280.

347 Martha E. Williams, Stephen W. Barth and Scott E. Preece. "Summary of Statistics for Five Years of the MARC Data Base," *Journal of Library Automation* 12:4 (December 1979), 314-337. (**28, 48, 49**)

348 Susan U. Golden and Gary A. Golden. "Access to Periodicals: Search Key versus Keyword," *Information Technology and Libraries* 2:1 (March 1983), 26-32. (**179**)

349 Ray R. Larson and Vicki Graham. "Monitoring and Evaluating MELVYL," *Information Technology and Libraries* 2:1 (March 1983), 93-104. (**138, 162, 163, 192, 193, 194, 196**)

350   Barbara E. Carr. "Improving the Periodicals Collection through an Index Correlation Study," *Reference Services Review* 9:4 (October/December 1981), 27-31.

351   I.N. Sengupta. "Impact of Scientific Serials on the Advancement of Medical Knowledge: An Objective Method of Analysis," *International Library Review* 4:2 (April 1972), 169-195.

352   June L. Stewart. "The Literature of Politics: A Citation Analysis," *International Library Review* 2:3 (July 1970), 329-353.

353   I.N. Sengupta. "The Literature of Microbiology," *International Library Review* 6:3 (July 1974), 353-369.

354   I.N. Sengupta. "The Literature of Pharmacology," *International Library Review* 6:4 (October 1974), 483-504.

355   A.W. Hafner. "Citation Characteristics of Physiology Literature, 1970-72," *International Library Review* 8:1 (January 1976), 85-115.

356   Hans Hanan Wellisch. "Script Conversion Practices in the World's Libraries," *International Library Review* 8:1 (January 1976), 55-84. **(94, 95, 96, 97, 142, 151, 174, 175, 176)**

357   Christine Anderson Brock and Gayle Smith Edelman. "Teaching Practices of Academic Law Librarians," *Law Library Journal* 71:1 (February 1978), 96-107.

358   Charles B. Wolfe. "Current Problems Facing State Law Libraries," *Law Library Journal* 71:1 (February 1978), 108-114).

359   Mindy J. Myers. "The Impact of Lexis on the Law Firm Library: A Survey," *Law Library Journal* 71:1 (February 1978), 158-169.

360   Nancy P. Johnson. "Legal Periodical Usage Survey: Method and Application," *Law Library Journal* 71:1 (February 1978), 177-186.

361   Ann M. Carter. "Budgeting in Private Law Firm Libraries," *Law Library Journal* 71:1 (February 1978), 187-194.

362   James F. Bailey, III and Oscar M. Trelles, II. "Autonomy, Librarian Status, and Librarian Tenure in Law School Libraries: The State of the Art, 1978," *Law Library Journal* 71:3 (August 1978), 425-462. **(82, 86)**

363   Frank Wm. Goudy. "Funding Local Public Libraries: FY 1966 to FY 1980," *Public Libraries* 21:2 (Summer 1982), 52-54.

364   Guy Garrison. "A Look At Research on Public Library Problems in the 1970's," *Public Libraries* 19:1 (Spring 1980), 4-8.

365   Terry L. Weech. "School and Public Library Cooperation—What We Would Like To Do, What We Do," *Public Libraries* 18:2 (Summer 1979), 33-34.

366 Patricia L. Piper and Cecilia Hing Ling Kwan. "Cataloging and Classification Practices in Law Libraries: Results of a Questionnaire," *Law Library Journal* 71:3 (August 1978), 481-483. **(8, 9, 34, 36, 81, 86, 104, 117, 120, 129, 130, 131, 132, 133, 141, 144, 145, 150, 166, 168)**

367 Christian M. Boissonnas. "The Quality of OCLC Bibliographic Records: The Cornell Law Library Experience," *Law Library Journal* 72:1 (Winter 1979), 80-85. **(14, 18, 19, 20, 22, 50, 52, 53, 71, 73, 99, 101)**

368 Kent Schrieffer and Linnea Christiani. "Ballots at Boalt," *Law Library Journal* 72:3 (Summer 1979), 497-512. **(8, 9, 10, 50, 53)**

369 Ermina Hahn. "Survey of Technical Services Practices at Fifty Large Law School Libraries," *Law Library Journal* 73:3 (Summer 1980), 715-725. **(35, 36, 40, 41, 143, 144, 145, 148, 150, 167, 168)**

370 Lana Caswell Garcia. "Legal Services Law Librarianship—An Investigation of Salary and Benefits in a Pioneer Field," *Law Library Journal* 73:3 (Summer 1980), 731-733.

371 Reynold J. Kosek. "Faculty Status and Tenure for Nondirector, Academic Law Librarians" a section within "Status of Academic Law Librarians," *Law Library Journal* 73:4 (Fall 1980), 892-905.

372 Martha C. Adamson and Gloria J. Zamora. "Authorship Characteristics in *Law Library Journal*: A Comparative Study," *Law Library Journal* 74:3 (Summer 1981), 527-533.

373 David G. Badertscher. "An Examination of the Dynamics of Change in Information Technology as Viewed from Law Libraries and Information Centers," *Law Library Journal* 75:2 (Spring 1982), 198-211.

374 Donald J. Dunn. "The Law Librarian's Obligation To Publish," *Law Library Journal* 75:2 (Spring 1982), 225-231.

375 Audio-Visual Committee, American Association of Law Libraries. "Summary of Audio-Visual Materials Used in Legal Education: Audio-Visual Committee Report—June 1967," *Law Library Journal* 60:3 (August 1967), 272-276.

376 Cameron Allen. "Duplicate Holding Practices of Approved American Law School Libraries." *Law Library Journal* 62:2 (May 1969), 191-200.

377 Margaret Shediac. "Private Law Libraries Special Interest Section 1980 Salary Survey," *Law Library Journal* 74:2 (Spring 1981), 444-457.

378 Bettie H. Scott. "Price Index for Legal Publications," *Law Library Journal* 75:1 (Winter 1982), 171-174.

379 Silvia A. Gonzalez. "County Law Library Survey," *Law Library Journal* 74:3 (Summer 1981), 654-691. **(167)**

380 Silvia A. Gonzalez. "Survey of State Law Libraries," *Law Library Journal* 74:1 (Winter 1981), 160-201.

381   Silvia A. Gonzalez. "Survey of Court Law Libraries," *Law Library Journal* 74:2 (Spring 1981), 458-494.

382   David A. Thomas. "1980 Statistical Survey of Law School Libraries and Librarians," *Law Library Journal* 74:2 (Spring 1981), 359-443.

383   Marija Hughes. "Sex-Based Discrimination in Law Libraries," *Law Library Journal* 64:1 (February 1971), 13-22.

384   Oscar M. Trelles. "Law Libraries and Unions," *Law Library Journal* 65:2 (May 1972), 158-180.

385   Claudia Sumler, Kristine Barone and Art Goetz. "Getting Books Faster and Cheaper: A Jobber Acquisitions Study," *Public Libraries* 19:4 (Winter 1980), 103-105.

386   Vernon A. Rayford. "A Black Librarian Takes a Look at Discrimination: by a Law School Library Survey," *Law Library Journal* 65:2 (May 1972), 183-189.

387   Audio-Visual Committee, American Association of Law Libraries. "The Use of Audio-Visual Teaching Aids and Library Microforms in American Legal Education," *Law Library Journal* 66:1 (February 1973), 84-87.

388   Cameron Allen. "Whom We Shall Serve: Secondary Patrons of the University Law School Library," *Law Library Journal* 66:2 (May 1973), 160-171.

389   O. James Werner. "The Present Legal Status and Conditions of Prison Law Libraries," *Law Library Journal* 66:3 (August 1973), 259-269.

390   George S. Grossman. "Clinical Legal Education and the Law Library," *Law Library Journal* 67:1 (February 1974), 60-78.

391   Kurt Schwerin and Igor I. Kavass. "Foreign Legal Periodicals in American Law Libraries 1973 Union List," *Law Library Journal* 67:1 (February 1974), 120-126.

392   Bethany J. Ochal. "County Law Libraries," *Law Library Journal* 67:2 (May 1974), 177-234.

393   Peter Enyingi. "Subject Cataloging Practices in American Law Libraries: A Survey," *Law Library Journal* 68:1 (February 1975), 11-17.(**85, 86, 117, 118, 142, 143, 144, 150, 168**)

394   Sandra Sadow and Benjamin R. Beede. "Library Instruction in American Law Schools," *Law Library Journal* 68:1 (February 1975), 27-32.

395   Michael L. Richmond. "Attitudes of Law Librarians to Theft and Mutilation Control Methods," *Law Library Journal* 68:1 (February 1975), 60-81.

396 Ellin B. Christianson. "Mergers in the Publishing Industry, 1958-1970," *Journal of Library History, Philosophy and Comparative Librarianship* 7:1 (January 1972), 5-32.

397 Eugene E. Graziano. "Interlibrary Loan Analysis: Diagnostic for Scientific Serials Backfile Acquisitions," *Special Libraries* 53:5 (May/June 1962), 251-257.

398 John E. James. "Library Technician Program: The Library Technician Graduates' Point of View," *Special Libraries* 62:6 (July/August 1971), 268-278.

399 James M. Matarazzo. "Scientific Journals: Page or Price Explosion?" *Special Libraries* 63:2 (February 1972), 53-58.

400 Julie L. Moore. "Bibliographic Control of American Doctoral Dissertations," *Special Libraries* 63:7 (July 1972), 285-291.

401 Robert T. Bottle and William W. Chase. "Some Characteristics of the Literature on Music and Musicology," *Special Libraries* 63:10 (October 1972), 469-476.

402 William P. Koughan and John A. Timour. "Are Hospital Libraries Meeting Physicians' Information Needs?" *Special Libraries* 64:5/6 (May/June 1972), 222-227.

403 Jean M. Ray. "Who Borrows Maps from a University Library Map Collection —And Why?" *Special Libraries* 65:3 (March 1974), 104-109.

404 Ching-Chih Chen. "How Do Scientists Meet Their Information Needs?" *Special Libraries* 65:7 (July 1974), 272-280.

405 Katherine C. Owen. "Productive Journal Titles in the Pharmaceutical Industry," *Special Libraries* 65:10/11 (October/November 1974), 430-439.

406 Stanley A. Elman. "Cost Comparison of Manual and On-Line Computerized Literature Searching," *Special Libraries* 66:1 (January 1975), 12-18.

407 Jerome P. Fatcheric. "Survey of Users of a Medium-Sized Technical Library," *Special Libraries* 66:5/6 (May/June 1975), 245-251.

408 Bahaa El-Hadidy. "Bibliographic Control among Geoscience Abstracting and Indexing Services," *Special Libraries* 66:5/6 (May/June 1975), 260-265.

409 Ruth W. Wender. "Hospital Journal Title Usage Study," *Special Libraries* 66:11 (November 1975), 532-537.

410 Thelma Freides. "Bibliographic Gaps in the Social Science Literature," *Special Libraries* 67:2 (February 1976), 68-75.

411 Eileen E. Hitchingham. "MEDLINE Use in a University without a School of Medicine," *Special Libraries* 67:4 (April 1976), 188-194.

412 David Hull and Henry D. Fearnley. "The Museum Library in the United States: A Sample," *Special Libraries* 67:7 (July 1976), 289-298.

413 Amelia Breiting, Marcia Dorey and Deirdre Sockbeson. "Staff Development in College and University Libraries," *Special Libraries* 67:7 (July 1976), 305-309.

414 Arley L. Ripin and Dorothy Kasman. "Education for Special Librarianship: A Survey of Courses Offered in Accredited Programs," *Special Libraries* 67:11 (November 1976), 504-509.

415 George W. Black, Jr. "Selected Annaul Bound Volume Production," *Special Libraries* 67:11 (November 1976), 534-536.

416 Howard Fosdick. "An SDC-Based On-Line Search Service: A Patron Evaluation Survey and Implications," *Special Libraries* 68:9 (September 1977), 305-312.

417 Diane M. Nelson. "Methods of Citation Analysis in the Fine Arts," *Special Libraries* 68:11 (November 1977), 390-395.

418 Annette Corth. "Coverage of Marine Biology Citations,"*Special Libraries* 68:12 (December 1977), 439-446.

419 Jean K. Martin. "Computer-Based Literature Searching: Impact on Interlibrary Loan Service," *Special Libaries* 69:1 (January 1978), 1-6.

420 Jean M. Ray. "Who Borrows Maps from a University Library Map Collection —and Why? Report II," *Special Libraries* 69:1 (January 1978), 13-20.

421 Robert Goehlert. "Periodical Use in an Academic Library: A Study of Economists and Political Scientists," *Special Libraries* 69:2 (February 1978), 51-60.

422 Sandra J. Springer, Robert A. Yokel, Nancy M. Lorenzi, Leonard T. Sigell and E. Don Nelson. "Drug Information to Patient Care Areas via Television: Preliminary Evaluation of Two Years' Experience," *Special Libraries* 69:4 (April 1978), 155-163. **(161)**

423 Martha J. Bailey. "Requirement for Middle Managerial Positions," *Special Libraries* 69:9 (September 1978), 323-331.

424 Carolyn L. Warden. "An Industrial Current Awareness Service: A User Evaluation Study," *Special Libraries* 69:12 (December 1978), 459-467.

425 Charles H. Davis. "Programming Aptitude as a Function of Undergraduate Major," *Special Libraries* 69:12 (December 1978), 482-485.

426 Jean Mace Schmidt. "Translation of Periodical Literature in Plant Pathology," *Special Libraries* 70:1 (January 1979), 12-17.

427 Susan Dingle-Cliff and Charles H. Davis. "Collection Overlap in Canadian Addictions Libraries," *Special Libraries* 70:2 (February 1979), 76-81.

428 John J. Knightly. "Overcoming the Cirterion Problem in the Evaluation of Library Performance," *Special Libraries* 70:4 (April 1979), 173-178.

429 Ruth W. Wender. "Counting Journal Title Usage in the Health Sciences," *Special Libraries* 70:5/6 (May/June 1975), 219-226.

430 John Steuben. "Interlibrary Loan of Photocopies of Articles under the New Copyright Law," *Special Libraries* 70:5/6 (May/June 1979), 227-232.

431 John Kok and Edward G. Strable. "Moving Up: Librarians Who Have Become Officers of Their Organization," *Special Libraries* 71:1 (January 1980), 5-12.

432 Rebecca J. Jensen, Herbert D. Asbury and Radford G. King. "Costs and Benefits to Industry of Online Literature Searches," *Special Libraries* 71:7 (July 1980), 291-299.

433 C. Margaret Bell. "The Applicability of OCLC and Inforonics in Special Libraries," *Special Libraries* 71:9 (September 1980), 398-404. **(10, 76, 77)**

434 A. Neil Yerkey. "The Psychological Climate of Librarianship: Values of Special Librarians," *Special Libraries* 72:3 (July 1981), 195-200.

435 Virgil P. Diodato. "Author Indexing," *Special Libraries* 72:4 (October 1981), 361-369.

436 Judith M. Pask. "Bibliographic Instruction in Business Libraries," *Special Libraries* 72:4 (October 1981), 370-378.

437 Ann T. Dodson, Paul P. Philbin and Kunj B. Rastogi. "Electronic Interlibrary Loan in the OCLC Library: A Study of its Effectiveness," *Special Libraries* 73:1 (January 1982), 12-20.

438 Gloria J. Zamora and Martha C. Adamson. "Authorship Characteristics in *Special Libraries*: A Comparative Study," *Special Libraries* 73:2 (April 1982), 100-107.

439 Robert K. Poyer. "Time Lag in Four Indexing Services," *Special Libraries* 73:2 (April 1982), 142-146.

440 Pauline R. Hodges. "Keyword in Title Indexes: Effectiveness of Retrieval in Computer Searches," *Special Libraries* 74:1 (January 1983), 56-60.

441 D.K. Varma. "Increased Subscription Costs and Problems of Resource Allocation," *Special Libraries* 74:1 (January 1983), 61-66.

442 Michael Halperin and Ruth A. Pagell. "Searchers' Perceptions of Online Database Vendors," *Special Libraries* 74:2 (April 1973), 119-126.

443 Michael E.D. Koenig. "Education for Special Librarianship," *Special Libraries* 74:2 (April 1983), 182-196.

444 Powell Niland and William H. Kurth. "Estimating Lost Volumes in a University Library Collection," *College and Research Libraries* 37:2 (March 1976), 128-136.

445 Rush G. Miller. "The Influx of Ph.D.s into Librarianship: Intrusion or Transfusion?" *College and Research Libraries* 37:2 (March 1976), 158-165.

446 Steven Leach. "The Growth Rates of Major Academic Libraries: Rider and Purdue Reviewed," *College and Research Libraries* 37:6 (November 1976), 531-542.

447 T. Saracevic, W.M. Shaw, Jr. and P.B. Kantor. "Causes and Dynamics of User Frustration in an Academic Library," *College and Research Libraries* 38:1 (January 1977), 7-18.

448 R.W. Meyer and Rebecca Panetta. "Two Shared Cataloging Data Bases: A Comparison," *College and Research Libraries* 38:1 (January 1977), 19-24. **(7, 23, 75)**

449 Peter Hernon and Maureen Pastine. "Student Perceptions of Academic Librarians," *College and Research Libraries* 38:2 (March 1977), 129-139.

450 Catherine V. Von Schon. "Inventory 'By Computer'," *College and Research Libraries* 38:2 (March 1977), 147-152.

451 David C. Genaway and Edward B. Stanford. "Quasi-Departmental Libraries," *College and Research Libraries* 38:3 (May 1977), 187-194.

452 Elizabeth W. Matthews. "Trends Affecting Community College Library Administrators," *College and Research Libraries* 38:3 (May 1977), 210-217. **(30, 34, 39, 54, 157, 166)**

453 Lawrence J. Perk. "Secondary Publications in Education: A Study of Duplication," *College and Research Libraries* 38:3 (May 1977), 221-226.

454 Geraldine Murphy Wright. "Current Trends in Periodical Collections," *College and Research Libraries* 38:3 (May 1977), 234-240.

455 Lawrence J. Perk and Noelle Van Pulis. "Periodical Usage in an Education-Psychology Library," *College and Research Libraries* 38:4 (July 1977), 304-308.

456 Egill A. Halldorsson and Marjorie E. Murfin. "The Performance of Professionals and Nonprofessionals in the Reference Interview," *College and Research Libraries* 38:5 (September 1977), 385-395.

457 Susan A. Lee. "Conflict and Ambiguity in the Role of the Academic Library Director," *College and Research Libraries* 38:5 (September 1977), 396-403.

458 Glenn R. Wittig. "Dual Pricing of Periodicals," *College and Research Libraries* 38:5 (September 1977), 412-418.

459 Miriam A. Drake. "Attribution of Library Costs," *College and Research Libraries* 38:6 (November 1977), 514-519.

460 Harry M. Kriz. "Subscriptions vs. Books in a Constant Dollar Budget," *College and Research Libraries* 39:2 (March 1978), 105-109.

461 Charles J. Popovich. "The Characteristics of a Collection for Research in Business/Management," *College and Research Libraries* 39:2 (March 1978), 117.

462 Jean A. Major. "The Visually Impaired Reader in the Academic Library," *College and Research Libraries* 39:3 (May 1978), 191-196.

463 Herbert S. White and Karen Momenee. "Impact of the Increase in Library Doctorates," *College and Research Libraries* 39:3 (May 1978), 207-214.

464 James Michalko and Toby Heidtmann. "Evaluating the Effectiveness of an Electronic Security System," *College and Research Libraries* 39:4 (July 1978), 263-267.

465 William M. McClellan. "Judging Music Libraries," *College and Research Libraries* 39:4 (July 1978), 281-286.

466 Rita Hoyt Smith and Warner Granade. "User and Library Failures in an Undergraduate Library," *College and Research Libraries* 39:6 (November 1978), 467-473.

467 Linda Ann Hulbert and David Stewart Curry. "Evaluation of an Approval Plan," *College and Research Libraries* 39:6 (November 1978), 485-491.

468 Julia F. Baldwin and Robert S. Rudolph. "The Comparative Effectiveness of a Slide/Tape Show and a Library Tour," *College and Research Libraries* 40:1 (January 1979), 31-35.

469 Melissa D. Trevvett. "Characteristics of Interlibrary Loan Requests at the Library of Congress," *College and Research Libraries* 40:1 (January 1979), 36-43.

470 Elaine Zaremba Jennerich and Bessie Hess Smith. "A Bibliographic Instruction Program in Music," *College and Research Libraries* 40:3 (May 1979), 226-233.

471 William J. Maher and Benjamin F. Shearer. "Undergraduate Use Patterns of Newspapers on Microfilm," *College and Research Libraries* 40:3 (May 1979), 254-260.

472 Larry Hardesty, Nicholas P. Lovrich, Jr. and James Mannon. "Evaluating Library-Use Instruction," *College and Research Libraries* 40:4 (July 1979), 309-317.

473 Seymour H. Sargent. "The Uses and Limitations of Trueswell," *College and Research Libraries* 40:5 (September 1979), 416-425.

474 Patricia Stenstrom and Ruth B. McBride." Serial Use by Social Science Faculty: A Survey," *College and Research Libraries* 40:5 (September 1979), 426-431.

475 Elaine C. Clever. "Using Indexes as 'Memory Assists'," *College and Research Libraries* 40:5 (September 1979), 444-449.

476 William E. McGrath, Donald J. Simon and Evelyn Bullard. "Ethnocentricity and Cross-Disciplinary Circulation," *College and Research Libraries* 40:6 (November 1979), 511-518.

477 Michael Gorman and Jami Hotsinpiller. "ISBD: Aid or Barrier to Understanding," *College and Research Libraries* 40:6 (November 1979), 519-526. **(152)**

478 Jinnie Y. Davis and Stella Bentley. "Factors Affecting Faculty Perceptions of Academic Libraries," *College and Research Libraries* 40:6 (November 1979), 527-532.

479 Dennis J. Reynolds. "Regional Alternatives for Interlibrary Loan: Access to Unreported Holdings," *College and Research Libraries* 41:1 (January 1980), 33-42.

480 Ronald Rayman and Frank William Goudy. "Research and Publication Requirements in University Libraries," *College and Research Libraries* 41:1 (January 1980), 43-48.

481 John N. Olsgaard and Jane Kinch Olsgaard. "Authorship in Five Library Periodicals," *College and Research Libraries* 41:1 (January 1980), 49-53.

482 Albert F. Maag. "Design of the Library Director Interview: The Candidate's Perspective," *College and Research Libraries* 41:2 (March 1980), 112-121.

483 Thomas M. Gaughan. "Resume Essentials for the Academic Librarian," *College and Research Libraries* 41:2 (March 1980), 122-127.

484 Harold B. Shill. "Open Stacks and Library Performance," *College and Research Libraries* 41:3 (May 1980), 220-225.

485 Robert L. Turner, Jr. "Femininity and the Librarian—Another Test," *College and Research Libraries* 41:3 (May 1980), 235-241.

486 Ray L. Carpenter. "College Libraries: A Comparative Analysis in Terms of the ACRL Standards," *College and Research Libraries* 42:1 (January 1981), 7-18.

487 George V. Hodowanec. "An Acquisition Rate Model for Academic Libraries," *College and Research Libraries* 39:6 (September 1978), 439-442.

488 Roland Person. "Long-Term Evaluation of Bibliographic Instruction: Lasting Encouragement," *College and Research Libraries* 42:1 (January 1981), 19-25.

489 Laslo A. Nagy and Martha Lou Thomas. "An Evaluation of the Teaching Effectiveness of Two Library Instructional Videotapes," *College and Research Libraries* 42:1 (January 1981), 26-30.

490 David N. King and John C. Ory. "Effects of Library Instruction on Student Research: A Case Study," *College and Research Libraries* 42:1 (January 1981), 31-41.

491 Herbert S. White. "Perceptions by Educators and Administrators of the Ranking of Library School Programs," *College and Research Libraries* 42:3 (May 1981), 191-202.

492 Russ Davidson, Connie Capers Thorson and Margo C. Trumpeter. "Faculty Status for Librarians in the Rocky Mountain Region: A Review and Analysis," *College and Research Libraries* 42:3 (May 1981), 203-213.

493 M. Kathy Cook. "Rank, Status, and Contribution of Academic Librarians as Perceived by the Teaching Faculty at Southern Illinois University, Carbondale," *College and Research Libraries* 42:3 (May 1981), 214-223.

494 John N. Olsgaard and Jane Kinch Olsgaard. "Post-MLS Educational Requirements for Academic Librarians," *College and Research Libraries* 42:3 (May 1981), 224-228.

495 Ronald Rayman. "Employment Opportunities for Academic Librarians in the 1970's: An Analysis of the Past Decade," *College and Research Libraries* 42:3 (May 1981), 229-234.

496 Martha C. Adamson and Gloria J. Zamora. "Publishing in Library Science Journals: A Test of the Olsgaard Profile," *College and Research Libraries* 42:3 (May 1981), 235-241.

497 Charles Sage, Janet Klass, Helen H. Spalding and Tracey Robinson. "A Queueing Study of Public Catalog Use," *College and Research Libraries* 42:4 (July 1981), 317-325. **(134, 195)**

498 Doris Cruger Dale. "Cataloging and Classsification Practices in Community College Libraries," *College and Research Libraries* 42:4 (July 1981), 333-339. **(9, 11, 30, 31, 35, 39, 40, 45, 54, 55, 59, 82, 99, 110, 112, 117, 157, 166, 167)**

499 Dana Weiss. "Book Theft and Book Mutilation in a Large Urban University Library," *College and Research Libraries* 42:4 (July 1981), 341-347.

500 Raymond L. Carpenter. "Two-Year College Libraries: A Comparative Analysis in Terms of the ACRL Standards," *College and Research Libraries* 42:5 (September 1981), 407-415.

501 Paul D. Luyben, Leonard Cohen, Rebecca Conger and Selby U. Gration. "Reducing Noise in a College Library," *College and Research Libraries* 42:5 (September 1981), 470-481.

502 Prabha Sharma. "A Survey of Academic Librarians and Their Opinions Related to Nine-Month Contracts and Academic Status Configurations in Alabama, Georgia and Mississippi," *College and Research Libraries* 42:6 (November 1981), 561-570.

503 Priscilla Geahigan, Harriet Nelson, Stewart Saunders and Lawrence Woods. "Acceptability of Non-Library/Information Science Publications in the Promotion and Tenure of Academic Librarians," *College and Research Libraries* 42:6 (November 1981), 571-575.

504 Barbara Moore, Tamara J. Miller and Don L. Tolliver. "Title Overlap: A Study of Duplication in the University of Wisconsin System Libraries," *College and Research Libraries* 43:1 (January 1982), 14-21.

505 Gary A. Golden, Susan U. Golden and Rebecca T. Lenzini. "Patron Approaches to Serials: A User Study," *College and Research Libraries* 43:1 (January 1982), 22-30. **(134, 135, 136, 191, 194, 203)**

506 Thomas T. Surprenant. "Learning Theory, Lecture, and Programmed Instruction Text: An Experiment in Bibliographic Instruction," *College and Research Libraries* 43:1 (January 1982), 31-37.

507 Larry Hardesty, Nicholas P. Lovrich, Jr. and James Mannon. "Library-Use Instruction: Assessment of the Long-Term Effects," *College and Research Libraries* 43:1 (January 1982), 38-46.

508 Robert Swisher and Peggy C. Smith. "Journals Read by ACRL Academic Librarians, 1973 and 1978," *College and Research Libraries* 43:1 (January 1982), 51-58.

509 William Caynon. "Collective Bargaining and Professional Development of Academic Librarians," *College and Research Libraries* 43:2 (March 1982), 133-139.

510 Barbara J. Smith. "Background Characteristics and Education Needs of a Group of Instruction Librarians in Pennsylvania," *College and Research Libraries* 43:3 (May 1982), 199-207.

511 Gloria S. Cline. "*College and Research Libraries*: Its First Forty Years," *College and Research Libraries* 43:3 (May 1982), 208-232.

512 John B. Harer and C. Edward Huber. "Copyright Policies in Virginia Academic Library Reserve Rooms," *College and Research Libraries* 43:3 (May 1982), 233-241.

513 Laurie S. Linsley. "Academic Libraries in an Interlibrary Loan Network," *College and Research Libraries* 43:4 (July 1982), 292-299.

514 Timothy D. Jewell. "Student Reactions to a Self-Paced Library Skills Workbook Program: Survey Evidence," *College and Research Libraries* 43:5 (September 1982), 371-378.

515 Mary Baier Wells. "Requirements and Benefits for Academic Librarians: 1959-1979," *College and Research Libraries* 43:6 (November 1982), 450-458.

516 Marjorie A. Benedict, Jacquelyn A. Gavryck and Hanan C. Selvin. "Status of Academic Librarians in New York State," *College and Research Libraries* 44:1 (January 1983), 12-19.

517 Carol Truett. "Services to Developmental Education Students in the Community College: Does the Library Have a Role?" *College and Research Libraries* 44:1 (January 1983), 20-28.

518 Gene K. Rinkel and Patricia McCandless. "Application of a Methodology Analyzing User Frustration," *College and Research Libraries* 44:1 (January 1983), 29-37.

519 Jo Bell Whitlatch. "Library Use Patterns Among Full- and Part-Time Faculty and Students," *College and Research Libraries* 44:2 (March 1983), 141-152.

520 Madeleine Stern. "Characteristics of the Literature of Literary Scholarship," *College and Research Libraries* 44:4 (July 1983), 199-209.

521 Philip Schwarz. "Demand-Adjusted Shelf Availability Parameters: A Second Look," *College and Research Libraries* 44:4 (July 1983), 210-219.

522 Paul M. Anderson and Ellen G. Miller. "Participative Planning for Library Automation: The Role of the User Opinion Survey," *College and Research Libraries* 44:4 (July 1983), 245-254. **(136)**

523 Raymond W. Barber and Jacqueline C. Mancall. "The Application of Bibliometric Techniques to the Analysis of Materials for Young Adults," *Collection Management* 2:3 (Fall 1978), 229-245.

524 Kenneth C. Kirsch and Albert H. Rubenstein. "Converting from Hard Copy to Microfilm: An Administrative Experiment," *Collection Management* 2:4 (Winter 1978), 279-302.

525 Herbert Goldhor. "U.S. Public Library Adult Non-Fiction Book Collections in the Humanities," *Collection Management* 3:1 (Spring 1979), 31-43.

526 Sally F. Williams. "Construction and Application of a Periodical Price Index," *Collection Management* 2:4 (Winter 1978), 329-344.

527 Mary Jane Pobst Reed. "Identification of Storage Candidates among Monographs," *Collection Management* 3:2/3 (Summer/Fall 1979), 203-214.

528 Ung Chon Kim. "Participation of Teaching Faculty in Library Book Selection," *Collection Management* 3:4 (Winter 1979), 333-352.

529 Glenn R. Lowry. "A Heuristic Collection Loss Rate Determination Methodology: An Alternative to Shelf-Reading," *Collection Management* 4:1/2 (Spring/Summer 1982), 73-83.

240 BIBLIOGRAPHY OF ARTICLES

530 Stewart Saunders. "Student Reliance on Faculty Guidance in the Selection of Reading Materials: The Use of Core Collections," *Collection Management* 4:4 (Winter 1982), 9-23.

531 Ralph M. Daehn. "The Measurement and Projection of Shelf Space," *Collection Management* 4:4 (Winter 1982), 25-39.

532 Igor I. Kavass. "Foreign and International Law Collections in Selected Law Libraries of the United States: Survey, 1972-73," *International Journal of Law Libraries* 1:3 (November 1973), 117-133. (**29, 31, 33, 36, 38, 39, 40, 41**)

533 Robert J. Garen. "Library Orientation on Television," *Canadian Library Journal* 24:2 (September 1967), 124-126.

534 D.W. Miller. "Non-English Books in Canadian Public Libraries," *Canadian Library Journal* 27:2 (March/April 1970), 123-129. (**11, 83**)

535 Robert H. Blackburn. "Canadian Content in a Sample of Photocopying," *Canadian Library Journal* 27:5 (September/October 1970), 332-340.

536 Peter H. Wolters and Jack E. Brown. "CAN/SDI System: User Reaction to a Computer Information Retrieval System for Canadian Scientists and Technologists," *Canadian Library Journal* 28:1 (January/ February), 20-23.

537 M. Jamil Qureshi. "Academic Status, Salaries and Fringe Benefits in Community College Libraries of Canada," *Canadian Library Journal* 28:1 (January/February 1971), 41-45.

538 George J. Snowball. "Survey of Social Sciences and Humanities Monograph Circulation by Random Sampling of the Stack," *Canadian Library Journal* 28:5 (September/October 1971), 352-361.

539 Roop K. Sandhu and Harjit Sandhu. "Job Perception of University Librarians and Library Students," *Canadian Library Journal* 28:6 (November/ December 1971), 438-445.

540 Brian Dale and Patricia Dewdney. "Canadian Public Libraries and the Physically Handicapped," *Canadian Library Journal* 29:3 (May/June 1972), 231-236.

541 R.G. Wilson. "Interlibrary Loan Experiments at the University of Calgary," *Canadian Library Journal* 30:1 (January/February 1973), 38-40.

542 Peter Simmons. "Studies in the Use of the Card Catalogue in a Public Library," *Canadian Library Journal* 31:4 (August 1974), 323-337. (**196,197,204**)

543 L.J. Amey and R.J. Smith. "Combination School and Public Libraries: An Attitudinal Study," *Canadian Library Journal* 33:3 (June 1976), 251-261.

544 John Wilkinson. "The Library Market for Canadian Juvenile Fiction: A Further Analysis," *Canadian Library Journal* 34:1 (February 1977), 5-15.

545 Larry Orten and John Wiseman. "Library Service to Part-time Students," *Canadian Library Journal* 34:1 (February 1977), 23-27.

546 Esther L. Sleep. "Whither the ISSN? A Practical Experience," *Canadian Library Journal* 34:4 (August 1977), 265-270.

547 Sarah Landy. "Why Johnny Can Read...but Doesn't," *Canadian Library Journal* 34:5 (October 1977), 379-387.

548 Sharon Mott. "An Edmonton High School Reduces Book Losses," *Canadian Library Journal* 35:1 (February 1978), 45-49.

549 Fotoula Pantazis. "Library Technicians in Ontario Academic Libraries," *Canadian Library Journal* 35:2 (April 1978), 77-91.

550 Dorothy Ryder. "Canadian Reference Sources—A 10 Year Overview," *Canadian Library Journal* 35:4 (August 1978), 289-293.

551 Laurent-G. Denis. "Full-time Faculty Survey Describes Educators," *Canadian Library Journal* 36:3 (June 1979), 107-121.

552 Marie Foster. "Philosophy of Librarianship," *Canadian Library Journal* 36:3 (June 1979), 131-137.

553 Kenneth H. Plate and Jacob P. Seigel. "Career Patterns of Ontario Librarians," *Canadian Library Journal* 36:3 (June 1979), 143-148.

554 Mavis Cariou. "Liaison Where Field and Faculty Meet," *Canadian Library Journal* 36:3 (June 1979), 155-163.

555 Norman Horrocks. "Encyclopedias and Public Libraries: A Canadian Survey," *Canadian Library Journal* 38:2 (April 1981), 79-83.

556 Stephen B. Lawton. "Diffusion of Automation in Post-Secondary Institutions," *Canadian Library Journal* 38:2 (April 1980), 93-97. **(140, 160, 161)**

557 Mary Ann Wasylycia-Coe. "Profile: Canadian Chief Librarians by Sex," *Canadian Library Journal* 38:3 (June 1981), 159-163.

558 Margaret Currie, Elaine Goettler and Sandra McCaskill. "Evaluating the Relationship between Library Skills and Library Instruction," *Canadian Library Journal* 39:1 (February 1982), 35-37.

559 Esther L. Sleep. "Periodical Vandalism: A Chronic Condition," *Canadian Library Journal* 39:1 (February 1982), 39-42.

560 Kenneth Setterington. "The Ph.D. in Library Administration: A Report of Research," *Library Research* (after Spring 1983 called *Library and Information Science Research*) 5:2 (Summer 1983), 177-194.

561 Robert F. Rose. "Identifying a Core Collection of Business Periodicals for Academic Libraries," *Collection Management* 5:1/2 (Spring/Summer 1983), 73-87.

562 Raymond Kilpela. "A Profile of Library School Deans, 1960-81," *Journal of Education for Librarianship* 23:3 (Winter 1983), 173-191.

563 Charlene Renner and Barton M. Clark. "Professional and Nonprofessional Staffing Patterns in Departmental Libraries," *Library Research* 1 (1979), 153-170.

564 Jacqueline C. Mancall and M. Carl Drott. "Materials Used by High School Students in Preparing Independent Study Projects: A Bibliometric Approach," *Library Research* 1 (1979), 223-236.

565 Alan R. Samuels. "Assessing Organizational Climate in Public Libraries," *Library Research* 1 (1979), 237-254.

566 Diane Mittermeyer and Lloyd J. Houser. "The Knowledge Base for the Administration of Libraries," *Library Research* 1 (1979), 255-276.

567 Michael V. Sullivan, Betty Vadeboncoeur, Nancy Shiotani and Peter Stangl. "Obsolescence in Biomedical Journals: Not an Artifact of Literature Growth," *Library Research* 2 (1980-81), 29-46.

568 Robert V. Williams. "Sources of the Variability in Level of Public Library Development in the United States: A Comparative Analysis," *Library Research* 2 (1980-81), 157-176.

569 Bluma C. Peritz. "The Methods of Library Science Research: Some Results from a Bibliometric Survey," *Library Research* 2 (1980-81), 251-268.

570 Nancy Van House DeWath. "Fees for Online Bibliographic Search Services in Publicly-Supported Libraries," *Library Research* 3 (1981), 29-45.

571 Bluma C. Peritz. "Citation Characteristics in Library Science: Some Further Results from a Bibliometric Survey," *Library Research* 3 (1981), 47-65.

572 Gary Moore. "Library Long-Range Planning: A Survey of Current Practices," *Library Research* 3 (1981), 155-165.

573 Larry Hardesty. "Use of Library Materials at a Small Liberal Arts College," *Library Research* 3 (1981), 261-282.

574 Stewart Saunders, Harriet Nelson and Priscilla Geahigan. "Alternatives to the Shelflist Measure for Determining the Size of a Subject Collection," *Library Research* 3 (1981), 383-391. (**31, 35, 36, 40, 101**)

575 P. Robert Paustian. "Collection Size and Interlibrary Loan in Large Academic Libraries," *Library Research* 3 (1981), 393-400.

576 Daniel O. O'Connor. "Evaluating Public Libraries Using Standard Scores: The Library Quotient," *Library Research* 4 (1982), 51-70.

577 Snunith Shoham. "A Cost-Preference Study of the Decentralization of Academic Library Services," *Library Research* 4 (1982), 175-194.

578 A.S. Pickett. "San Franscisco State College Library Technical Services Time Study," *Library Resources and Technical Services* 4:1 (Winter 1960), 45-46. **(107)**

579 Rosamond H. Danielson. "Cornell's Area Classification: A Space-Saving Device for Less-Used Books," *Library Resources and Technical Services* 5:2 (Spring 1961), 139-141.

580 Miriam C. Maloy. "Reclassification for the Divisional Plan," Library Resources and Technical Services 6:3 (Summer 1962), 239-242. **(102, 103)**

581 Andre Nitecki. "Costs of a Divided Catalog," *Library Resources and Technical Services* 6:4 (Fall 1962), 351-355. **(131, 136, 145, 153, 164, 165)**

582 Donald V. Black. "Automatic Classification and Indexing, for Libraries?" *Library Resources and Technical Services* 9:1 (Winter 1965), 35-52.**(100, 101, 114, 115)**

583 Perry D. Morrison. "Use of Library of Congress Classsification Decisions in Academic Libraries—An Empirical Study," *Library Resources and Technical Services* 9:2 (Spring 1965), 235-242. **(13, 19, 32)**

584 Manuel D. Lopez. "Subject Catalogers Equal to the Future?" *Library Resources and Technical Services* 9:3 (Summer 1965), 371-375. **(101, 113, 115)**

585 Ashby J. Fristoe. "The Bitter End," *Library Resources and Technical Services* 10:1 (Winter 1966), 91-95.

586 Ole V. Groos. "Less-Used Titles and Volumes of Science Journals: Two Preliminary Notes," *Library Resources and Technical Services* 10:3 (Summer 1966), 289-290.

587 Paula M. Strain. "A Study of the Usage and Retention of Technical Periodicals," *Library Resources and Technical Services* 10:3 (Summer 1966), 295-304.

588 William R. Nugent. "Statistics of Collection Overlap at the Libraries of the Six New England State Universities," *Library Resources and Technical Services* 12:1 (Winter 1968), 31-36.

589 Walter R. Stubbs and Robert N. Broadus. "The Value of the Kirkus Service for College Libraries," *Library Resources and Technical Services* 13:2 (Spring 1969), 203-205.

590 Barton R. Burkhalter and LaVerne Hoag. "Another Look at Manual Sorting and Filing: Backwards and Forwards," *Library Resources and Technical Services* 14:3 (Summer 1970), 445-454. **(131, 132)**

591 "More on DC Numbers on LC Cards: Quantity and Quality," *Library Resources and Technical Services* 14:4 (Fall 1970), 517-527. **(27, 28)**

592 Carol A. Nemeyer. "Scholarly Reprint Publishing in the United States: Selected Findings from a Recent Survey of the Industry," *Library Resources and Technical Services* 15:1 (Winter 1971), 35-48.

593 Betty J. Mitchell and Carol Bedoian. "A Systematic Approach to Performance Evaluation of Out-of-Print Book Dealers: The San Fernando Valley State College Experience," *Library Resources and Technical Services* 15:2 (Spring 1971), 215-222.

594 Barbara Schrader and Elaine Orsini. "British, French and Australian Publications in the National Union Catalog: A Study of NPAC's Effectiveness," *Library Resources and Technical Services* 15:3 (Summer 1971), 345-353.

595 Joel Levis. "Canadian Publications in the English Language: CBI vs. *Canadiana*," *Library Resources and Technical Services* 15:3 (Summer 1971), 354-358.

596 Zubaidah Isa. "The Entry-Word in Indonesian Names and Titles," *Library Resources and Technical Services* 15:3 (Summer 1971), 393-398. (46, 79)

597 Richard J. Hyman. "Access to Library Collections: Summary of a Documentary and Opinion Survey on the Direct Shelf Approach and Browsing," *Library Resources and Technical Services* 15:4 (Fall 1971), 479-491. (113)

598 Robert L. Mowery. "The Cryptic Other," *Library Resources and Technical Services* 16:1 (Winter 1972), 74-78. (29, 30, 33, 34, 38)

599 Ann Craig Turner. "Comparative Card Production Methods," *Library Resources and Technical Services* 16:3 (Summer 1972), pp. 347-358. (11, 12)

600 Edmund G. Hamann. "Expansion of the Public Card Catalog in a Large Library," *Library Resources and Technical Services* 16:4 (Fall 1972), 488-496. (136, 137)

601 Ernest R. Perez. "Acquisitions of Out-of-Print Materials," *Library Resources and Technical Services* 17:1 (Winter 1973), 42-59.

602 E. Dale Cluff and Karen Anderson. "LC Card Order Experiment Conducted at University of Utah Marriott Library," *Library Resources and Technical Services* 17:1 (Winter 1973), 70-72. (11)

603 Betty J. Mitchell. "Methods Used in Out-of-Print Acquisition; A Survey of Out-of-Print Book Dealers," *Library Resources and Technical Services* 17:2 (Spring 1973), 211-215.

604 George Piternick. "University Library Arrearages," *Library Resources and Technical Services* 13:1 (Winter 1969), 102-114. (6)

605 Nancy E. Brodie. "Evaluation of a KWIC Index for *Library Literature*," *Journal of the American Society for Information Science* 21:1 (January-February 1970), 22-28.

606 William S. Cooper. "The Potential Usefulness of Catalog Access Points Other than Author, Title and Subject," *Journal of the American Society for Information Science* 21:2 (March-April 1970), 112-127. **(197, 198, 201)**

607 Barbara F. Frick and John M. Ginski. "Cardiovascular Serial Literature: Characteristics, Productive Journals, and Abstracting/Indexing Coverage," *Journal of the American Society for Information Science* 21:5 (September-October 1970), 338-344.

608 Ching-Chih Chen. "The Use Patterns of Physics Journals in a Large Academic Research Library," *Journal of the American Society for Information Science* 23:4 (July-August 1972), 254-265.

609 Janet Friedlander. "Clinician Search for Information," *Journal of the American Society for Information Science* 24:1 (January-February 1973), 65-69.

610 Tefko Saracevic and Lawrence J. Perk. "Ascertaining Activities in a Subject Area through Bibliometric Analysis," *Journal of the American Society for Information Science* 24:3 (March-April 1973), 120-134.

611 Ruth Kay Maloney. "Title versus Title/Abstract Text Searching in SDI Systems," *Journal of the American Society for Information Science* 25:6 (November-December 1974), 370-373.

612 Gladys B. Dronberger and Gerald T. Kowitz. "Abstract Readability as a Factor in Information Systems," *Journal of the American Society for Information Science* 26:2 (March-April 1975), 108-111.

613 Jerry R. Byrne. "Relative Effectiveness of Titles, Abstracts and Subject Headings for Machine Retrieval from the COMPENDEX Services," *Journal of the American Society for Information Science* 26:4 (July-August 1975), 223-229.

614 Joseph D. Smith and James E. Rush. "The Relationship between Author Names and Author Entries in a Large On-Line Union Catalog as Retrieved Using Truncated Keys," *Journal of the American Society for Information Science* 28:2 (March 1977), 115-120. **(178)**

615 Marcia J. Bates. "Factors Affecting Subject Catalog Search Success," *Journal of the American Society for Information Science* 28:3 (May 1977), 161-169. **(182, 198, 199, 201, 202)**

616 Terry Noreault, Matthew Koll and Michael J. McGill. "Automatic Ranked Output from Boolean Searches in SIRE," *Journal of the American Society for Information Science* 28:6 (November 1977), 333-339.

617 Chai Kim and Eui Hang Shin. "Sociodemographic Correlates of Intercounty Variations in the Public Library Output," *Journal of the American Society for Information Science* 28:6 (November 1977), 359-365.

618 Harold E. Bamford, Jr. "Assessing the Effect of Computer Augmentation on Staff Productivity," *Journal of the American Society for Information Science* 30:3 (May 1979), 136-142.

619 Charles H. Davis and Deborah Shaw. "Collection Overlap as a Function of Library Size: A Comparison of American and Canadian Public Libraries," *Journal of the American Society for Information Science* 30:1 (January 1979), 19-24.

620 M. Carl Drott and Belver C. Griffith. "An Empirical Examination of Bradford's Law and the Scattering of Scientific Literature," *Journal of the American Society for Information Science* 29:5 (September 1978), 238-246.

621 James D. Anderson. "*Ad hoc* and Selective Translations of Scientific and Technical Journal Articles: Their Characteristics and Possible Predictability," *Journal of the American Society for Information Science* 29:3 (May 1978), 130-135.

622 Richard C. Anderson, Francis Narin and Paul McAllister. "Publication Ratings versus Peer Ratings of Universities," *Journal of the American Society for Information Science* 29:2 (March 1978), 91-103.

623 Dennis R. Eichesen. "Cost-Effectiveness Comparison of Manual and On-line Retrospective Bibliographic Searching," *Journal of the American Society for Information Science* 29:2 (March 1978), 56-66.

624 Topsy N. Smalley. "Comparing *Psychological Abstracts* and *Index Medicus* for Coverage of the Journal Literature in a Subject Area in Psychology," *Journal of the American Society for Information Science* 31:3 (May 1980), 144-146.

625 Paul R. McAllister, Richard C. Anderson and Francis Narin. "Comparison of Peer and Citation Assessment of the Influence of Scientific Journals," *Journal of the American Society for Information Science* 31:3 (May 1980), 148-152.

626 Jerry Specht. "Patron Use of an Online Circulation System in Known-Item Searching," *Journal of the American Society for Information Science* 31:5 (September 1980), 335-346. **(191, 194, 202, 203)**

627 Guilbert C. Hentschke and Ellen Kehoe. "Serial Acquisition as a Capital Budgeting Problem," *Journal of the American Society for Information Science* 31:5 (September 1980), 357-362.

628 G. Edward Evans and Claudia White Argyres. "Approval Plans and Collection Development in Academic Libraries," *Library Resources and Technical Services* 18:1 (Winter 1974), 35-50.

629 Doris E. New and Retha Zane Ott. "Interlibrary Loan Analysis as a Collection Development Tool," *Library Resources and Technical Services* 18:3 (Summer 1974), 275-283.

630 H. William Axford. "The Validity of Book Price Indexes for Budgetary Projections," *Library Resources and Technical Services* 19:1 (Winter 1975), 5-12.

631 Geza A. Kosa. "Book Selection Tools for Subject Specialists in a Large Research Library: An Analysis," *Library Resources and Technical Services* 19:1 (Winter 1975), 13-18.

632 George P. D'Elia. "The Determinants of Job Satisfaction among Beginning Librarians," *Library Quarterly* 49:3 (July 1979), 283-302.

633 Tim LaBorie and Michael Halperin. "Citation Patterns in Library Science Dissertations," *Journal of Education for Librarianship* 16:4 (Spring 1976), 271-283.

634 Anne Woodsworth and Victor R. Neufeld. "A Survey of Physician Self-education Patterns in Toronto. Part 1: Use of Libraries," *Canadian Library Journal* 29:1 (January-February 1972), 38-44.

635 Richard Eggleton. "The ALA Duplicates Exchange Union—A Study and Evaluation," *Library Resources and Technical Services* 19:2 (Spring 1975), 148-163.

636 Katherine H. Packer and Dagobert Soergel. "The Importance of SDI for Current Awareness in Fields with Severe Scatter of Information," *Journal of the American Society for Information Science* 30:3 (May 1979), 125-135.

637 Doris M. Carson. "The Act of Cataloging," *Library Resources and Technical Services* 20:2 (Spring 1976), 149-153. (**98, 110**)

638 Robert L. Mowery. "The Cutter Classification: Still at Work," *Library Resources and Technical Services* 20:2 (Spring 1976), 154-156. (**27**)

639 Kelly Patterson, Carol White and Martha Whittaker. "Thesis Handling in University Libraries," *Library Resources and Technical Services* 21:3 (Summer 1977), 274-285. (**30, 34, 39, 81, 82, 103, 104**)

640 Sandra L. Stokley and Marion T. Reid. "A Study of Performance of Five Book Dealers Used by Louisiana State University Library," *Library Resources and Technical Services* 22:2 (Spring 1978), 117-125.

641 Hans H. Wellisch. "Multiscript and Multilingual Bibliographic Control: Alternatives to Romanization," *Library Resources and Technical Services* 22:2 (Spring 1978), 179-190. (**97, 176, 177**)

642 Bert R. Boyce and Mark Funk. "Bradford's Law and the Selection of High Quality Papers," *Library Resources and Technical Services* 22:4 (Fall 1978), 390-401.

643 Susan Dingle-Cliff and Charles H. Davis. "Comparison of Recent Acquisitions and OCLC Find Rates for Three Canadian Special Libraries," *Journal of the American Society for Information Science* 32:1 (January 1981), 65-69. (**77**)

644 Rose Mary Juliano Longo and Ubaldino Dantas Machado. "Characterization of Databases in the Agricultural Sciences," *Journal of the American Society for Information Science* 32:2 (March 1981), 83-91.

645 Edward S. Warner. "The Impact of Interlibrary Access to Periodicals on Subscription Continuation/Cancellation Decision Making," *Journal of the American Society for Information Science* 32:2 (March 1981), 93-95.

646 Charles T. Payne and Robert S. McGee. "Comparisons of LC Proofslip and MARC Tape Arrival Dates at the University of Chicago Library," *Journal of Library Automation* 3:2 (June 1970), 115-121. **(49)**

647 Wanda V. Dole and David Allerton. "University Collections: A Survey of Costs," *Library Acquistions: Practice and Theory* 6:2 (1982), 25-32.

648 Silvia A. Gonzalez. "1976 Statistical Survey of Law Libraries Serving a Local Bar," *Law Library Journal* 70:2 (May 1977), 222-237.

649 Carole J. Mankin and Jacqueline D. Bastille. "An Analysis of the Differences between Density-of-Use Ranking and Raw-Use Ranking of Library Journal Use," *Journal of the American Society for Information Science* 32:3 (May 1981), 224-228.

650 Katherine W. McCain and James E. Bobick. "Patterns of Journal Use in a Departmental Library: A Citation Analysis," *Journal of the American Society for Information Science* 32:4 (July 1981), 257-267.

651 Manfred Kochen, Victoria Reich and Lee Cohen. "Influence on [sic] Online Bibliographic Services on Student Behavior," *Journal of the American Society for Information Science* 32:6 (November 1981), 412-420.

652 Mark P. Carpenter and Francis Narin. "The Adequacy of the *Science Citation Index* (SCI) as an Indicator of International Scientific Activity," *Journal of the American Society for Information Science* 32:6 (November 1981), 430-439.

653 Chai Kim. "Retrieval Languages of Social Sciences and Natural Sciences: A Statistical Investigation," *Journal of the American Society for Information Science* 33:1 (January 1982), 3-7.

654 Ann H. Schabas. "Postcoordinate Retrieval: A Comparison of Two Indexing Languages," *Journal of the American Society for Information Science* 33:1 (January 1982), 32-37. **(114, 180)**

655 Miranda Lee Pao. "Collaboration in Computational Musicology," *Journal of the American Society for Information Science* 33:1 (January 1982), 38-43.

656 Robert K. Poyer. "*Science Citation Index*'s Coverage of the Preclinical Science Literature," *Journal of the American Society for Information Science* 33:5 (September 1982), 333-337.

657 Stephen M. Lawani and Alan E. Bayer. "Validity of Citation Criteria for Assessing the Influence of Scientific Publications: New Evidence with Peer Assessment," *Journal of the American Society for Information Science* 34:1 (January 1983), 59-66.

658 Edward G. Summers, Joyce Matheson and Robert Conry. "The Effect of Personal, Professional and Psychological Attributes, and Information Seeking Behavior on the Use of Information Sources by Educators," *Journal of the American Society for Information Science* 34:1 (January 1983), 75-85.

659 Bluma C. Peritz. "A Note on 'Scholarliness' and 'Impact,'" *Journal of the American Society for Information Science* 34:5 (September 1983), 360-362.

660 Michael D. Cooper. "Response Time Variations in an Online Search System," *Journal of the American Society for Information Science* 34:6 (November 1983), 374-380.

661 Richard S. Marcus. "An Experimental Comparison of the Effectiveness of Computers and Humans as Search Intermediaries," *Journal of the American Society for Information Science* 34:6 (November 1983), 381-404.

662 Michael J. Simonds, "Work Attitudes and Union Membership," *College and Research Libraries* 36:2 (March 1975), 136-142.

663 Jerold Nelson. "Faculty Awareness and Attitudes toward Academic Library Reference Services: A Measure of Communication," *College and Research Libraries* 34:5 (September 1973), 268-275.

664 Andre Nitecki, "Polish Books in America and the Farmington Plan," *College and Research Libraries* 27:6 (November 1966), 439-449.

665 Leslie R. Morris. "Projections of the Number of Library School Graduates," *Journal of Education for Librarianship* 22:4 (Spring 1982), 283-291.

666 Thomas J. Galvin and Allen Kent. "Use of a University Library Collection," *Library Journal* 102:20 (November 1977), 2317-2320. [For further and more complete information see Allen Kent, et al. *Use of Library Materials: The University of Pittsburgh Study.* New York: Marcel Dekker, 1979.]

667 Allen Kent. "Library Resource Sharing Networks: How To Make a Choice," *Library Acquisitions: Practice and Theory* 2 (1978), 69-76. [For further and more complete information see Allen Kent, et al. *Use of Library Materials: The University of Pittsburgh Study.* New York: Marcel Dekker, 1979.]

668 Leigh S. Estabrook and Kathleen M. Heim. "A Profile of ALA Personal Members," *American Libraries* 11:11 (December 1980), 654-659. [For a fuller and more complete description of this study see Kathleen M. Heim and Leigh S. Estabrook. *Career Profiles and Sex Discrimination in the Library Profession.* Chicago: American Library Association, 1983.]

669 Mary Lee DeVilbiss. "The Approval-Built Collection in the Medium-Sized Academic Library," *College and Research Libraries* 36:6 (November 1975), 487-492.

670 Thomas P. Fleming and Frederick G. Kilgour. "Moderately and Heavily Used Biomedical Journals," *Bulletin of the Medical Library Association* 52:1 (January 1964), 234-241.

671 Richard J. Hyman. "Medical Interlibrary Loan Patterns," *Bulletin of the Medical Library Association* 53:2 (April 1965), 215-224.

672 L. Miles Raisig, Meredith Smith, Renata Cuff and Frederick G. Kilgour. "How Biomedical Investigators Use Library Books," *Bulletin of the Medical Library Association* 54:2 (April 1966), 104-107.

673 Helen Crawford. "Centralization vs. Decentralization in Medical School Libraries," *Bulletin of the Medical Library Association* 54:2 (April 1966), 199-205.

674 Peter Stangl and Frederick G. Kilgour. "Analysis of Recorded Biomedical Book and Journal Use in the Yale Medical Library," *Bulletin of the Medical Library Association* 55:3 (July 1967), 290-300.

675 Peter Stangl and Frederick G. Kilgour. "Analysis of Recorded Biomedical Book and Journal Use in the Yale Medical Library," *Bulletin of the Medical Library Association* 55:3 (July 1967), 301-315.

676 Gwendolyn S. Cruzat. "Keeping Up with Biomedical Meetings," *Bulletin of the Medical Library Association* 56:2 (April 1968), 132-137.

677 Joan B. Woods, Sam Pieper and Shervert H. Frazier. "Basic Psychiatric Literature: I. Books," *Bulletin of the Medical Library Association* 56:3 (July 1968), 295-309.

678 Joan B. Woods, Sam Pieper and Shervert H. Frazier. "Basic Psychiatric Literature: II. Articles and Article Sources," *Bulletin of the Medical Library Association* 56:4 (October 1968), 404-427.

679 Reva Pachefsky. "Survey of the Card Catalog in Medical Libraries," *Bulletin of the Medical Library Association* 57:1 (January 1969), 10-20. **(115, 117, 143, 144, 146, 148, 165, 166, 181, 183, 184, 187)**

680 Janet Barlup. "Mechanization of Library Procedures in the Medium-sized Medical Library: VII. Relevancy of Cited Articles in Citation Indexing," *Bulletin of the Medical Library Association* 57:3 (July 1969), 260-263.

681 Wilhelm Moll. "Basic Journal List for Small Hospital Libraries," *Bulletin of the Medical Library Association* 57:3 (July 1969), 267-271.

682 Lois Ann Colainni and Robert F. Lewis. "Reference Services in U.S. Medical School Libraries," *Bulletin of the Medical Library Association* 57:3 (July 1969), 272-274.

683 Vern M. Pings and Joyce E. Malin. "Access to the Scholarly Record of Medicine by the Osteopathic Physicians of Southeastern Michigan," *Bulletin of the Medical Library Association* 58:1 (January 1970), 18-22.

684 D.J. Goode, J.K. Penry and J.F. Caponio. "Comparative Analysis of *Epilepsy Abstracts* and a MEDLARS Bibliography," *Bulletin of the Medical Library Association* 58:1 (January 1970), 44-50.

685 Robert Oseasohn. "Borrower Use of a Modern Medical Library by Practicing Physicians," *Bulletin of the Medical Library Association* 59:1 (January 1970), 58-59.

686 Joan M.B. Smith. "A Periodical Use Study at Children's Hospital of Michigan," *Bulletin of the Medical Library Association* 58:1 (January 1970), 65-67.

687 Jean K. Miller. "Mechanization of Library Procedures in the Medium-sized Medical Library: XI. Two Methods of Providing Selective Dissemination of Information to Medical Scientists," *Bulletin of the Medical Library Association* 58:3 (July 1970), 378-397.

688 Stella S. Gomes. "The Nature and the Use and Users of the Midwest Regional Medical Library," *Bulletin of the Medical Library Association* 58:4 (October 1970), 559-577.

689 Donald A. Windsor. "Publications on a Drug before the First Report of Its Administration to Man," *Bulletin of the Medical Library Association* 59:3 (July 1971), 433-437.

690 Charles L. Bowden and Virginia M. Bowden. "A Survey of Information Sources Used by Psychiatrists," *Bulletin of the Medical Library Association* 59:4 (October 1971), 603-608.

691 Ruth E. Fenske. "Mechanization of Library Procedures in the Medium-sized Medical Library: XIV. Correlations between National Library of Medicine Classification Numbers and MeSH Headings," *Bulletin of the Medical Library Association* 60:2 (April 1972), 319-324. (**80, 83, 84**)

692 Anne Brearley Piternick. "Measurement of Journal Availability in a Biomedical Library," *Bulletin of the Medical Library Association* 60:4 (October 1972), 534-542.

693 Isabel Spiegel and Janet Crager. "Comparison of SUNY and MEDLINE Searches," *Bulletin of the Medical Library Association* 61:2 (April 1973), 205-209.

694 Fred W. Roper. "Special Programs in Medical Library Education, 1957-1971: Part II: Analysis of the Programs," *Bulletin of the Medical Library Association* 61:4 (October 1973), 387-395.

695 Norma Jean Lodico. "Physician's Referral Letter Bibliographic Service: A New Method of Disseminating Medical Information," *Bulletin of the Medical Library Association* 61:4 (October 1973), 422-432.

696 Wilhelm Moll. "MEDLINE Evaluation Study," *Bulletin of the Medical Library Association* 62:1 (January 1974), 1-5.

697 Pamela Tibbetts. "A Method for Estimating the In-House Use of the Periodical Collection in the University of Minnesota Bio-Medical Library," *Bulletin of the Medical Library Association* 62:1 (January 1974), 37-48.

698 Joan Ash. "Library Use of Public Health Materials: Description and Analysis," *Bulletin of the Medical Library Association* 62:2 (April 1974), 95-104.

699 Ching-Chih Chen. "Current Status of Biomedical Book Reviewing: Part I. Key Biomedical Reviewing Journals with Quantitative Significance," *Bulletin of the Medical Library Association* 62:2 (April 1974), 105-112.

700 Ching-Chih Chen. "Current Status of Biomedical Book Reviewing: Part II. Time Lag in Biomedical Book Reviewing," *Bulletin of the Medical Library Association* 62:2 (April 1974), 113-119.

701 George Scheerer and Lois E. Hines. "Classification Systems Used in Medical Libraries," *Bulletin of the Medical Library Association* 62:3 (July 1974), 272-280. (**36, 37, 41, 42, 84, 102**)

702 Jo Ann Bell. "The Academic Health Sciences Library and Serial Selection," *Bulletin of the Medical Library Association* 62:3 (July 1974), 281-290.

703 Ching-Chih Chen. "Current Status of Biomedical Book Reviewing: Part III. Duplication Patterns in Biomedical Book Reviewing," *Bulletin of the Medical Library Association* 62:3 (July 1974), 296-301.

704 Ching-Chih Chen. "Current Status of Biomedical Book Reviewing: Part IV. Major American and British Biomedical Book Publishers," *Bulletin of the Medical Library Association* 62:3 (July 1974), 302-308.

705 M. Sandra Wood and Robert S. Seeds. "Development of SDI Services from a Manual Current Awareness Service to SDILINE," *Bulletin of the Medical Library Association* 62:4 (October 1974), 374-384.

706 Margaret Butkovich and Robert M. Braude. "Cost-Performance of Cataloging and Card Production in a Medical Center Library," *Bulletin of the Medical Library Association* 63:1 (January 1975), 29-34. (**12, 13, 43, 44, 107, 108**)

707 Donald A. Windsor. "Science-Speciality Literatures: Their Legendary-Contemporary Parity, Based on the Transmission of Information between Generations," *Bulletin of the Medical Library Association* 63:2 (April 1975), 209-215.

708 Helen J. Brown, Jean K. Miller and Diane M. Pinchoff. "Study of the Information Dissemination Service—Health Sciences Library, State University of New York at Buffalo," *Bulletin of the Medical Library Association* 63:3 (July 1975), 259-271.

709 Rachel K. Goldstein and Dorothy R. Hill. "The Status of Women in the Administration of Health Science Libraries," *Bulletin of the Medical Library Association* 63:4 (October 1975), 386-395.

710 Janet G. Schnall and Joan W. Wilson. "Evaluation of a Clinical Medical Librarianship Program at a University Health Sciences Library," *Bulletin of the Medical Library Association* (July 1976), 278-283.

711 Anne B. Piternick. "Effects of Binding Policy and Other Factors on the Availability of Journal Issues," *Bulletin of the Medical Library Association* 64:3 (July 1976), 284-292.

712 Richard B. Fredericksen and Helen N. Michael. "Subject Cataloging Practices in North American Medical School Libraries," *Bulletin of the Medical Library Association* 64:4 (October 1976), 356-366. **(17, 18, 19, 22, 80, 81, 84, 85, 90, 115, 116, 117, 118, 119, 120, 146, 147, 148, 149, 150, 154, 155, 156, 157, 166, 167, 168, 169, 170, 171, 172, 173, 174, 181, 183, 184, 185, 186, 187, 188, 189, 190)**

713 Paul M. McIlvaine and Malcolm H. Brantz. "Audiovisual Materials: A Survey of Bibliographic Controls in Distributors' Catalogs," *Bulletin of the Medical Library Association* 65:1 (January 1977), 17-21.

714 Bette Greenberg, Robert Breedlove and Wendy Berger. "MEDLINE Demand Profiles: An Analysis of Requests for Clinical and Research Information," *Bulletin of the Medical Library Association* 65:1 (January 1977), 22-28.

715 Renata Tagliacozzo. "Estimating the Satisfaction of Information Users," *Bulletin of the Medical Library Association* 65:2 (April 1977), 243-249.

716 Ruth W. Wender, Ester L. Fruehauf, Marilyn S. Vent and Constant D. Wilson. "Determination of Continuing Medical Education Needs of Clinicians from a Literature Search Study: Part I. The Study," *Bulletin of the Medical Library Association* 65:3 (July 1977), 330-337.

717 Ruth W. Wender, Ester L. Fruehauf, Marilyn S. Vent and Constant D. Wilson. "Determination of Continuing Medical Education Needs of Clinicians from a Literature Search Study: Part II. Questionnaire Results," *Bulletin of the Medical Library Association* 65:3 (July 1977), 338-341.

718 Donald J. Morton. "Analysis of Interlibrary Requests by Hospital Libraries for Photocopied Journal Articles," *Bulletin of the Medical Library Association* 65:4 (October 1977), 425-432.

719 Patrick W. Brennen and W. Patrick Davey. "Citation Analysis in the Literature of Tropical Medicine," *Bulletin of the Medical Library Association* 66:1 (January 1978), 24-30.

720 Theresa C. Strasser. "The Information Needs of Practicing Physicians in Northeastern New York State," *Bulletin of the Medical Library Association* 66:2 (April 1978), 200-209.

721 Inci A. Bowman, Elizabeth K. Eaton and J. Maurice Mahan. "Are Health Science Faculty Interested in Medical History? An Evaluative Case Study," *Bulletin of the Medical Library Association* 66:2 (April 1978), 228-231.

722 Maurice C. Leatherbury and Richard A. Lyders. "Friends of the Library Groups in Health Sciences Libraries," *Bulletin of the Medical Library Association* 66:3 (July 1978), 315-318.

723 Bette Greenberg, Sara Battison, Madeleine Kolisch and Martha Leredu. "Evaluation of a Clinical Medical Librarian Program at the Yale Medical Library," *Bulletin of the Medical Library Association* 66:3 (July 1978), 319-326.

724 Gloria Werner. "Use of On-Line Bibliographic Retrieval Services in Health Sciences Libraries in the United States and Canada," *Bulletin of the Medical Library Association* 67:1 (January 1979), 1-14.

725 B. Tommie Usdin. "Core Lists of Medical Journals: A Comparison," *Bulletin of the Medical Library Association* 67:2 (April 1979), 212-217.

726 John A. Timour. "Brief Communications: Use of Selected Abstracting and Indexing Journals in Biomedical Resource Libraries," *Bulletin of the Medical Library Association* 67:3 (July 1979), 330-335.

727 Rachel K. Goldstein and Dorothy R. Hill. "The Status of Women in the Administration of Health Sciences Libraries: A Five-Year Follow-Up Study, 1972-1977," *Bulletin of the Medical Library Association* 68:1 (January 1980), 6-15.

728 Richard T. West and Maureen J. Malone. "Communicating the Results of NLM Grant-supported Library Projects," *Bulletin of the Medical Library Association* 68:1 (January 1980), 33-39.

729 James A. Thompson and Michael R. Kronenfeld. "The Effect of Inflation on the Cost of Journals on the Brandon List," *Bulletin of the Medical Library Association* 68:1 (January 1980), 47-52.

730 Carol C. Spencer. "Random Time Sampling with Self-observation for Library Cost Studies: Unit Costs of Reference Questions," *Bulletin of the Medical Library Association* 68:1 (January 1980), 53-57.

731 Justine Roberts. "Circulation versus Photocopy: Quid pro Quo?" *Bulletin of the Medical Library Association* 68:3 (July 1980), 274-2 7.

732 Dick R. Miller and Joseph E. Jensen. "Dual Pricing of Health Sciences Periodicals: A Survey," *Bulletin of the Medical Library Association* 68:4 (October 1980), 336-347.

733 Jacqueline D. Bastille. "A Simple Objective Method for Determining a Dynamic Journal Collection," *Bulletin of the Medical Library Association* 68:4 (October 1980), 357-366.

734 Mary H. Mueller. "An Examination of Characteristics Related to Success of Friends Groups in Medical School Rare Book Libraries," *Bulletin of the Medical Library Association* 69:1 (January 1981), 9-13.

735 Scott Davis, Lincoln Polissar and Joan W. Wilson. "Continuing Education in Cancer for the Community Physician: Design and Evaluation of a Regional

Table of Contents Service," *Bulletin of the Medical Library Association* 69:1 (January 1981), 14-20.

736   Gary D. Byrd. "Copyright compliance in Health Sciences Libraries: A Status Report Two Years after the Implementation of PL 94-553," *Bulletin of the Medical Library Association* 69:2 (April 1981), 224-230.

737   Ester L. Baldinger, Jennifer P.S. Nakeff-Plaat and Margaret S. Cummings. "An Experimental Study of the Feasibility of Substituting Chemical Abstracts Online for the Printed Copy in a Medium-Sized Medical Library," *Bulletin of the Medical Library Association* 69:2 (April 1981), 247-251.

738   Doris R.F. Dunn. "Dissemination of the Published Results of an Important Clinical Trial: An Analysis of the Citing Literature," *Bulletin of the Medical Library Association* 69:3 (July 1981), 301-306.

739   Cynthia H. Goldstein. "A Study of Weeding Policies in Eleven TALON Resource Libraries," *Bulletin of the Medical Library Association* 69:3 (July 1981), 311-316.

740   K. Suzanne Johnson and E. Guy Coffee. "Veterinary Medical School Libraries in the United States and Canada, 1977-78," *Bulletin of the Medical Library Association* 70:1 (January 1982), 10-20.

741   Suzanne F. Grefsheim, Robert H. Larson, Shelley A. Bader and Nina W. Matheson. "Automation of Internal Library Operations in Academic Health Sciences Libraries: A State of the Art Report," *Bulletin of the Medical Library Association* 70:2 (April 1982), 191-200. (**9, 10, 52, 53, 61, 63, 140, 141, 161, 164**)

742   Elizabeth R. Lenz and Carolyn F. Walz. "Nursing Educators' Satisfaction with Library Facilities," *Bulletin of the Medical Library Association* 70:2 (April 1982), 201-206.

743   Ruth Traister Morris, Edwin A. Holtum and David S. Curry. "Being There: The Effect of the User's Presence on MEDLINE Search Results," *Bulletin of the Medical Library Association* 70:3 (July 1982), 298-304.

744   James K. Cooper, Diane Cooper and Timothy P. Johnson. "Medical Library Support in Rural Areas," *Bulletin of the Medical Library Association* 71:1 (January 1983), 13-15.

745   Susan Crawford. "Health Science Libraries in the United States: I. Overview of the Post-World War II Years," *Bulletin of the Medical Library Association* 71:1 (January 1983), 16-20.

746   Susan Crawford and Alan M. Rees. "Health Sciences Libraries in the United States: II. Medical School Libraries, 1960-1980," *Bulletin of the Medical Library Association* 71:1 (January 1983), 21-29.

747   Susan Crawford. "Health Science Libraries in the United States: III. Hospital Health Science Libraries, 1969-1979," *Bulletin of the Medical Library Association* 71:1 (January 1983), 30-36.

748   Mark E. Funk and Carolyn Anne Reid. "Indexing Consistency in MED-LINE," *Bulletin of the Medical Library Association* 71:2 (April 1983), 176-183. **(87, 88, 100)**

749   Michael R. Kronenfeld and Sarah H. Gable. "Real Inflation of Journal Prices: Medical Journals, U.S. Journals and Brandon List Journals," *Bulletin of the Medical Library Association* 71:4 (October 1983), 375-379.

750   Jane McCarthy. "Survey of Audiovisual Standards and Practices in Health Sciences Libraries," *Bulletin of the Medical Library Association* 71:4 (October 1983), 391-395. **(56, 57, 120)**

751   Rajia C. Tobia and David A. Kronick. "A Clinical Information Consultation Service at a Teaching Hospital," *Bulletin of the Medical Library Association* 71:4 (October 1983), 396-399.

752   Elizabeth R. Ashin. "Library Service to Dental Practitioners," *Bulletin of the Medical Library Association* 71:4 (October 1983), 400-402.

753   Peter P. Olevnik. "Non-Formalized Point-of-Use Library Instruction: A Survey," *Catholic Library World* 50:5 (December 1978), 218-220.

754   Susan A. Stussy. "Automation in Catholic College Libraries," *Catholic Library World* 53:3 (October 1981), 109-111. **(61)**

755   R.M. Longyear. "Article Citations and 'Obsolescence' in Musicological Journals," *Notes* 33:3 (March 1977), 563-571.

756   Ann Basart. "Criteria for Weeding Books in a University Music Library," *Notes* 36:4 (June 1980), 819-836.

757   Richard P. Smiraglia and Arsen R. Papakhian. "Music in the OCLC Online Union Catalog: A Review," *Notes* 38:2 (December 1981), 257-274. **(17, 18, 19, 21, 22, 23, 24, 52, 53, 54, 63, 64, 69, 70, 72, 73, 74, 75, 93, 94, 158, 159, 199, 200)**

758   William Gray Potter. "When Names Collide: Conflict in the Catalog and AACR 2," *Library Resources and Technical Services* 24:1 (Winter 1980), 3-16. **(4, 127, 130, 152)**

759   Rose Mary Magrill and Constance Rinehart. "Selection for Preservation: A Service Study," *Library Resources and Technical Services* 24:1 (Winter 1980), 44-57.

760   Sally Braden, John D. Hall and Helen H. Britton. "Utilization of Personnel and Bibliographic Resources for Cataloging by OCLC Participating Librar-ies," *Library Resources and Technical Services* 24:2 (Spring 1980), 135-154. **(8, 14, 15, 16, 30, 34, 35, 39, 46, 49, 50, 58, 81, 91, 92, 98, 99, 106, 109, 110, 111, 112, 121)**

761   Cynthia C. Ryans. "Cataloging Administrators' Views on Cataloging Educa-tion," *Library Resources and Technical Services* 24:4 (Fall 1980), 343-351.

762   Thomas Schadlich. "Changing from Sears to LC Subject Headings," *Library Resources and Technical Services* 24:4 (Fall 1980), 361-363. **(114)**

763 Elizabeth L. Tate. "For Our 25th Anniversary...," *Library Resources and Technical Services* 25:1 (January/March 1981), 3-7.

764 Barbara Moore. "Patterns in the Use of OCLC by Academic Library Cataloging Departments," *Library Resources and Technical Services* 25:1 (January/March 1981), 30-39. (**7, 9, 12, 13, 20, 21, 50, 51, 55, 56, 59, 60, 68, 72, 92, 99**)

765 Judith J. Johnson and Clair S. Josel. "Quality Control and the OCLC Data Base: A Report on Error Reporting," *Library Resources and Technical Services* 25:1 (January/March 1981), 40-47. (**21, 43, 51, 52, 60, 68, 69, 82**)

766 Edward T. O'Neill and Rao Aluri. "Library of Congress Subject Heading Patterns in OCLC Monographic Records," *Library Resources and Technical Services* 25:1 (January/March 1981), 63-80. (**121, 122**)

767 Elizabeth H. Groot. "A Comparison of Library Tools for Monograph Verification," *Library Resources and Technical Services* 25:2 (April/June 1981), 149-161.

768 Elizabeth G. Mikita. "Monographs in Microform: Issues in Cataloging and Bibliographic Control," *Library Resources and Technical Services* 25:4 (October/December 1981), 352-361. (**7, 23, 24, 75, 76**)

769 Lee R. Nemchek. "Problems of Cataloging and Classification in Theater Librarianship," *Library Resources and Technical Services* 25:4 (October/December 1981), 374-385. (**28, 32, 37, 79, 80, 103**)

770 John Hostage. "AACR 2, OCLC, and the Card Catalog in the Medium-Sized Library," *Library Resources and Technical Services* 26:1 (January/March 1982), 12-20. (**4, 5, 46, 47, 62, 63, 122, 123, 127, 128, 155**)

771 Robert H. Hassell. "Revising the Dewey Music Schedules: Tradition vs. Innovation," *Library Resources and Technical Services* 26:2 (April/June 1982), 192-203. (**26, 27, 28, 29**)

772 Patricia Dwyer Wanninger. "Is the OCLC Database Too Large? A Study of the Effect of Duplicate Records in the OCLC System," *Library Resources and Technical Services* 26:4 (October/December 1982), 353-361. (**57, 58, 179**)

773 Stephen R. Salmon. "Characteristics of Online Public Catalogs," *Library Resources and Technical Services* 27:1 (January/March 1983), 36-67. (**153, 159, 160, 180**)

774 Thomas E. Nisonger. "A Test of Two Citation Checking Techniques for Evaluating Political Science Collections in University Libraries," *Library Resources and Technical Services* 27:2 (April/June 1983), 163-176.

775 John Rutledge and Willy Owen. "Changes in the Quality of Paper in French Books, 1860-1914: A Study of Selected Holdings of the Wilson Library, University of North Carolina," *Library Resources and Technical Services* (April/June 1983), 177-187.

776 Jim Williams and Nancy Romero. "A Comparison of the OCLC Database and *New Serial Titles* as an Information Resource for Serials," *Library Resources and Technical Services* 27:2 (April/June 1983), 177-187.

777 Mary E. Clack and Sally F. Williams. "Using Locally and Nationally Produced Periodical Price Indexes in Budget Preparation," *Library Resources and Technical Services* 27:4 (October/December 1983), 345-356.

778 Victoria Cheponis Lessard and Jack Hall. "Vocational Technical Collection Building: Does it Exist?" *Collection Building* 4:2 (1982), 6-18.

779 Virginia Witucke. "The Reviewing of Children's Science Books," *Collection Building* 4:2 (1982) 19-30.

780 Margaret F. Stieg. "The Information Needs of Historians," *College and Research Libraries* 42:6 (November 1981), 549-560.

781 Howard D. White. "Library Censorship and the Permissive Minority," *Library Quarterly* 51:2 (1981), 192-207.

782 Judith Serebnick. "Book Reviews and the Selection of Potentially Controversial Books in Public Libraries," *Library Quarterly* 51:4 (1981), 390-409.

783 Richard W. Scamell and Bette Ann Stead. "A Study of Age and Tenure as it Pertains to Job Satisfaction," *Journal of Library Administration* 1:1 (Spring 1980), 3-18.

784 Robert M. Hayes. "Citation Statistics as a Measure of Faculty Research Productivity," *Journal of Education for Librarianship* 23:3 (Winter 1983), 151-172.

785 William Skeh Wong and David S. Zubatsky. "The First-Time Appointed Academic Library Director 1970-1980: A Profile," *Journal of Library Administration* 4:1 (Spring 1983), 41-70.

786 James Rice, Jr. "An Assessment of Student Preferences for Method of Library Orientation," *Journal of Library Administration* 4:1 (Spring 1983), 87-93.

787 Frank William Goudy. "Affirmative Action and Library Science Degrees: A Statistical Overview, 1973-74 through 1980-81," *Journal of Library Administration* 4:3 (Fall 1983), 51-60.

788 Thomas G. English. "Librarian Status in the Eighty-Nine U.S. Academic Institutions of the Association of Research Libraries: 1982," *College and Research Libraries* 44:3 (May 1983), 199-211.

789 Nathan M. Smith and Veneese C. Nelson. "Burnout: A Survey of Academic Reference Librarians," *College and Research Libraries* 44:3 (May 1983), 245-250.

790 Floris W. Wood. "Reviewing Book Review Indexes," *Reference Services Review* (April/June 1980), 47-52.

791 Herbert Goldhor. "Public Library Circulation up 3%; Spending Jumps 11%," *American Libraries* 14:8 (September 1983), 534.

792 Laura N. Gasaway and Steve Margeton. "Continuing Education for Law Librarianship," *Law Library Journal* 70:1 (February 1977), 39-52.

793 Michael L. Renshawe. "The Condition of the Law Librarian in 1976," *Law Library Review* 69:4 (November 1976), 626-640.

794 Susanne Patterson Wahba. "Women in Libraries," *Law Library* Journal 69:2 (May 1976), 223-231.

795 Jean Finch and Lauri R. Flynn. "An Update on Faculty Libraries," *Law Library Journal* 73:1 (Winter 1980), 99-106.

796 Robert D. Swisher, Peggy C. Smith and Calvin J. Boyer. "Educational Change Among ACRL Academic Librarians," *Library Research* (*Library and Information Science Research* since Spring 1983) 5:2 (Summer 1983), 195-205.

797 Michael D. Cooper. "Economies of Scale in Academic Libraries," *Library Research* (*Library and Information Science Research* after Spring 1983) 5:2 (Summer 1983), 207-219.

798 Virgil Diodato. "Faculty Workload: A Case Study," *Journal of Education for Librarianship* 23:4 (Spring 1983), 286-295.

799 Jerry D. Saye. "Continuing Education and Library School Faculty," *Journal of Education for Librarianship* 24:1 (Summer 1983), 3-16.

800 Maurice P. Marchant and Carolyn F. Wilson. "Developing Joint Graduate Programs for Librarians," *Journal of Education for Librarianship* 24:1 (Summer 1983), 30-37.

801 Barbara L. Stein and Herman L. Totten. "Cognitive Styles: Similarities Among Students," *Journal of Education for Librarianship* 24:1 (Summer 1983), 38-43.

802 Marilyn J. Markham, Keith H. Stirling and Nathan M. Smith. "Librarian Self-Disclosure and Patron Satisfaction in the Reference Interview," *RQ* 22:4 (Summer 1983), 369-374.

803 June L. Engle and Elizabeth Futas. "Sexism in Adult Encyclopedias," *RQ* 23:1 (Fall 1983), 29-39.

804 David F. Kohl. "Circulation Professionals: Management Information Needs and Attitudes," *RQ* 23:1 (Fall 1983), 81-86.

805 Kevin Carey. "Problems and Patterns of Periodical Literature Searching at an Urban University Research Library," *RQ* 23:2 (Winter 1983), 211-218.

806 Beverly P. Lynch and Jo Ann Verdin. "Job Satisfaction in Libraries: Relationships of the Work Itself, Age, Sex, Occupational Group, Tenure, Supervisory Level, Career Commitment and Library Department," *Library Quarterly* 53:4 (October 1983), 434-447.

807 Louise W. Diodato and Virgil P. Diodato. "The Use of Gifts in a Medium Sized Academic Library," *Collection Management* 5:1/2 (Spring/Summer 1983), 53-71.

AUTHOR INDEX
TO BIBLIOGRAPHY OF ARTICLES

Note: The index is arranged alphabetically, word by word. All characters or groups of characters separated by spaces, dashes, hyphens, diagonal slashes or periods are treated as separate words. Acronyms not separated by spaces or punctuation are alphabetized as though they are single words, while initials separated by spaces or punctuation are treated as if each letter is a complete word. Personal names beginning with capital Mc, M' and Mac are all listed under Mac as though the full form were used, and St. is alphabetized as if spelled out.

ABOUT THE AUTHORS

DAVID F. KOHL is currently Undergraduate Librarian and Assistant Director for Undergraduate Libraries and Instructional Services at the University of Illinois-Urbana, with the rank of Associate Professor. Dr. Kohl did his graduate work at the University of Chicago. He has taught library administration at the University of Illinois Graduate School of Library and Information Science and has published numerous articles and monographs on library management and automation. His wide range of service in library management includes active participation in the ARL/OMS Library Consultant Program, the Washington State University's Managing for Productivity Program, and the Assessment Center Program for Potential Managers, sponsored jointly by the University of Washington Graduate Library School and the Washington State Library.

SANFORD BERMAN, Head Cataloger at Hennepin County Library (Minnetonka, Minnesota) since 1973, has authored *Prejudices and Antipathies: A Tract on the LC Subject Heads Concerning People* (Scarecrow Press, 1971) and *The Joy of Cataloging* (Oryx Press, 1981), as well as editing *Subject Cataloging: Critiques and Innovations* (Haworth Press, 1984). He also contributes "Consumer, Beware!" and "Alternatives" columns to *Technicalities* and *Collection Building,* and serves on the editorial advisory board for *The Reference Librarian.* In 1981, Berman won the American Library Association's Margaret Mann Citation for "outstanding achievement in cataloging and classification."